D0368686

4

Decisions
of the
United States
Supreme Court

1998-99 TERM

---

by
The Editorial Staff
United States Supreme Court Reports,
Lawyers' Edition

701 East Water Street
Charlottesville, VA 22902

ISBN 0-327-09962-3

7683511

CONTENTS

PREFACE

This volume is designed to serve as a quick-reference guide to the work of the United States Supreme Court during its 1998–1999 Term. Its important features are described below.

The Court's Personnel. A list of the Justices of the Supreme Court is accompanied by photographs and biographical sketches of each Justice serving during the Term.

Survey of the Term. A succinct narrative statement outlines the high spots of the Term.

Summaries of Decisions. Every important decision of the Supreme Court is individually summarized. These summaries (reprinted from Vols. 142–144 L Ed 2d) describe the manner in which the case came before the Court, the facts involved and issues presented, the holding of the Court and the reasons supporting that holding, the name of the Justice who wrote the opinion of the majority, and the names and views of those of the Justices who concurred or dissented.

The Summaries are printed in the order in which the cases were decided by the Court. Notations to Summaries indicate the volume and page at which the full opinion of the Court may be found in the official reports (US) published by the Federal Government, and the privately published United States Supreme Court Reports, Lawyers' Edition (L Ed 2d), and Supreme Court Reporter (S Ct).

Following each Summary is a listing of the attorneys who argued in behalf of the litigants.

Glossary. A glossary of common legal terms defines, in simple, nontechnical language, various legal words and phrases frequently used in the Supreme Court's decisions.

Table of Cases. A complete Table of Cases makes possible the location of the Summary of any case through the name of a party litigant.

Index. A detailed, alphabetical word index makes possible the location of the Summary of any case by consulting the index entries for appropriate factual and conceptual terms.

THE COURT'S PERSONNEL

JUSTICES

OF THE

SUPREME COURT OF THE UNITED STATES

1998–99 Term

Chief Justice

HON. WILLIAM H. REHNQUIST

Associate Justices

HON. JOHN P. STEVENS

HON. SANDRA DAY O'CONNOR

HON. ANTONIN SCALIA

HON. ANTHONY M. KENNEDY

HON. DAVID H. SOUTER

HON. CLARENCE THOMAS

HON. RUTH BADER GINSBURG

HON. STEPHEN BREYER

BIOGRAPHIES OF THE JUSTICES

Chief Justice Rehnquist was born in Milwaukee, Wisconsin, on October 1, 1924, the son of William B.

and Margery P. Rehnquist. He married Natalie Cornell in 1953. They have three children, James, Janet, and Nancy.

Chief Justice Rehnquist attended public schools in Shorewood, Wisconsin, and received his B.A. degree, with great distinction, and an M.A. degree from Stanford University in 1948. He also earned an M.A. degree from Harvard University in 1950, and then returned to Stanford University, where he received his LL.B. degree in 1952.

From 1952 to 1953, he served as law clerk for Justice Robert H. Jackson, Supreme Court of the United States. From 1953 to 1969, Chief Justice Rehnquist engaged in private practice in Phoenix, Arizona, and in 1969, he was appointed Assistant Attorney General, Office of Legal Counsel, by President Nixon.

Chief Justice Rehnquist served in the United States Army Air Corps in this country and overseas from 1943 to 1946, and was discharged with the rank of sergeant.

Chief Justice Rehnquist was nominated to the position of Associate Justice of the United States Supreme Court by President Nixon on October 21, 1971, and took office on January 7, 1972. On June 17, 1986, he was nominated Chief Justice by President Reagan, and on September 26, 1986, he was sworn in as Chief Justice.

Chief Justice Rehnquist's professional activities have included membership in the American Bar Association, the Arizona Bar Association, the Maricopa County (Arizona) Bar Association (President, 1963), the National Conference of Lawyers and Realtors, the National Conference of Commissioners of Uniform State Laws, and the Council of the Administrative Conference of the United States.

Justice Stevens was born in Chicago, Illinois, on April 20, 1920. He is married to Maryan Mulholland Stevens

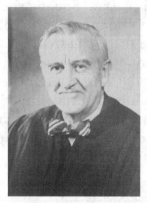

and has four children, John Joseph, Kathryn Stevens Tedlicka, Elizabeth Jane, and Susan Roberta.

Justice Stevens received an A.B. degree from the University of Chicago in 1941 and a J.D. degree, magna cum laude, from Northwestern University School of Law in 1947.

During the 1947–1948 Term of the United States Supreme Court, he was a law clerk to Justice Wiley Rutledge, and in 1949, he was admitted to practice law in Illinois. In 1951 and 1952, Justice Stevens was Associate Counsel to the Subcommittee on the Study of Monopoly Power of the Judiciary Committee of the United States House of Representatives, and from 1953 to 1955 he was a member of the Attorney General's National Committee to Study Anti-trust Law. From 1970 to 1975 he served as a Judge of the United States Court of Appeals for the Seventh Circuit.

Justice Stevens served in the United States Navy from 1942 to 1945.

Justice Stevens was appointed to the position of Associate Justice of the United States Supreme Court by President Ford on December 1, 1975, and took his seat on December 19, 1975.

Justice Stevens is a member of the Illinois Bar Association, Chicago Bar Association, Federal Bar Association, American Law Institute, and American Judicature Society.

Justice O'Connor was born in El Paso, Texas, on March 26, 1930, the daughter of Harold A. Day and Ada  Mae Wilkey Day. She married John Jay O'Connor III in 1952. They have three children, Scott, Brian, and Jay.

Justice O'Connor graduated from Stanford University in 1950 with a B.A. degree, magna cum laude. She earned her LL.B. degree at Stanford in 1952.

Justice O'Connor served as a deputy county attorney in San Mateo County, California, from 1952 to 1953, and as a civilian attorney for the Quartermaster Market Center in Frankfurt, Germany, from 1954 to 1957. She was in the private practice of law in Maryvale, Arizona, from 1958 to 1960, and served as an Assistant Attorney General in Arizona from 1965 to 1969.

Justice O'Connor was a member of the Arizona State Senate from 1969 to 1975. She was a judge of the Maricopa County Superior Court in Phoenix, Arizona, from 1975 to 1979, and served on the Arizona Court of Appeals from 1979 to 1981.

Justice O'Connor was appointed to the position of Associate Justice of the United States Supreme Court by President Reagan on July 7, 1981, and took office on September 25, 1981.

Justice Scalia was born on March 11, 1936 in Trenton, New Jersey. He married Maureen McCarthy, September 10, 1960. They have  nine children: Ann Forrest, Eugene, John Francis, Catherine Elisabeth, Mary Clare, Paul David, Matthew, Christopher James, and Margaret Jane.

Justice Scalia attended Georgetown University and University of Fribourg (Switzerland), receiving his A.B. degree in 1957. He earned his LL.B. degree in 1960 from Harvard University.

Justice Scalia was admitted to the Ohio Bar, 1962, and the Virginia Bar, 1970. He was in private practice with Jones, Day, Cockley and Reavis, Cleveland, Ohio, from 1961 to 1967.

He served as general counsel, Office of Telecommunications Policy, Executive Office of the President, 1971 to 1972; chairman, Administrative Conference of the United States, 1972 to 1974; Assistant Attorney General, Office of Legal Counsel, U. S. Department of Justice, 1974 to 1977.

Justice Scalia was a professor of law at the University of Virginia from 1967 to 1974, a scholar in residence at the American Enterprise Institute in 1977, visiting professor of law at Georgetown University in 1977, professor of law at the University of Chicago from 1977 to 1982, and visiting professor of law at Stanford University from 1980 to 1981.

From 1982 to 1986, Justice Scalia served as a Judge of the United States Court of Appeals for the District of Columbia Circuit. He was nominated by President

Reagan as Associate Justice of the United States Supreme Court, and he took the oath of office on September 26, 1986.

Justice Kennedy was born in Sacramento, California, on July 23, 1936. He married Mary Davis on June 29,

1963, and they have three children, Justin Anthony, Gregory Davis, and Kristin Marie.

Justice Kennedy attended Stanford University and the London School of Economics, receiving a B.A. from Stanford in 1958. He then earned an LL.B. from Harvard Law School in 1961. From 1960 to 1961, he was on the board of student advisors, Harvard Law School.

Justice Kennedy was admitted to the California bar in 1962 and the United States Tax Court bar in 1971. From 1961 to 1963, he was an associate at Thelen, Marrin, Johnson & Bridges, San Francisco, then practiced as a sole practitioner in Sacramento from 1963 to 1967, and was a partner in Evans, Jackson & Kennedy, Sacramento, from 1967 to 1975. He was nominated to be a judge of the United States Court of Appeals for the Ninth Circuit by President Ford, and took the oath of office on May 30, 1975. In addition, Justice Kennedy has been a professor of constitutional law at McGeorge School of Law, University of the Pacific, from 1965 to 1988.

He has served in the California Army National Guard, 1961; the Judicial Conference of the United States Advisory Panel on Financial Disclosure Reports and Judicial Activities (subsequently renamed the Advisory Committee on Codes of Conduct), 1979 to 1987; and the board of the Federal Judicial Center, 1987 to 1988. He has been on the Committee on Pacific Territories, 1979 to 1988, and was named chairman 1982. He is a member of the American Bar Association,

Sacramento County Bar Association, State Bar of California, and Phi Beta Kappa.

Justice Kennedy was nominated by President Reagan as an Associate Justice of the Supreme Court, and took the oath of office on February 18, 1988.

Justice Souter was born in Melrose, Massachusetts on September 17, 1939, the son of Joseph Alexander and  Helen Adams Hackett Souter.

He graduated from Harvard College in 1961 with an A.B. degree. After two years as a Rhodes Scholar, Justice Souter received an A.B. in Jurisprudence from Oxford University in 1963. He earned an LL.B. degree from Harvard Law School in 1966 and an M.A. degree from Oxford University in 1989.

Justice Souter was an associate at the law firm of Orr and Reno in Concord, New Hampshire from 1966 to 1968. He then became an Assistant Attorney General of New Hampshire. In 1971, he became Deputy Attorney General, and in 1976, Attorney General of New Hampshire. Justice Souter was named Associate Justice of the Superior Court of New Hampshire in 1978. In 1983, he was appointed as an Associate Justice of the Supreme Court of New Hampshire.

On May 25, 1990, Justice Souter became a Judge of the United States Court of Appeals for the First Circuit. He was nominated by President Bush as an Associate Justice of the United States Supreme Court, and he took his seat on October 9, 1990.

Justice Souter is a member of the National Association of Attorneys General, the New Hampshire Bar Association, and the American Bar Association.

Justice Thomas was born in Pinpoint, Georgia on June 23, 1948. He married Virginia Lamp on May 30, 1987, and has one child, Jamal Adeen.

Justice Thomas attended Conception Seminary and Holy Cross College, receiving an A.B. degree, cum laude, from Holy Cross in 1971. He earned a J.D. degree from Yale Law School in 1974.

He was admitted to the Missouri Bar in 1974, and after serving as Assistant Attorney General of Missouri from 1974 to 1977, he was an attorney for the Monsanto Company from 1977 to 1979.

Justice Thomas served as a legislative assistant to Senator John C. Danforth of Missouri from 1979 to 1981, before serving as Assistant Secretary for Civil Rights for the United States Department of Education from 1981 to 1982 and Chairman of the United States Equal Employment Opportunity Commission from 1982 to 1990.

On March 12, 1990, Justice Thomas became a Judge of the United States Court of Appeals for the District of Columbia Circuit. He was nominated by President Bush as Associate Justice of the United States Supreme Court, and he took the oath of office on October 23, 1991.

Justice Ginsburg was born in Brooklyn, New York, on March 15, 1933, the daughter of Nathan Bader and  Celia Amster Bader. She married Martin D. Ginsburg in 1954, and they have two children, Jane and James.

She received a B.A. degree, with high honors in Government and distinction in all subjects, from Cornell University in 1954. She attended Harvard Law School and Columbia Law School, receiving her L.L.B. degree from Columbia in 1959.

Justice Ginsburg was admitted to the New York Bar in 1959 and the District of Columbia Bar in 1975. She served as a law clerk for Judge Edmund L. Palmieri of the United States District Court for the Southern District of New York from 1959 to 1961.

Justice Ginsburg was a professor at the Rutgers University School of Law from 1963 to 1972 and at Columbia Law School from 1972 to 1980. In addition, she served the American Civil Liberties Union as general counsel from 1973 to 1980 and as a member of the national board of directors from 1974 to 1980.

On June 30, 1980, Justice Ginsburg became a Judge of the United States Court of Appeals for the District of Columbia Circuit. She was nominated by President Clinton as an Associate Justice of the United States Supreme Court, and she took the oath of office on August 10, 1993.

Justice Breyer was born in San Francisco, California, on August 15, 1938. He married Joanna Hare on

September 4, 1967, and they have three children, Chloe, Nell, and Michael.

Justice Breyer received an A.B. degree, with Great Distinction, from Stanford University in 1959. He attended Oxford University as a Marshall Scholar and received a B.A. degree, with 1st Class Honors, in 1961. He earned his LL.B. degree from Harvard Law School, magna cum laude, in 1964.

During the 1964-1965 Term of the United States Supreme Court, he served as clerk to Justice Arthur Goldberg. He served as Special Assistant to the Assistant Attorney General (Antitrust), Department of Justice, 1965 to 1967; Assistant Special Prosecutor, Watergate Special Prosecution Force, 1973; Special Counsel to the U.S. Senate Judiciary Committee, 1974 to 1975; and Chief Counsel to the U.S. Senate Judiciary Committee, 1979 to 1980.

At Harvard University, Justice Breyer was an assistant professor from 1967 to 1970, a professor of law from 1970 to 1980, a professor at the Kennedy School of Government from 1977 to 1980, and a lecturer since 1980. He was a visiting professor at the College of Law, Sydney, Australia, in 1975, and the University of Rome in 1993.

He was appointed to the United States Court of Appeals for the First Circuit in 1980, and served as Chief Judge of that Court from 1990 to 1994. He was nominated by President Clinton as Associate Justice of the United States Supreme Court and took office on August 4, 1994.

SURVEY OF THE 1998-99 TERM

by

John A. Frey, J.D.

---

§ 1. Generally; statistics

The Supreme Court's 1998-99 Term began on October 5, 1998. The court took a recess from June 24 until October 4, 1999, at which time the 1998-99 Term adjourned.

Statistics released by the Office of the Clerk of the Supreme Court reveal that (1) 8,083 cases appeared on the Supreme Court's docket for the 1998-99 Term, and (2) of these, 974 were carried over from the prior term, and 7,109 were docketed during the 1998-99 Term.

Of the 8,083 cases on the docket during the 1998-99 Term, 6,866 nonoriginal cases were disposed of by (1) the court's denial of review, (2) the court's dismissal, or (3) withdrawal. Another 55 nonoriginal cases were summarily decided. A total of 1,038 cases, including 5 original cases, were not acted upon, or remained undisposed of.

There were 124 cases available for argument during the 1998-99 Term, of which 90 cases were argued and 4 were dismissed or remanded without argument, leaving 30 cases still available for argument. Of the 90 cases which were argued, 84 were disposed of by signed opinion, 4 were disposed of by per curiam opinion, and 2 were set for reargument.

§ 2. Landmark decisions

During the 1998-99 Term, the United States Supreme Court handed down a number of well-publicized landmark decisions. Three cases involved states' sovereign immunity. The court held that (1) Congress' powers under the Federal Constitution's Article I do not include the power to subject nonconsenting states to private suits for damages in state courts, and (2) Maine did not waive sovereign immunity with regard to state court actions filed under the Fair Labor Standards Act of 1938 (29 USCS §§ 201 et seq.) (Alden v Maine (1999, US) 144 L Ed 2d 636, 119 S Ct 2240, infra § 47). With respect to a patent infringement suit against a Florida state entity, the Supreme Court held that the abrogation of states' sovereign immunity in the Patent and Plant Variety Protection Remedy Clarification Act (35 USCS §§ 271(h), 296(a)) was invalid, as such abrogation could not be sustained as legislation enacted to enforce the guarantees of the due process clause of the Constitution's Fourteenth Amendment (Florida Prepaid Postsecondary Educ. Expense Bd. v College Sav. Bank (1999, US) 144 L Ed 2d 575, 119 S Ct 2199, infra § 47). The Supreme Court also held that the federal courts had no jurisdiction over a suit brought under § 43(a) of the Lanham Act (15 USCS § 1125(a)) against a Florida state entity which allegedly made misstatements about the entity's tuition savings plans in brochures and annual reports, as Florida's sovereign immunity was neither (1) validly abrogated by the Trademark Remedy Clarification Act (106 Stat 3567), nor (2) voluntarily waived by Florida's activities in interstate commerce (College Sav. Bank v Florida Prepaid Postsecondary Educ. Expense Bd. (1999, US) 144 L Ed 2d 605, 119 S Ct 2219, infra § 47).

The Supreme Court decided cases concerning the Americans with Disabilities Act of 1990 (ADA) (42 USCS §§ 12101 et seq.) during the Term. In one case, the court held that (1) the determination whether an individual's impairment substantially limited one or more major life activities, within the meaning of a provision of the ADA (42 USCS §§ 12102(2)(A)), was to be made with reference to the mitigating measures that the individual employed, and (2) the individual was not "regarded" as disabled, for purposes of another ADA provision (42 USCS § 12102(2)(C)), on account of high blood pressure (Murphy v UPS (1999, US) 144 L Ed 2d 484, 119 S Ct 2133, infra § 4). In another case, it was held that the antidiscrimination provision of Title II of the ADA (42 USCS § 12132) requires states to place mentally disabled persons in community settings rather than institutions, where (1) the state's treatment professionals determine that such placement is appropriate, (2) transfer to such a setting is not opposed by the affected individual, and (3) the placement can be reasonably accommodated, given the resources available to the state and the needs of others with mental disabilities (Olmstead v L. C. by Zimring (1999, US) 144 L Ed 2d 540, 119 S Ct 2176, infra § 4). In addition, the court held that individuals who were severely myopic, and who were denied employment as global airline pilots, failed to allege that they were disabled, within the meaning of relevant provisions of the ADA (42 USCS §§ 12102(2)(A), 12102(2)(C)), where corrective lenses allowed such individuals to function identically to individuals without a similar impairment (Sutton v United Air Lines, Inc. (1999, US) 144 L Ed 2d 450, 119 S Ct 2139, infra § 4).

In other cases concerning the construction of federal statutes, the court held that (1) the federal carjacking statute (18 USCS § 2119, later amended) defined three separate offenses by specification of distinct elements, rather than defining a single crime with a choice of three maximum penalties (Jones v United States (1999, US) 143 L Ed 2d 311, 119 S Ct 1215, infra § 11); (2) with respect to two forms of statistical sampling that the United States Census Bureau proposed to use in the year 2000 decennial census, the Census Act (13 USCS §§ 1 et seq.) prohibited the proposed uses of sampling in calculating the population for purposes of congressional apportionment (DOC v United States House of Representatives (1999, US) 142 L Ed 2d 797, 119 S Ct 765, infra § 12); and (3) a hospital patient need not prove that the hospital acted with an improper motive, in failing to stabilize the patient, in order to recover in a suit alleging a violation of the Emergency Medical Treatment and Active Labor Act (42 USCS § 1395dd(b)) (Roberts v Galen of Virginia (1999, US) 142 L Ed 2d 648, 119 S Ct 685, infra § 17).

With respect to the rights guaranteed by the Federal Constitution's First Amendment, the court held in one case that the First Amendment was violated by Colorado requirements that (1) initiative petition circulators be registered voters and wear badges bearing the circulators' names, and (2) an initiative's proponents report the names and addresses of paid circulators and the amounts that the circulators were paid (Buckley v American Constitutional Law Found. (1999, US) 142 L Ed 2d 599, 119 S Ct 636, infra § 16). In another case, the court held that the free speech clause of the First Amendment was violated by 18 USCS § 1304 and 47

CFR § 73.1211, as applied to prohibit private casino gambling advertisements broadcast by radio or television stations which were located in a state where such gambling was legal (Greater New Orleans Broad. Ass'n v United States (1999, US) 144 L Ed 2d 161, 119 S Ct 1923, infra § 25).

The court also decided significant cases concerning the Federal Constitution's Fourth Amendment. It was held that (1) a "media ride-along"—in which a print reporter and a photographer accompanied federal and county police officers during an attempt to execute arrest warrants in a private home—violated the Fourth Amendment, but (2) the officers were entitled to qualified immunity from damages liability, under the rule of Bivens v Six Unknown Named Agents of Federal Bureau of Narcotics (1971) 403 US 388, 29 L Ed 2d 619, 91 S Ct 1999, because the state of the law was not clearly established at the time that the entry of the home took place (Wilson v Layne (1999, US) 143 L Ed 2d 818, 119 S Ct 1692, infra § 43). Similarly, the court held that (1) a complaint—asserting that members of the news media had accompanied federal officials during a 1993 execution of a search warrant at a ranch—alleged a violation of the Fourth Amendment, under the Supreme Court's decision in Wilson v Layne, supra, but (2) the officials were entitled to qualified immunity from damages liability under the rule of Bivens v Six Unknown Named Agents of Federal Bureau of Narcotics, supra (Hanlon v Berger (1999, US) 143 L Ed 2d 978, 119 S Ct 1706, infra § 43). With respect to police observation of apartment visitors' drug transaction, it was held that because some persons had no legitimate expectation of privacy in another's apartment used for a purely business transaction, any search that may have occurred there did not violate the persons' rights under the Fourth Amendment (Minnesota v Carter

(1998, US) 142 L Ed 2d 373, 119 S Ct 469, infra § 43).
In cases concerning police searches of automobiles, the
court held that (1) the full search of an automobile, as
authorized by Iowa law, by a police officer who stopped
the automobile's driver for speeding and issued the
driver a citation—rather than arresting the driver, as
also authorized by state law—violated the Fourth
Amendment, where the officer conceded that the
officer had neither the driver's consent nor probable
cause to search the automobile (Knowles v Iowa (1998,
US) 142 L Ed 2d 492, 119 S Ct 484, infra § 44); (2)
police officers with probable cause to conduct a warrantless search of a car for contraband did not violate
the Fourth Amendment by searching a passenger's
personal belongings in the car that were capable of
concealing contraband (Wyoming v Houghton (1999,
US) 143 L Ed 2d 408, 119 S Ct 1297, infra § 44); and (3)
the automobile exception to the search warrant requirement of the Fourth Amendment does not require
a separate finding of exigency in addition to a probable
cause finding (Maryland v Dyson (1999, US) 144 L Ed
2d 442, 119 S Ct 2013, infra § 44).

The Supreme Court held that in an employment
discrimination suit under Title VII of the Civil Rights
Act of 1964 (42 USCS §§ 2000e et seq.), (1) an employer's conduct need not be independently "egregious" in
order to satisfy the requirements for a punitive damages
award under a provision of the Civil Rights Act of 1991
(42 USCS § 1981a(b)(1)); and (2) in the punitive
damages context, an employer may not be held vicariously liable for the discriminatory employment decisions of managerial agents, where these decisions are
contrary to the employer's good-faith efforts to comply
with Title VII (Kolstad v ADA (1999, US) 144 L Ed 2d
494, 119 S Ct 2118, infra § 18).

It was held that Chicago's "gang congregation" ordinance, which prohibited loitering together in any public place by two or more people, of whom at least one was a "criminal street gang member"—where the ordinance (1) defined "loitering" as remaining in any one place with no apparent purpose, and (2) criminalized any person's disobeying of a dispersal order given by a police officer pursuant to the ordinance—was impermissibly vague, in violation of the due process clause of the Federal Constitution's Fourteenth Amendment (City of Chicago v Morales (1999, US) 144 L Ed 2d 67, 119 S Ct 1849, § 34).

With respect to a private action brought under Title IX of the Education Amendments of 1972 (20 USCS §§ 1681 et seq.), the court held that such an action may lie against a public school board for sex discrimination where the board acted with deliberate indifference to acts of student-on-student sexual harassment which were so severe, pervasive, and objectively offensive as to effectively bar the harassment victim's access to an educational benefit or activity (Davis v Monroe County Bd. of Educ. (1999, US) 143 L Ed 2d 839, 119 S Ct 1661, infra § 46).

Finally, the court held that (1) California's durational residency requirement—which limited a family that had resided in California for less than 12 months to the welfare benefit level paid by the family's state of former residence—violated the right to travel guaranteed by § 1 of the Federal Constitution's Fourteenth Amendment; and (2) the requirement's constitutionality was not resuscitated by a change in federal welfare law (codified at 42 USCS § 604(c)) that approved durational residency requirements (Saenz v Roe (1999, US) 143 L Ed 2d 689, 119 S Ct 1518, infra § 51).

§ 3. Airline Passenger Injuries

The Supreme Court held that under the Warsaw Convention (49 Stat 3000 et seq.), an airline passenger could not maintain a personal injury damages action against an airline under local law—such as, in the case at hand, New York state tort law—where the passenger's claim did not satisfy the Convention's conditions for liability with respect to international air transportation. [El Al Isr. Airlines v Tsui Yaun Tseng (1999, US) 142 L Ed 2d 576, 119 S Ct 662.]

§ 4. Americans with Disabilities Act

It was held that a general arbitration clause in a collective bargaining agreement did not require a longshore worker to use the arbitration procedure for an alleged violation of the Americans with Disabilities Act of 1990 (42 USCS §§ 12101 et seq.), as (a) the asserted cause of action was not subject to a presumption of arbitrability, and (b) the agreement did not contain a clear and unmistakable waiver of the covered employees' rights to a judicial forum for federal claims of employment discrimination. [Wright v Universal Maritime Service Corp. (1998, US) 142 L Ed 2d 361, 119 S Ct 391.]

The court held that individuals who were severely myopic, and who were denied employment as global airline pilots, failed to allege that they were disabled, within the meaning of relevant provisions of the Americans with Disabilities Act of 1990 (42 USCS §§ 12102(2)(A), 12102(2)(C)), where corrective lenses allowed such individuals to function identically to individuals without a similar impairment. [Sutton v United Air Lines, Inc. (1999, US) 144 L Ed 2d 450, 119 S Ct 2139.]

The Supreme Court held that (1) the determination whether an individual's impairment substantially limited one or more major life activities, within the meaning of a provision of the Americans with Disabilities Act of 1990 (ADA) (42 USCS §§ 12102(2)(A)), was to be made with reference to the mitigating measures that the individual employed; and (2) the individual was not "regarded" as disabled, for purposes of another ADA provision (42 USCS § 12102(2)(C)), on account of high blood pressure. [Murphy v UPS (1999, US) 144 L Ed 2d 484, 119 S Ct 2133.]

The court held that (1) under the Americans with Disabilities Act (ADA) (42 USCS §§ 12101 et seq.), an employer who required as a job qualification that the employee meet an otherwise applicable federal safety regulation that tended to exclude persons with disabilities did not have to justify enforcing the regulation solely because the standard could be waived experimentally in an individual case; and (2) an employer was entitled under the ADA to enforce a federal visual acuity standard (49 CFR § 391.41(b)(10)) against an employee truckdriver who had obtained a waiver of the standard under an experimental federal program. [Albertson's, Inc. v Kirkingburg (1999, US) 144 L Ed 2d 518, 119 S Ct 2162.]

It was held that the antidiscrimination provision of Title II of the Americans with Disabilities Act of 1990 (42 USCS § 12132) requires states to place mentally disabled persons in community settings rather than institutions, where (1) the state's treatment professionals determine that such placement is appropriate; (2) transfer to such a setting is not opposed by the affected individual; and (3) the placement can be reasonably accommodated, given the resources available to the state and the needs of others with mental disabilities. [Olmstead v L. C. by Zimring (1999, US) 144 L Ed 2d 540, 119 S Ct 2176.]

§ 5. Antitrust law

The Supreme Court held that the antitrust rule that group boycotts are per se violations of § 1 of the Sherman Act (15 USCS § 1) did not apply to the decision by a single buyer of telephone equipment removal services to buy from one seller rather than another. [NYNEX Corp. v Discon, Inc. (1998, US) 142 L Ed 2d 510, 119 S Ct 493.]

§ 6. Appeal of sentence

The failure of a Federal District Court to advise a defendant of his right to appeal his sentence, which failure to so advise was error in violation of former Rule 32(a)(2) of the Federal Rules of Criminal Procedure, was held not to entitle the defendant to postconviction relief under 28 USCS § 2255, where the defendant knew of his right and hence suffered no prejudice from the omission. [Peguero v United States (1999, US) 143 L Ed 2d 18, 119 S Ct 961.]

§ 7. Appellate jurisdiction

It was held that the United States Court of Appeals for the Armed Forces lacked jurisdiction, under the All Writs Act (28 USCS § 1651(a)), to enjoin the President and various other executive branch officials from dropping a United States Air Force major, who had been convicted by a court-martial, from the rolls of the Air Force. [Clinton v Goldsmith (1999, US) 143 L Ed 2d 720, 119 S Ct 1538.]

See Cunningham v Hamilton County (1999, US) 144 L Ed 2d 184, 119 S Ct 1915, infra § 9, in which it was held that a Federal District Court order that imposed sanctions on an attorney pursuant to Rule 37(a)(4) of the Federal Rules of Civil Procedure for failure to comply with discovery orders was not a final decision appealable under 28 USCS § 1291—which grants the

Federal Courts of Appeals jurisdiction of appeals from all final decisions of the Federal District Courts—even where the attorney no longer represented a party in the case.

§ 8. Asbestos litigation

The Supreme Court held that lower courts had erred in certifying and affirming the certification of a mandatory settlement class on a limited fund theory under Rule 23(b)(1)(B) of the Federal Rules of Civil Procedure in asbestos personal injury litigation. [Ortiz v Fibreboard Corp. (1999, US) 144 L Ed 2d 715, 119 S Ct 2295.]

§ 9. Attorneys

The court held that two county prosecutors did not violate an attorney's right, under the Federal Constitution's Fourteenth Amendment, to practice his profession when the prosecutors caused the attorney to be searched at the same time that his client was testifying before a grand jury. [Conn v Gabbert (1999, US) 143 L Ed 2d 399, 119 S Ct 1292.]

It was held that a Federal District Court order that imposed sanctions on an attorney pursuant to Rule 37(a)(4) of the Federal Rules of Civil Procedure for failure to comply with discovery orders was not a final decision appealable under 28 USCS § 1291—which grants the Federal Courts of Appeals jurisdiction of appeals from all final decisions of the Federal District Courts—even where the attorney no longer represented a party in the case. [Cunningham v Hamilton County (1999, US) 144 L Ed 2d 184, 119 S Ct 1915.]

§ 10. Bankruptcy

The Supreme Court held that 11 USCS § 1129(b)(2)(B)(ii) disqualified a debtor's prebankruptcy equity holders, over the objection of a senior class of impaired creditors, from contributing new capital and receiving ownership interests in the reorganized entity, where that ownership opportunity was given exclusively to such holders under a plan adopted without consideration of alternatives. [Bank of Am. Nat'l Trust & Sav. Ass'n v 203 N. LaSalle St. Pshp. (1999, US) 143 L Ed 2d 607, 119 S Ct 1411.]

§ 11. Carjacking

The court held that the phrase "intent to cause death or serious bodily harm," as used in the federal carjacking statute (18 USCS § 2119), did not require proof of an unconditional intent to kill or harm, but merely required proof of an intent to kill or harm if necessary to effect a carjacking. [Holloway v United States (1999, US) 143 L Ed 2d 1, 119 S Ct 966.]

It was held that the federal carjacking statute (18 USCS § 2119, later amended) defined three separate offenses by specification of distinct elements, rather than defining a single crime with a choice of three maximum penalties. [Jones v United States (1999, US) 143 L Ed 2d 311, 119 S Ct 1215.]

§ 12. Census

With respect to two forms of statistical sampling that the United States Census Bureau proposed to use in the year 2000 decennial census, the Census Act (13 USCS §§ 1 et seq.) was held to prohibit the proposed uses of sampling in calculating the population for purposes of congressional apportionment. [DOC v United States House of Representatives (1999, US) 142 L Ed 2d 797, 119 S Ct 765.]

§ 13. Confessions

It was held that (1) an accused's rights under the confrontation clause of the Federal Constitution's Sixth

Amendment were violated by the introduction at trial of his accomplice's confession which incriminated the accused for murder, and (2) the case would be remanded for a determination whether the error was harmless. [Lilly v Virginia (1999, US) 144 L Ed 2d 117, 119 S Ct 1887.]

§ 14. Customs

The Supreme Court held that (1) a customs classification regulation for imported goods (19 CFR § 10.16(c)) was subject to analysis under Chevron U. S. A. v Natural Resources Defense Council (1984) 467 US 837, 81 L Ed 2d 694, 104 S Ct 2778, and (2) if the regulation was a reasonable interpretation and implementation of an ambiguous statutory provision, it was required to be given judicial deference. [United States v Haggar Apparel Co. (1999, US) 143 L Ed 2d 480, 119 S Ct 1392.]

§ 15. Death penalty

It was held that the Supreme Court would decline to exercise its original jurisdiction to allow Germany to challenge Arizona's scheduled execution of a German citizen, given (1) the tardiness of Germany's pleas, and (2) the jurisdictional barriers that they implicated. [F.R.G. v United States (1999, US) 143 L Ed 2d 192, 119 S Ct 1016.]

The court held that an accused had (1) waived his claim that execution by lethal gas violated the prohibition, under the Federal Constitution's Eighth Amendment, against cruel and unusual punishment, and (2) procedurally defaulted that claim and the claim of ineffective assistance of counsel that the accused had raised in his habeas corpus petition. [Stewart v LaGrand (1999, US) 143 L Ed 2d 196, 119 S Ct 1018.]

The Supreme Court held that (1) a state did not violate the rule of Brady v Maryland (1963) 373 US 83, 10 L Ed 2d 215, 83 S Ct 1194, and its progeny, by failing to disclose exculpatory evidence to an accused, where the accused, who was sentenced to death, could not show prejudice; and (2) the accused therefore was not entitled to federal habeas corpus relief. [Strickler v Greene (1999, US) 144 L Ed 2d 286, 119 S Ct 1936.]

It was held that (1) an accused who was facing a possible death sentence was not entitled, under the Federal Constitution's Eighth Amendment, to have the sentencing jury instructed as to the consequences of the jurors' failure to agree on a verdict; and (2) where a death sentence was imposed, an alleged error in allowing the sentencing jury to consider various aggravating factors, allegedly in violation of the Eighth Amendment, was harmless. [Jones v United States (1999, US) 144 L Ed 2d 370, 119 S Ct 2090.]

See Calderon v Coleman (1998, US) 142 L Ed 2d 521, 119 S Ct 500, infra § 26, in which the court held that that with respect to a Federal Court of Appeals' ruling that an accused, who was under a California death sentence, was entitled to habeas corpus relief based on a claimed error in a capital sentencing instruction—which had informed the jury of the governor's power to commute a sentence of life imprisonment without possibility of parole—even if it were assumed that this instruction did not meet federal constitutional standards, the Court of Appeals had erred by failing to apply the harmless-error analysis required by a prior Supreme Court decision.

§ 16. Elections and voting

It was held that the Federal Constitution's First Amendment was violated by Colorado requirements that (1) initiative petition circulators be registered voters and wear badges bearing the circulators' names, and (2) an initiative's proponents report the names and addresses of paid circulators and the amounts that the circulators were paid. [Buckley v American Constitutional Law Found. (1999, US) 142 L Ed 2d 599, 119 S Ct 636.]

The Supreme Court held that a California county that was a covered jurisdiction for purposes of § 5 of the Voting Rights Act of 1965 (42 USCS § 1973c) was obligated to seek federal preclearance under § 5 before giving effect to changes affecting the voting in the county's judicial elections, notwithstanding that (1) such changes were required by California law and were nondiscretionary, and (2) California itself was not a covered jurisdiction for purposes of § 5. [Lopez v Monterey County (1999, US) 142 L Ed 2d 728, 119 S Ct 693.]

Some plaintiffs—who claimed, in a suit brought in a Federal District Court, that a North Carolina congressional district constituted a racial gerrymander in violation of the equal protection clause of the Federal Constitution's Fourteenth Amendment—were held not to be entitled to summary judgment on this claim, because North Carolina's motivation in drawing the district was in dispute. [Hunt v Cromartie (1999, US) 143 L Ed 2d 731, 119 S Ct 1545.]

§ 17. Emergency medical treatment

The court held that a hospital patient—in order to recover in a suit alleging a violation of the Emergency Medical Treatment and Active Labor Act (42 USCS § 1395dd(b))—need not prove that the hospital acted with an improper motive in failing to stabilize the patient. [Roberts v Galen of Virginia (1999, US) 142 L Ed 2d 648, 119 S Ct 685.]

§ 18. Employment

The Supreme Court held that with respect to a corporation's former at-will employee, who alleged that corporate officers had conspired to bring about the employee's termination to retaliate for the employee's obeying a federal subpoena and to deter the employee from testifying at a federal criminal trial, the harm allegedly occasioned stated a claim for damages under 42 USCS § 1985(2), which provided civil liability for conspiring to injure a party or witness "in his person or property" on account of that person's having attended or testified in a court of the United States. [Haddle v Garrison (1998, US) 142 L Ed 2d 502, 119 S Ct 489.]

The court held that (1) the pursuit and receipt of Social Security Disability Insurance benefits did not estop, or create a strong presumption against the success of, a recipient's employment discrimination claim under § 102(a) of the Americans with Disabilities Act (ADA) (42 USCS § 12112(a)), but (2) the recipient was required to explain why her Social Security claim—that she was unable to work—was consistent with her ADA claim that she could perform her job's essential functions. [Cleveland v Policy Mgmt. Sys. Corp. (1999, US) 143 L Ed 2d 966, 119 S Ct 1597.]

The Equal Employment Opportunity Commission was held to possess the legal authority to require federal agencies to pay compensatory damages when such agencies discriminate in employment in violation of Title VII of the Civil Rights Act of 1964 (42 USCS §§ 2000e et seq.). [West v Gibson (1999, US) 144 L Ed 2d 196, 119 S Ct 1906.]

The Supreme Court held that in an employment discrimination suit under Title VII of the Civil Rights Act of 1964 (42 USCS §§ 2000e et seq.), (1) an employer's conduct need not be independently "egregious" in order to satisfy the requirements for a punitive damages award under a provision of the Civil Rights Act of 1991 (42 USCS § 1981a(b)(1)); and (2) in the punitive damages context, an employer may not be held vicariously liable for the discriminatory employment decisions of managerial agents, where these decisions are contrary to the employer's good-faith efforts to comply with Title VII. [Kolstad v ADA (1999, US) 144 L Ed 2d 494, 119 S Ct 2118.]

As to claims of employment discrimination under the Americans with Disabilities Act of 1990 (42 USCS §§ 12101 et seq.), see § 4, supra.

§ 19. Expert testimony

It was held that a federal trial judge's gatekeeping obligation under the Federal Rules of Evidence—which assign to the trial judge the task of insuring that an expert witness' testimony rests on a reliable foundation and is relevant to the task at hand—applies not only to testimony based on scientific knowledge, but also to testimony based on technical and other specialized knowledge. [Kumho Tire Co. v Carmichael (1999, US) 143 L Ed 2d 238, 119 S Ct 1167.]

§ 20. Federal judges

The court held that (1) a county's suits to collect an occupational tax from federal judges were properly removed to a federal court under 28 USCS § 1442(a)(3); (2) federal adjudication of the suits was not barred by the Tax Injunction Act (28 USCS § 1341); and (3) imposition of the tax, which operated as a nondiscriminatory tax on the judges' compensation, was consented to by the Public Salary Tax Act of 1939 (4 USCS § 111). [Jefferson County v Acker (1999, US) 144 L Ed 2d 408, 119 S Ct 2069.]

§ 21. Federal sovereign immunity

The Supreme Court held that § 10(a) of the Administrative Procedure Act (5 USCS § 702) did not waive the Federal Government's sovereign immunity from a subcontractor's claim for an "equitable lien" on certain funds allegedly held by the Army with respect to an Army project. [Department of the Army v Blue Fox, Inc. (1999, US) 142 L Ed 2d 718, 119 S Ct 687.]

§ 22. Federal Trade Commission

It was held that (1) the jurisdiction of the Federal Trade Commission (FTC) extended to a nonprofit association that provided substantial economic benefits to its for-profit members, and (2) the FTC's "quick look" at the association's advertising restrictions on members was insufficient to justify a finding that the restrictions were anticompetitive in violation of 15 USCS § 45. [California Dental Ass'n v FTC (1999, US) 143 L Ed 2d 935, 119 S Ct 1604.]

§ 23. Firearms

Venue in a prosecution under 18 USCS § 924(c)(1) for using or carrying a firearm during and in relation to a crime of violence was held to be proper in any federal judicial district where the underlying crime of violence was committed. [United States v Rodriguez-Moreno (1999, US) 143 L Ed 2d 388, 119 S Ct 1239.]

§ 24. Fraud

The Supreme Court held that (1) a Federal District Court's refusal, with respect to criminal charges of tax fraud, to submit the issue of materiality to the jury was subject to harmless-error analysis under Rule 52(a) of the Federal Rules of Criminal Procedure, and (2) the materiality of falsehood is an element of offenses under the federal mail fraud statute (18 USCS § 1341), the federal wire fraud statute (18 USCS § 1343), and the federal bank fraud statute (18 USCS § 1344). [Neder v United States (1999, US) 144 L Ed 2d 35, 119 S Ct 1827.]

§ 25. Free speech

The court held that the free speech clause of the Federal Constitution's First Amendment was violated by 18 USCS § 1304 and 47 CFR § 73.1211, as applied to prohibit private casino gambling advertisements broadcast by radio or television stations which were located in a state where such gambling was legal. [Greater New Orleans Broad. Ass'n v United States (1999, US) 144 L Ed 2d 161, 119 S Ct 1923.]

§ 26. Habeas corpus

It was held that with respect to a Federal Court of Appeals' ruling that an accused, who was under a California death sentence, was entitled to habeas corpus relief based on a claimed error in a capital sentencing instruction—which had informed the jury of the governor's power to commute a sentence of life imprisonment without possibility of parole—even if it were assumed that this instruction did not meet federal constitutional standards, the Court of Appeals had erred by failing to apply the harmless-error analysis required by a prior Supreme Court decision. [Calderon v Coleman (1998, US) 142 L Ed 2d 521, 119 S Ct 500.]

The Supreme Court held that an Illinois state prisoner who sought federal habeas corpus relief had not exhausted state remedies, as required by 28 USCS § 2254, as to claims that had not been raised in the prisoner's petition for discretionary review in Illinois' highest court. [O'Sullivan v Boerckel (1999, US) 144 L Ed 2d 1, 119 S Ct 1728.]

§ 27. Illegal gratuity

It was held that in order to establish a violation of the federal illegal gratuity statute (18 USCS § 201(c)(1)(A))—which makes it a criminal offense to give anything of value to a public official "for or because of any official act performed or to be performed" by the official—the government must prove a link between a thing of value conferred upon a public official and a specific official act for or because of which the thing was given. [United States v Sun-Diamond Growers (1999, US) 143 L Ed 2d 576, 119 S Ct 1402.]

§ 28. Immigration law

The Supreme Court held that a provision of the Illegal Immigration Reform and Immigrant Responsibility Act of 1996 (IIRIRA) (8 USCS § 1252(g)), which severely restricted judicial review of deportation proceedings, deprived the federal courts of jurisdiction over a deportation-related selective enforcement claim that was pending on the IIRIRA's effective date. [Reno v American-Arab Anti-Discrimination Comm. (1999, US) 142 L Ed 2d 940, 119 S Ct 936.]

The court held that in requiring the Board of Immigration Appeals (BIA) to supplement its weighing test for determining an alien's entitlement to withholding of deportation under 8 USCS § 1253(h)(2)(C), a Federal Court of Appeals had failed to accord to the BIA's interpretation of § 1253(h)(2)(C) the deference required under the rule of Chevron U. S. A. v Natural Resources Defense Council (1994) 467 US 837, 81 L Ed 2d 694, 104 S Ct 2778. [INS v Aguirre-Aguirre (1999, US) 143 L Ed 2d 590, 1999 S Ct 1439.]

§ 29. Indian tribes

It was held that several Chippewa Indian Bands retained hunting, fishing, and gathering rights on land in present-day Minnesota that they ceded to United States in an 1837 Treaty with the Chippewa (7 Stat 536). [Minnesota v Mille Lacs Band of Chippewa Indians (1999, US) 143 L Ed 2d 270, 119 S Ct 1187.]

The Supreme Court held that the judicially created doctrine of tribal court exhaustion, requiring a Federal District Court to stay its hand while an Indian tribal court determines its own jurisdiction, did not require a District Court to abstain from deciding whether the Price-Anderson Amendments Act of 1988 (42 USCS §§ 2011 et seq.)—which in 42 USCS § 2210(n)(2) grants District Courts original and removal jurisdiction over all public liability actions arising out of nuclear incidents—applied to tribe members' claims against uranium mine operators for damages allegedly suffered as a result of mining operations. [El Paso Natural Gas Co. v Neztsosie (1999, US) 143 L Ed 2d 635, 119 S Ct 1430.]

The court held that the term "coal," as used in the Coal Lands Act of 1909 (30 USCS § 81) and the Coal Lands Act of 1910 (30 USCS §§ 83 et seq.), does not encompass coalbed methane (CBM) gas and thus does not give ownership of CBM gas to the Southern Ute Tribe, which owns coal rights reserved under the Acts. [AMOCO Prod. Co. v Southern Ute Indian Tribe (1999, US) 144 L Ed 2d 22, 119 S Ct 1719.]

§ 30. In forma pauperis proceedings

The Supreme Court (1) denied in forma pauperis status for an extraordinary writ to a petitioner who had filed numerous frivolous petitions for certiorari and for extraordinary writs, and (2) entered an order denying the petitioner in forma pauperis status as to prospective filings of such petitions in noncriminal cases. [In re Kennedy (1999, US) 142 L Ed 2d 573, 119 S Ct 635.]

It was held that (1) a person who, on a single day earlier in the current Supreme Court Term, had been denied leave to proceed in forma pauperis with respect to four petitions for certiorari—where the denials were based on Supreme Court Rule 39.8, which authorized the court to deny such leave with respect to frivolous petitions—would be denied leave to proceed in forma pauperis on two certiorari petitions, and (2) an order would be entered barring the person's future in forma pauperis filings of noncriminal certiorari petitions. [Schwarz v NSA (1999, US) 143 L Ed 2d 203, 119 S Ct 1109.]

The Supreme Court (1) invoked Supreme Court Rule 39.8 to deny leave to proceed in forma pauperis to an individual who was twice previously denied leave to proceed in forma pauperis, and (2) directed the Clerk of the Supreme Court not to accept any further petitions for certiorari or for extraordinary writs in noncriminal matters from the individual unless he complied with Supreme Court Rules 33.1 and 38. [Rivera v Florida Dep't of Corrections (1999, US) 143 L Ed 2d 235, 119 S Ct 1166.]

The court (1) invoked Supreme Court Rule 39.8 to deny an individual's request for leave to proceed in forma pauperis with respect to four petitions for certiorari that the court determined to be frivolous, and (2) directed the Clerk of the Supreme Court not to accept any further petitions for certiorari or for extraordinary writs in noncriminal matters from the individual unless he complied with Supreme Court Rules 33.1 and 38. [Lowe v Pogue (1999, US) 143 L Ed 2d 384, 119 S Ct 1238.]

The Supreme Court (1) invoked Supreme Court Rule 39.8 to deny an individual's request for leave to proceed in forma pauperis with respect to 2 petitions that the court determined to be frivolous, and (2) directed the Clerk of the Supreme Court not to accept any further petitions for certiorari in noncriminal matters from the individual—who had previously filed 10 other frivolous petitions—unless he complied with Supreme Court Rules 33.1 and 38. [Cross v Pelican Bay State Prison (1999, US) 143 L Ed 2d 982, 119 S Ct 1596.]

The court denied a person leave to proceed in forma pauperis on all future certiorari petitions in noncriminal cases, where the person had filed many frivolous in forma pauperis petitions in the Supreme Court. [Fertel-Rust v Milwaukee County Mental Health Ctr. (1999, US) 144 L Ed 2d 447, 119 S Ct 1997.]

Similarly, the court denied another person leave to proceed in forma pauperis on all future certiorari and extraordinary writ petitions in noncriminal cases, where the person had filed many frivolous in forma pauperis petitions in the Supreme Court. [Whitfield v Texas (1999, US) 144 L Ed 2d 764, 119 S Ct 2333.]

§ 31. Injunctions

The Supreme Court held that a Federal District Court had no authority—in a contract action brought by note holders against a note issuer for money damages—to issue a preliminary injunction preventing the note issuer from disposing of assets in which the note holders claimed no lien or equitable interest. [Grupo Mexicano de Desarrollo, S.A. v Alliance Bond Fund, Inc. (1999, US) 144 L Ed 2d 319, 119 S Ct 1961.]

§ 32. Jury unanimity

It was held that a jury in a federal criminal case under 21 USCS § 848—which forbids any person from engaging in a continuing criminal enterprise and defines "continuing criminal enterprise" as a violation of the drug statutes where such violation is part of a continuing series of violations—must unanimously agree not only (1) that an accused committed a continuing series of violations, but also (2) as to which specific violations made up that continuing series. [Richardson v United States (1999, US) 143 L Ed 2d 985, 119 S Ct 1707.]

§ 33. Labor law

The court held that (1) a labor union did not breach its duty of fair representation by negotiating a union security clause that tracked language of § 8(a)(3) of the National Labor Relations Act (29 USCS § 158(a)(3)) concerning such clauses without expressly explaining the Supreme Court's interpretation of that language in prior cases, and (2) an employee's challenge to a particular union security clause's provision allowing new employees a 30-day grace period before joining the union was within the National Labor Relations Board's primary jurisdiction. [Marquez v Screen Actors Guild (1998, US) 142 L Ed 2d 242, 119 S Ct 292.]

The Supreme Court held that a provision of the Federal Service Labor-Management Relations Statute (5 USCS § 7114(a)(4)) which requires federal agencies and the unions that represent the agencies' employees to "meet and negotiate in good faith for the purposes of arriving at a collective bargaining agreement" delegates to the Federal Labor Relations Authority the legal power to determine whether the parties must engage in midterm bargaining—that is, bargaining while the basic comprehensive labor contract is in effect—about subjects not included in the basic contract. [National Fed'n of Fed. Emples., Local 1309 v DOI (1999, US) 143 L Ed 2d 171, 119 S Ct 1003.]

An Ohio statute's exemption of state university faculties' instructional workload standards from collective bargaining was held not to violate the equal protection clause of the Federal Constitution's Fourteenth

Amendment. [Central State Univ. v American Ass'n of Univ. Professors, Cent. State Univ. Chapter (1999, US) 143 L Ed 2d 227, 119 S Ct 1162.]

The court held that an investigator employed by the Office of Inspector General of the National Aeronautics and Space Administration (NASA) was a representative of NASA when examining a NASA employee, so that the employee could invoke the right to union representation at the examination under a provision of the Federal Service Labor-Management Relations Statute (5 USCS § 7114(a)(2)(B)). [NASA v Federal Labor Rels. Auth. (1999, US) 144 L Ed 2d 258, 119 S Ct 1979.]

§ 34. Loitering

It was held that Chicago's "gang congregation" ordinance, which prohibited loitering together in any public place by two or more people, of whom at least one was a "criminal street gang member"—where the ordinance (1) defined "loitering" as remaining in any one place with no apparent purpose, and (2) criminalized any person's disobeying of a dispersal order given by a police officer pursuant to the ordinance—was impermissibly vague, in violation of the due process clause of the Federal Constitution's Fourteenth Amendment. [City of Chicago v Morales (1999, US) 144 L Ed 2d 67, 119 S Ct 1849.]

§ 35. Medicare

The Supreme Court held that neither the Medicare Provider Reimbursement Review Board nor the federal courts had jurisdiction to review a fiscal intermediary's refusal to reopen its decision that had determined the amount of a health services provider's reimbursement from the Secretary of Health and Human Services for the provider's covered Medicare services for a particular year. [Your Home Visiting Nurse Servs., Inc. v Shalala (1999, US) 142 L Ed 2d 919, 119 S Ct 930.]

§ 36. Patents

It was held that under 35 USCS § 102(b)—which provides that no person may patent an invention that has been "on sale" for more than 1 year before the filing of a patent application—an inventor's patent on a computer chip socket was invalid, as the 1-year period began to run when the inventor accepted a purchase order for the socket more than 1 year before applying for the patent, rather than when the inventor reduced the socket to practice less than 1 year before applying for the patent. [Pfaff v Wells Elecs. (1998, US) 142 L Ed 2d 261, 119 S Ct 304.]

The court held that when, under 35 USCS § 141, the United States Court of Appeals for the Federal Circuit (CAFC) directly reviews findings of fact made by the Patent and Trademark Office, the CAFC must use the "court/agency" framework for reviewing a federal agency's factual findings that is set forth in an Administrative Procedure Act provision (5 USCS § 706), rather than the traditionally stricter "court/court" standard of reviewing for clear error, which standard has previously been used by the CAFC and is of the type set forth in Rule 52(a) of the Federal Rules of Civil Procedure for appellate court review of factual findings by a Federal District Court judge. [Dickinson v Zurko (1999, US) 144 L Ed 2d 143, 119 S Ct 1816.]

§ 37. Pensions and retirement funds

It was held that two amendments by an employer to an employee retirement plan—to provide for an early retirement program and a noncontributory benefit structure—did not violate the Employee Retirement Income Security Act of 1974 (ERISA) (29 USCS §§ 1001 et seq.). [Hughes Aircraft Co. v Jacobson (1999, US) 142 L Ed 2d 881, 119 S Ct 755.]

The Supreme Court held that (1) California's notice-prejudice rule—under which an insurer cannot avoid liability although the proof of claim is untimely, unless the insurer shows that it suffered actual prejudice from the delay—is a "law . . . which regulates insurance" and is therefore saved from pre-emption by the Employee Retirement Income Security Act of 1974 (ERISA) (29 USCS §§ 1001 et seq.); but (2) California's agency rule—deeming an employer administering a health plan to be the insurer's agent—does not occupy ground outside ERISA's pre-emption clause. [UNUM Life Ins. Co. of Am. v Ward (1999, US) 143 L Ed 2d 462, 119 S Ct 1380.]

§ 38. Prison litigation

The court held that § 803(d)(3) of the Prison Litigation Reform Act of 1995 (42 USCS § 1997e(d)(3)) limited attorneys' fees for postjudgment monitoring services performed in prisoner suits after the Act's effective date, but did not limit such fees for monitoring performed before that date. [Martin v Hadix (1999, US) 144 L Ed 2d 347, 119 S Ct 1998.]

§ 39. Public schools

It was held, with respect to the Individuals with Disabilities Education Act (IDEA) (20 USCS §§ 1400 et seq.)—which authorized federal financial assistance to states that agreed to provide special education and related services to children with disabilities—that the definition of "related services" in an IDEA provision (20 USCS § 1401(a)(17)) required a public school district to provide a ventilator-dependent student with the continuous one-on-one nursing services that the student needed during school hours in order to remain in school. [Cedar Rapids Community Sch. Dist. v Garret F. by Charlene F. (1999, US) 143 L Ed 2d 154.]

See Davis v Monroe County Bd. of Educ. (1999, US) 143 L Ed 2d 839, 119 S Ct 1661, infra § 46, in which it was held that a private action, under Title IX of the Education Amendments of 1972 (20 USCS §§ 1681 et seq.), may lie against a public school board for sex discrimination where the board acted with deliberate indifference to acts of student-on-student sexual harassment which were so severe, pervasive, and objectively offensive as to effectively bar the harassment victim's access to an educational benefit or activity.

§ 40. Racketeer Influenced and Corrupt Organizations Act (RICO)

The Supreme Court held that because the Racketeer Influenced and Corrupt Organizations Act (RICO) (18 USCS §§ 1961 et seq.) advanced Nevada's interest in combating insurance fraud and did not frustrate any articulated state policy or disturb the state's administrative regime, recourse by insurance beneficiaries in Nevada to RICO was not blocked by § 2(b) of the McCarran-Ferguson Act (15 USCS § 1012(b)). [Humana Inc. v Forsyth (1999, US) 142 L Ed 2d 753, 119 S Ct 710.]

§ 41. Removal of state case

The court held that under 28 USCS § 1446(b), a named defendant's time to remove a case from state court to federal court is triggered by simultaneous service of the summons and complaint—or by receipt of the complaint, through service or otherwise, after and apart from service of the summons—and not by mere receipt of the complaint unattended by any formal service. [Murphy Bros., Inc. v Michetti Pipe Stringing, Inc. (1999, US) 143 L Ed 2d 448, 119 S Ct 1322.]

It was held that in cases removed from a state court to a federal court, as in cases originating in a federal court, there is no unyielding jurisdictional hierarchy that would always require the federal court to resolve doubts about subject matter jurisdiction before inquiring about personal jurisdiction. [Ruhrgas AG v Marathon Oil Co. (1999, US) 143 L Ed 2d 760, 119 S Ct 1563.]

§ 42. Review by Supreme Court

The Supreme Court—after having been advised that an accused had died a few days earlier—vacated an order granting a writ of certiorari and dismissed the accused's petition for certiorari to review a Federal Court of Appeals' decision in a criminal case. [Mosley v United States (1998, US) 142 L Ed 2d 500, 119 S Ct 484.]

As to in forma pauperis proceedings in the Supreme Court, see § 30, supra.

§ 43. Search and seizure—generally

With respect to police observation of apartment visitors' drug transaction, it was held that because some persons had no legitimate expectation of privacy in another's apartment used for a purely business transaction, any search that may have occurred there did not violate the persons' rights under the Federal Constitution's Fourth Amendment. [Minnesota v Carter (1998, US) 142 L Ed 2d 373, 119 S Ct 469.]

The Supreme Court held that police officers, when seizing property for a criminal investigation, are not required by the due process clause of the Federal Constitution's Fourteenth Amendment to provide the owner with notice of state-law remedies for the return of property lawfully seized but no longer needed for a police investigation or criminal prosecution. [City of W. Covina v Perkins (1999, US) 142 L Ed 2d 636, 119 S Ct 678.]

It was held that (1) a "media ride-along"—in which a print reporter and a photographer accompanied federal and county police officers during an attempt to execute arrest warrants in a private home—violated the Federal Constitution's Fourth Amendment, but (2) the officers were entitled to qualified immunity from damages liability, under the rule of Bivens v Six Unknown Named Agents of Federal Bureau of Narcotics (1971) 403 US 388, 29 L Ed 2d 619, 91 S Ct 1999, because the state of the law was not clearly established at the time that the entry of the home took place. [Wilson v Layne (1999, US) 143 L Ed 2d 818, 119 S Ct 1692.]

The court held that (1) a complaint—asserting that members of the news media had accompanied federal officials during a 1993 execution of a search warrant at a ranch—alleged a violation of the Federal Constitution's Fourth Amendment, under the Supreme Court's decision in Wilson v Layne, supra, but (2) the officials were entitled to qualified immunity from damages liability under the rule of Bivens v Six Unknown Named Agents of Federal Bureau of Narcotics, supra. [Hanlon v Berger (1999, US) 143 L Ed 2d 978, 119 S Ct 1706.]

§ 44. —Automobile

The full search of an automobile, as authorized by Iowa law, by a police officer who stopped the automobile's driver for speeding and issued the driver a citation—rather than arresting the driver, as also authorized by state law—was held to violate the Federal Constitution's Fourth Amendment, where the officer conceded that the officer had neither the driver's consent nor probable cause to search the automobile. [Knowles v Iowa (1998, US) 142 L Ed 2d 492, 119 S Ct 484.]

The Supreme Court held that police officers with probable cause to conduct a warrantless search of a car for contraband did not violate the Federal Constitution's Fourth Amendment by searching a passenger's personal belongings in the car that were capable of concealing contraband. [Wyoming v Houghton (1999, US) 143 L Ed 2d 408, 119 S Ct 1297.]

The court held that the Federal Constitution's Fourth Amendment does not require police to obtain a warrant before seizing an automobile from a public place, where the police have probable cause to believe that the automobile is forfeitable contraband. [Florida v White (1999, US) 143 L Ed 2d 748, 119 S Ct 1555.]

It was held that the automobile exception to the search warrant requirement of the Federal Constitution's Fourth Amendment does not require a separate finding of exigency in addition to a probable cause finding. [Maryland v Dyson (1999, US) 144 L Ed 2d 442, 119 S Ct 2013.]

§ 45. Self-incrimination

The court held that under the Federal Constitution's Fifth Amendment (1) a guilty plea in a federal case does not act as a waiver of an accused's right to invoke the privilege against self-incrimination in the sentencing phase, and (2) a federal trial judge may not draw an adverse inference from the accused's silence in determining facts about the crime that bear on the severity of the sentence. [Mitchell v United States (1999, US) 143 L Ed 2d 424, 119 S Ct 1307.]

§ 46. Sex discrimination

The Supreme Court held that the fact that the National Collegiate Athletic Association (NCAA) received dues from federally funded member institutions did not suffice to subject the NCAA to suit under Title IX of the Education Amendments of 1972 (20 USCS §§ 1681 et seq.), where 20 USCS § 1681(a) proscribes sex discrimination in "any education program or activity receiving Federal financial assistance." [NCAA v Smith (1999, US) 142 L Ed 2d 929, 119 S Ct 924.]

It was held that a private action, under Title IX of the Education Amendments of 1972 (20 USCS §§ 1681 et seq.), may lie against a public school board for sex discrimination where the board acted with deliberate indifference to acts of student-on-student sexual harassment which were so severe, pervasive, and objectively offensive as to effectively bar the harassment victim's access to an educational benefit or activity. [Davis v Monroe County Bd. of Educ. (1999, US) 143 L Ed 2d 839, 119 S Ct 1661.]

§ 47. States' sovereign immunity

With respect to a patent infringement suit against a Florida state entity, the Supreme Court held that the abrogation of the states' sovereign immunity in the Patent and Plant Variety Protection Remedy Clarification Act (35 USCS §§ 271(h), 296(a)) was invalid, as such abrogation could not be sustained as legislation enacted to enforce the guarantees of the due process clause of the Federal Constitution's Fourteenth Amendment. [Florida Prepaid Postsecondary Educ. Expense Bd. v College Sav. Bank (1999, US) 144 L Ed 2d 575, 119 S Ct 2199.]

The Supreme Court held that the federal courts had no jurisdiction over a suit brought under § 43(a) of the Lanham Act (15 USCS § 1125(a)) against a Florida state entity which allegedly made misstatements about the entity's tuition savings plans in brochures and annual reports, as Florida's sovereign immunity was neither (1) validly abrogated by the Trademark Remedy Clarification Act (106 Stat 3567), nor (2) voluntarily waived by Florida's activities in interstate commerce. [College Sav. Bank v Florida Prepaid Postsecondary Educ. Expense Bd. (1999, US) 144 L Ed 2d 605, 119 S Ct 2219.]

The court held that (1) Congress' powers under the Federal Constitution's Article I do not include the power to subject nonconsenting states to private suits for damages in state courts; and (2) Maine did not waive sovereign immunity with regard to state court actions filed under the Fair Labor Standards Act of 1938 (29 USCS §§ 201 et seq.). [Alden v Maine (1999, US) 144 L Ed 2d 636, 119 S Ct 2240.]

§ 48. State taxes

It was held that absent a constitutional immunity or congressional exemption, a state was allowed to impose a nondiscriminatory transaction privilege tax on a private company's proceeds from contracts with the Federal Government, regardless of whether the contractor rendered its services on an Indian reservation. [Arizona Dep't of Revenue v Blaze Constr. Co. (1999, US) 143 L Ed 2d 27, 119 S Ct 957.]

The Supreme Court (1) held that an Alabama franchise tax discriminated against interstate commerce in violation of the Federal Constitution's commerce clause (Art I, § 8, cl 3), and (2) rejected Alabama's claims of res judicata or collateral estoppel. [South Cent. Bell Tel. Co. v Alabama (1999, US) 143 L Ed 2d 258, 119 S Ct 1180.]

§ 49. Telecommunications

The court held that (1) the Federal Communications Commission (FCC) had jurisdiction to implement the local-competition provisions of the Telecommunica-

tions Act of 1996 (47 USCS §§ 251 et seq.), and (2) the
FCC's implementing rules were, with one exception,
consistent with the Act. [AT&T Corp. v Iowa Utils. Bd.
(1999, US) 142 L Ed 2d 834, 119 S Ct 721.]

§ 50. Uncompensated taking

The Supreme Court held that a Federal District
Court did not err, under the Federal Constitution's
Seventh Amendment, in submitting to a jury the question of liability on an individual's claim, under 42 USCS
§ 1983, that a city's denial of his development proposal
was an uncompensated taking in violation of the takings clause of the Constitution's Fifth Amendment.
[City of Monterey v Del Monte Dunes, Ltd. (1999, US)
143 L Ed 2d 882, 119 S Ct 1624.]

§ 51. Welfare benefits

It was held that (1) California's durational residency
requirement—which limited a family that had resided
in California for less than 12 months to the welfare
benefit level paid by the family's state of former
residence—violated the right to travel guaranteed by
§ 1 of the Federal Constitution's Fourteenth Amendment; and (2) the requirement's constitutionality was
not resuscitated by a change in federal welfare law
(codified at 42 USCS § 604(c)) that approved durational residency requirements. [Saenz v Roe (1999, US)
143 L Ed 2d 689, 119 S Ct 1518.]

§ 52. Workers' compensation

The Supreme Court held that that (1) a decision by
a private insurer, pursuant to Pennsylvania's workers'
compensation statute, to withhold payment and seek
"utilization review" of the reasonableness and necessity
of a particular medical treatment for an employee's
work-related injury did not satisfy the state-action re-

quirement for finding a violation of the due process clause of the Federal Constitution's Fourteenth Amendment; and (2) the state's workers' compensation law did not confer upon employees a protected property interest, under the due process clause, in the payment of medical benefits for the employees' work-related injuries. [American Mfrs. Mut. Ins. Co. v Sullivan (1999, US) 143 L Ed 2d 130, 119 S Ct 977.]

SUMMARIES OF DECISIONS

NAOMI MARQUEZ, Petitioner

v

SCREEN ACTORS GUILD, INC., et al.

525 US 23, 142 L Ed 2d 242, 119 S Ct 292

[No. 97-1056]

Argued October 5, 1998.
Decided November 3, 1998.

Decision: Union held not to have breached duty of fair representation by negotiating union security clause that tracked language of § 8(a)(3) of National Labor Relations Act (29 USCS § 158(a)(3)) without including judicial interpretations.

SUMMARY

Section 8(a)(3) of the National Labor Relations Act (NLRA) (29 USCS § 158(a)(3)) permits unions and employers to negotiate a union security clause that requires union "membership" as a condition of employment for all employees "on or after the thirtieth day following the beginning of such employment." The United States Supreme Court has (1) interpreted a proviso to this language to mean that the only "membership" that a union can require is the payment of fees and dues; and (2) held that unions are allowed to collect and expend funds over the objection of nonmembers only to the extent that such funds are used for collective bargaining, contract administration, and grievance adjustment activities. A union and an entertainment production company signed a collective bargaining agreement that contained a standard union security clause which—in generally tracking the language of § 8(a)(3)—contained a term that interpreted the 30-day grace period provision to begin running with any employment in the motion picture industry. An actress who successfully auditioned for a role in an episode of a television series produced by the company understood from a company representative that pursuant to the security clause, the actress would be required to pay the union fees before she could begin work, because the actress had previously worked in the motion picture industry for more than 30 days. The actress attempted to negotiate an agreement with the union that would have allowed her to pay the union fees after she was paid for her work by the company. When these negotiations failed and the actress had not paid the fees by the day before her part was to be filmed, the company hired a different person to fill the part. In a suit filed against the company and the union in the United States District Court for the Western District of Washington, the actress alleged, among other matters, that (1) the union had breached the duty of fair representation by negotiating and enforcing a union security clause which did not contain language informing her of her right not to join the union and to pay for only the union's representational activities; and (2) the clause's grace period provision contravened the express language of § 8(a)(3). The District Court, in granting summary judgment to the company and the union on all claims, concluded that (1) the union had not breached the duty of fair representation by negotiating the union security clause, and (2) the challenge to the grace period provision was actually an unfair labor practice claim and was thus pre-empted by the exclusive jurisdiction of the National Labor Relations Board (NLRB) (1996 US Dist LEXIS 12602). The United States Court of Appeals for the Ninth Circuit, in affirming in part and reversing in part, (1) agreed that (a) the union had not breached the duty of fair representation by negotiating a union security clause that tracked the NLRA language, and (b) the challenge to the grace period provision was not a fair representation claim and thus did not fall within the District Court's jurisdiction; but (2) reversed the grant of summary judgment—and remanded the case for further proceedings—on the claim that the union had arbitrarily or in bad faith breached the duty of fair representation in the enforcement of the collective bargaining agreement (124 F3d 1034, 1997 US App LEXIS 22796). The Supreme Court granted certiorari to review the issues of the clause's facial validity and the NLRB's primary jurisdiction.

On certiorari, the Supreme Court affirmed. In an opinion by O'CONNOR, J., expressing the unanimous view of the court, it was held that (1) the union had not breached the duty of fair representation merely by negotiating the union security clause, as (a) it was not argued that the union's negotiation of the clause was discriminatory, (b) negotiation of such a clause was not arbitrary, and (c) the union's conduct in negotiating the clause was not in bad faith; and (2) the challenge to the grace period provision fell within the NLRB's primary jurisdiction, rather than federal court jurisdiction, for (a) the challenge was at base merely a claim that the union's conduct violated § 8(a)(3), and (b) this claim was not collateral to any independent basis for federal court jurisdiction.

KENNEDY, J., joined by THOMAS, J., concurring, expressed the view that the Supreme Court's opinion (1) reflected only the conclusion that the negotiation of a security clause containing the statutory language as to union membership did not necessarily, or in all circumstances, violate the duty of fair representation; and (2) was not inconsistent with the Court of Appeals' ruling that remand was necessary as to the question whether the union had misinformed the actress as to her membership obligations.

COUNSEL

Raymond J. LaJeunesse argued the cause for petitioner.

Leo Geffner argued the cause for respondents.

WAYNE K. PFAFF, Petitioner

v

WELLS ELECTRONICS, INC.

525 US 55, 142 L Ed 2d 261, 119 S Ct 304

[No. 97-1130]

Argued October 6, 1998.
Decided November 10, 1998.

Decision: Patent on computer chip socket held invalid
under "on sale" bar in 35 USCS § 102(b), where
invention was ready for patenting when inventor
accepted purchase order for sockets more than 1
year before he applied for patent, even though
invention had not yet been reduced to practice.

SUMMARY

Under a provision in § 102(b) of the Patent Act of
1952 (35 USCS § 102(b)), no person is entitled to
patent an invention that has been "on sale" more than
1 year before filing a patent application. In response to
a request from a manufacturer, an inventor commenced work on a computer chip socket. Prior to April
8, 1981, the inventor (1) provided the manufacturer
with detailed drawings, and (2) accepted a purchase
order from the manufacturer for 30,100 sockets at a
total price of about $91,000. However, the manufac-
turer took some time to develop the necessary tooling,
and the inventor did not fill the order until July 1981.
On April 19, 1982, the inventor filed a patent application for his socket. The patent was issued in 1985. Later,
the inventor brought, in the United States District
Court for the Northern District of Texas, a patent

infringement action against a competitor. Eventually, the District Court (1) concluded that (a) four of the inventor's patent claims were valid, and (b) three of these claims were infringed by various of the competitor's models; and (2) in adopting a special master's findings, rejected—on the basis that the inventor had filed his application less than 1 year after reducing his invention to practice—the competitor's defense under § 102(b)'s on-sale bar (1995 US Dist LEXIS 21747; 1995 US Dist LEXIS 21748). On appeal, the United States Court of Appeals for the Federal Circuit, in reversing in pertinent part, expressed the view that (1) as long as an invention is substantially complete at the time of sale, the 1-year period of § 102(b) begins to run, even though the invention has not yet been reduced to practice; and (2) under this test, four patent claims, which described the sockets sold through the purchase order, were invalid (124 F3d 1429, 1997 US App LEXIS 23562).

On certiorari, the United States Supreme Court affirmed. In an opinion by STEVENS, J., expressing the unanimous view of the court, it was held that (1) the on-sale bar in § 102(b) applies when two conditions are satisfied before the "critical date"—that is, the date 1 year prior to a patent application's filing—(a) the product must be the subject of a commercial offer for sale, and (b) the invention must be ready for patenting, a condition which may be satisfied in at least two ways, by (i) proof of reduction to practice before the critical date, or (ii) proof that prior to the critical date, the inventor prepared drawings or other descriptions of the invention that were sufficiently specific to enable a person skilled in the art to practice the invention; and (2) under this test, the inventor's patent was invalid, in that the invention was complete and ready for patenting when the inventor accepted the manufacturer's purchase order prior to April 8, 1981, as the drawings sent to the manufacturer fully disclosed the invention, even though the invention had not yet been reduced to practice.

COUNSEL

Jerry R. Selinger argued the cause for petitioner.

C. Randall Bain argued the cause for respondent.

Jeffrey P. Minear argued the cause for the United States, as amicus curiae, by special leave of court.

_____

CEASAR WRIGHT, Petitioner

v

UNIVERSAL MARITIME SERVICE CORPORATION
et al.

525 US 70, 142 L Ed 2d 361, 119 S Ct 391

[No. 97-889]

Argued October 7, 1998.
Decided November 16, 1998.

Decision: General arbitration clause in collective bargaining agreement held not to require longshore worker to use arbitration procedure for alleged violation of Americans with Disabilities Act of 1990 (42 USCS §§ 12101 et seq.).

SUMMARY

A longshore worker in South Carolina was subject to a collective bargaining agreement which (1) provided for arbitration of matters "under dispute"; (2) stated that the agreement was intended to cover all matters affecting wages, hours, and other terms and conditions of employment; and (3) declared that the intention and purpose of all parties was that no provision or part of the agreement would be violative of any federal or state law. In addition, the worker was subject to a seniority plan containing a grievance provision under which plan-related disputes were to be settled by labor and management representatives. After an injury in 1992, the worker sought compensation for permanent disability under the Longshore and Harbor Workers' Compensation Act (33 USCS §§ 901 et seq.) and ultimately settled the claim. With a doctor's approval, the
8

worker briefly returned to work for several stevedoring companies in 1995, but when the companies realized that the worker had previously settled a claim for permanent disability, the companies informed the worker's union that the worker would not be accepted for employment, on the ground that a person certified as permanently disabled was not qualified to perform longshore work under the collective bargaining agreement. The worker, rather than filing a grievance pursuant to the agreement, ultimately filed suit in the United States District Court for the District of South Carolina against a stevedoring companies' association and six individual companies. In the suit, the worker alleging that the companies and the association had violated the Americans with Disabilities Act of 1990 (ADA) (42 USCS §§ 12101 et seq.) by refusing the worker employment. The District Court, adopting a magistrate judge's report and recommendation, dismissed the case without prejudice on the ground that the worker had failed to pursue the grievance procedure provided by the collective bargaining agreement. The District Court subsequently rejected the worker's motion for reconsideration. The United States Court of Appeals for the Fourth Circuit affirmed (121 F3d 702, 1997 US App LEXIS 40568, reported in full at 1997 US App LEXIS 19299).

On certiorari, the United States Supreme Court vacated the Court of Appeals' judgment and remanded the case for further proceedings. In an opinion by SCALIA, J., expressing the unanimous view of the court, it was held that (1) the collective bargaining agreement's arbitration clause did not require the worker to use the arbitration procedure for the alleged ADA violation, as (a) the asserted cause of action was not subject to a presumption of arbitrability, and (b) the agreement did not contain a clear and unmistakable waiver of the covered employees' rights to a judicial forum for federal claims of employment discrimination; and (2) the employee seniority plan did not constitute such a waiver.

COUNSEL

Ray P. McClain argued the cause for petitioner.

Barbara D. Underwood argued the cause for the United States, as amicus curiae, by special leave of court.

Charles A. Edwards argued the cause for respondents.

MINNESOTA, Petitioner

v

THOMAS CARTER

MINNESOTA, Petitioner

v

MELVIN JOHNS

525 US 83, 142 L Ed 2d 373, 119 S Ct 469

[No. 97-1147]

Argued October 6, 1998.
Decided December 1, 1998.

Decision: With respect to police observation of apartment visitors' drug transaction, any search which might have occurred held not to violate visitors' Fourth Amendment rights, where visitors had no legitimate expectation of privacy in apartment.

SUMMARY

Two visitors came to a third person's apartment for the sole purpose of packaging cocaine. The visitors had never been to the apartment before and remained there for approximately $2^1/2$ hours. A police officer, investigating a tip from a confidential informant, looked into a window in the apartment through a gap in a closed blind and observed the visitors and the third person putting cocaine into bags. The visitors, who were ultimately arrested on drug charges and tried in a Minnesota trial court, sought to suppress all evidence obtained from the apartment, on the ground that the officer's initial observation of the visitors' activities was an unreasonable search in violation of the Federal

11

Constitution's Fourth Amendment. The trial court, in denying the visitors' motions to suppress, concluded that (1) the visitors had not been overnight social guests in the apartment and were thus not entitled to claim Fourth Amendment protection, and (2) the officer's observation was not a search within the meaning of the Fourth Amendment. The Court of Appeals of Minnesota affirmed the visitors' convictions (545 NW2d 695, 1996 Minn App LEXIS 401; 1996 Minn App LEXIS 685). The Supreme Court of Minnesota, in reversing, expressed the view that (1) the visitors had "standing" to claim Fourth Amendment protection because they had a legitimate expectation of privacy in the apartment, and (2) the observation constituted an unreasonable search of the apartment under the Fourth Amendment (569 NW2d 169, 1997 Minn LEXIS 691; 569 NW2d 180, 1997 Minn LEXIS 690).

On certiorari, the United States Supreme Court reversed and remanded. In an opinion by REHNQUIST, Ch. J., joined by O'CONNOR, SCALIA, KENNEDY, and THOMAS, JJ., it was held that any search which might have occurred did not violate the visitors' Fourth Amendment rights, for the visitors had no legitimate expectation of privacy in the apartment, as (1) the visitors were not overnight guests, but were in the apartment for only a matter of hours; (2) the visitors' transaction in the apartment was purely commercial in nature; (3) there was no suggestion that (a) the visitors had had a previous relationship with the apartment's occupant, or (b) there was any other purpose to the visit; (4) there was nothing similar to an overnight guest relationship to suggest a degree of acceptance of the visitors into the household; and (5) the visitors' situation was therefore closer to that of one who was simply permitted on the premises.

12

SCALIA, J., joined by THOMAS, J., concurring, expressed the view that (1) the meaning of the Fourth Amendment is that each person has the right to be secure against unreasonable searches and seizures in his own person, house, papers, and effects; and (2) although it was plausible to regard a person's overnight lodging as the person's temporary residence, it was impossible to give that characterization to an apartment used by the person to package cocaine.

KENNEDY, J., concurring, expressed the view that (1) almost all social guests have a legitimate expectation of privacy—and hence Fourth Amendment protection against unreasonable searches—in their host's home; but (2) such a rule was not applicable in the case at hand, as the visitors had established no meaningful tie or connection to the apartment, the apartment's owner, or the owner's expectation of privacy.

BREYER, J., concurring in the judgment, expressed the view that (1) the visitors could properly claim the Fourth Amendment's protection; but (2) the police officer's observation, made from a public area outside the curtilage of the residence, did not violate the visitors' Fourth Amendment rights.

GINSBURG, J., joined by STEVENS and SOUTER, JJ., dissenting, expressed the view that (1) when the owner or lessor of a home personally invites a guest into the home to share in a common endeavor, such as business purposes licit or illicit, that guest ought to share the host's Fourth Amendment shelter against unreasonable searches and seizures; and (2) the facts of the case at hand demonstrated that (a) the host had intended to share privacy with the visitors, and (b) the visitors had therefore entered into Fourth Amendment protection.

COUNSEL

James C. Backstrom argued the cause for petitioner.
Jeffrey A. Lamken argued the cause for the United States, as amicus curiae, by special leave of court.
Bradford Colbert argued the cause for respondents.

PATRICK KNOWLES, Petitioner

v

IOWA

525 US 113, 142 L Ed 2d 492, 119 S Ct 484

[No. 97-7597]

Argued November 3, 1998.
Decided December 8, 1998.

Decision: Full search of automobile, as authorized by
Iowa law, by police officer who issued speeding
citation—rather than making arrest, as authorized
by Iowa law—held to violate Federal Constitution's
Fourth Amendment.

SUMMARY

Iowa statutes, in addition to authorizing police officers to issue a citation to a person who violates a traffic
or motor vehicle equipment law, authorize police officers to arrest such a person. An Iowa police officer
stopped an automobile driver for speeding, issued the
driver a citation rather than arresting him, and, with
neither the driver's consent nor probable cause to
search the automobile, conducted a full automobile
search that revealed a bag of marijuana and a "pot
pipe." Before being tried in a state court for violating
state laws dealing with controlled substances, the driver,
arguing that the search violated the Federal Constitution's Fourth Amendment because the search was not
incident to an arrest, moved to suppress the evidence
obtained in the search. The trial court—on the basis of
the fact that an Iowa statutory provision that the
issuance of a citation in lieu of arrest "does not affect

the officer's authority to conduct an otherwise lawful search" had been interpreted by the Supreme Court of Iowa in prior cases as authorizing a full search of an automobile and driver incident to citation—denied the motion and found the driver guilty. The Supreme Court of Iowa affirmed the conviction (569 NW 2d 601).

On certiorari, the United States Supreme Court reversed and remanded. In an opinion by REHNQUIST, Ch. J., expressing the unanimous view of the court, it was held that the search of the automobile, authorized as it was by state law, nonetheless violated the Fourth Amendment, because neither of the two historical rationales for the authority to search incident to arrest—the need to disarm the suspect in order to take the suspect into custody, and the need to preserve evidence for later use at trial—was sufficient to justify the search in question, as (1) the threat to officer safety from issuing a traffic citation is a good deal less than in the case of a custodial arrest, (2) officers have bases other than authority for a full search incident to citation to search for weapons and protect themselves from danger, and (3) once the driver was stopped for speeding and was issued a citation, all the evidence necessary to prosecute that offense had been obtained.

COUNSEL

Paul Rosenberg argued the cause for petitioner.

Bridget A. Chambers argued the cause for respondent.

SYLVESTER MOSLEY, Petitioner

v

UNITED STATES

525 US 120, 142 L Ed 2d 500, 119 S Ct 484

[No. 97-7213]

Argued October 14, 1998.
Decided December 8, 1998.

Decision: Order granting writ of certiorari to review
decision against accused in criminal case vacated,
and accused's petition for certiorari dismissed,
where accused died after grant of certiorari.

SUMMARY

An accused was (1) convicted, in the United States
District Court for the District of New Jersey, on two
federal counts of bank robbery, and (2) sentenced to a
period of imprisonment followed by supervised release.
On appeal, the United States Court of Appeals for the
Third Circuit, in upholding the accused's conviction
and sentence, and in rejecting the accused's challenge
to the jury instructions, expressed the view that bank
larceny in violation of 18 USCS § 2113(b) is not a lesser
included offense of bank robbery in violation of 18
USCS § 2113(a) (126 F3d 200, 1997 US App LEXIS
25235). After the United States Supreme Court granted
the accused's petition for a writ of certiorari (523 US
——, 140 L Ed 2d 465, 118 S Ct 1298), and after the
case was argued before the Supreme Court, the accused
died.

The Supreme Court, in a per curiam opinion expressing the unanimous view of the court, (1) noted

that it had been advised that the accused had died a few days earlier, (2) vacated the order granting certiorari, and (3) dismissed the petition for certiorari.

COUNSEL

Donald J. McCauley argued the cause for petitioner. David C. Frederick argued the cause for respondent.

———————

MICHAEL A. HADDLE, Petitioner

v

JEANETTE G. GARRISON et al.

525 US 121, 142 L Ed 2d 502, 119 S Ct 489

[No. 97-1472]

Argued November 10, 1998.
Decided December 14, 1998.

Decision: Allegations as to termination of at-will employment held to state claim for damages under 42 USCS § 1985(2), where employer's officers allegedly conspired to bring about termination in order to intimidate and retaliate against employee.

SUMMARY

According to the allegations of a corporation's former at-will employee, (1) a federal grand jury indictment charged the corporation and two corporate officers with Medicare fraud; (2) the employee (a) cooperated with federal agents in the investigation that preceded the indictment, (b) appeared before the grand jury pursuant to a subpoena, and (c) was expected to appear as a witness in the criminal trial resulting from the indictment; (3) the two officers, although barred by a court from participating in the affairs of the corporation, conspired with one of the remaining officers to bring about the employee's termination in order to (a) intimidate the employee, and (b) retaliate against him for his attendance at the federal court proceedings. The employee—bringing a suit for damages in the United States District Court for the Southern District of Georgia—asserted, among other matters, a claim under 42 USCS § 1985(2), which provides, in pertinent part, for civil liability with respect to conspiracies to injure a party or witness "in his person or property" on account of that person's having attended or testified in a court of the United States. The District Court granted a motion to dismiss for failure to state a claim upon which relief could be granted, on the ground that (1) a terminated employee had to have suffered an actual injury in order to make out a cause of action under § 1985(2), and (2) an at-will employee had no constitutionally protected interest in continued employment. The United States Court of Appeals for the Eleventh Circuit affirmed in a decision without a published opinion (132 F3d 46, 1997 US App LEXIS 37603).

On certiorari, the United States Supreme Court reversed the Court of Appeals' judgment and remanded the case for further proceedings. In an opinion by REHNQUIST, Ch. J., expressing the unanimous view of the court, it was held that the harm alleged by the employee stated a claim for relief under § 1985(2), for (1) the fact that at-will employment was not a protected property interest for purposes of federal constitutional due process did not mean that loss of at-will employment might not injure the employee "in his person or property" for purposes of § 1985(2); and (2) there was no reason to ignore the tradition under which such harm, which was essentially third-party interference with at-will employment relationships, was a compensable injury under tort law.

COUNSEL

Charles C. Stebbins, III argued the cause for petitioner.

Matthew D. Roberts argued the cause for the United States, as amicus curiae, by special leave of court.

Phillip A. Bradley argued the cause for respondents.

———————

NYNEX CORPORATION, et al., Petitioners

v

DISCON, INCORPORATED

525 US 128, 142 L Ed 2d 510, 119 S Ct 493

[No. 96-1570]

Argued October 5, 1998.
Decided December 14, 1998.

Decision: Rule that group boycotts are per se violations
of § 1 of Sherman Act (15 USCS § 1) held not to
apply to single buyer's decision, not justifiable in
terms of ordinary competitive objectives, to buy
from one supplier rather than another.

SUMMARY

A local telephone company that had been buying
obsolete telephone equipment removal services from a
particular supplier switched its purchases of such services to a more expensive competitor of the supplier.
The supplier then brought against the company an
action alleging that the company's decision, not justifiable in terms of ordinary competitive objectives, to
switch to the competitor were unfair, improper, and
anticompetitive. After a Federal District Court dismissed the supplier's complaint for failure to state a
claim, the United States Court of Appeals for the
Second Circuit, affirming the dismissal with an exception (93 F3d 1055), determined that (1) the supplier
had alleged a cause of action under the rule of reason
and may have alleged a cause of action under the rule,
set forth in Klor's, Inc. v Broadway-Hale Stores, Inc.
(1959) 359 US 207, 3 L Ed 2d 741, 79 S Ct 705, that

group boycotts are per se violations of § 1 of the Sherman Act (15 USCS § 1), and (2) the supplier's complaint stated a valid claim of conspiracy to monopolize under the Act's § 2 (15 USCS § 2).

On certiorari, the United States Supreme Court vacated the Court of Appeals judgment and remanded the case for further proceedings. In an opinion by BREYER, J., expressing the unanimous view of the court, it was held that the rule that group boycotts are per se violations of § 1 did not apply to the telephone company's decision to buy removal services from the supplier's competitor, and thus the supplier had to allege and prove harm not just to itself, but to the competitive process, where (1) precedent limited the per se rule in the boycott context to cases involving horizontal agreements among direct competitors, (2) the instant case involved only a vertical agreement and a vertical restraint that deprived the supplier of a potential customer, and (3) the supplier's simple allegation of harm to itself did not automatically show injury to competition.

COUNSEL

James R. Young argued the cause for petitioners.

Lawrence G. Wallace argued the cause for the United States, as amicus curiae, by special leave of court.

Lawrence C. Brown argued the cause for respondent.

ARTHUR CALDERON, Warden, Petitioner

v

RUSSELL COLEMAN

525 US 141, 142 L Ed 2d 521, 119 S Ct 500

[No. 98-437]

Decided December 14, 1998.

Decision: Federal Court of Appeals held to have erred by failing to apply required harmless-error analysis, when court ruled that accused, who was under California death sentence, was entitled to habeas corpus relief based on claimed error in capital sentencing instruction.

SUMMARY

In Brecht v Abrahamson (1993) 507 US 619, 123 L Ed 2d 353, 113 S Ct 1710, the United States Supreme Court held that a federal court may grant habeas corpus relief on the basis of a state criminal trial error only when the error had a substantial and injurious effect or influence in determining the jury's verdict. An accused was convicted in a California court on charges including murder. The jury's findings made the accused eligible under state law for the death penalty. In the penalty phase, the accused was sentenced to death after the trial court's instructions to the jury included (1) a commutation instruction, which informed the jury of the governor's power to commute a sentence of life imprisonment without possibility of parole; and (2) an additional instruction, which told the jury that it was not to consider the governor's commutation power in reaching a verdict. On direct review, the California

Supreme Court, in upholding the death sentence, expressed the view that (1) the giving of the commutation instruction was error under state law, but (2) in view of the additional instruction, the error was not prejudicial (46 Cal 3d 749, 759 P2d 1260, 1988 Cal LEXIS 209). The accused then sought habeas corpus relief in the United States District Court for the Northern District of California. The District Court, in granting a writ of habeas corpus, expressed the view that (1) the commutation instruction's failure to mention a state-law limit on the governor's commutation power violated the Federal Constitution's Eighth and Fourteenth Amendments by giving the jury inaccurate information and potentially diverting the jury's attention from the mitigation evidence presented; and (2) in the context of the case, the instruction would likely have prevented the jury from giving due effect to the accused's mitigation evidence. On appeal, the United States Court of Appeals for the Ninth Circuit, in affirming, (1) agreed that the commutation instruction was unconstitutional; and (2) expressed the view that this error was not harmless under Brecht v Abrahamson, for when an inaccurate instruction undermined the jury's understanding of sentencing options, there was a reasonable likelihood that the jury had applied the challenged instruction in a way that prevented the consideration of constitutionally relevant evidence (150 F3d 1105, 1998 US App LEXIS 17074).

The United States Supreme Court granted a motion by the respondent accused for leave to proceed in forma pauperis, granted a warden's petition for a writ of certiorari, reversed the Court of Appeals' judgment, and remanded the case for further proceedings. In a per curiam opinion expressing the view of REHNQUIST, Ch. J., and O'CONNOR, SCALIA, KENNEDY, and THOMAS, JJ., it was held that even if it were assumed that the commutation instruction did not meet constitutional standards, the Court of Appeals had erred by failing to apply the harmless-error analysis required by Brecht v Abrahamson, as the reasonable-likelihood test which the Court of Appeals had applied was not a harmless-error test at all, but rather, the test for determining, in the first instance, whether constitutional error had occurred.

STEVENS, J., joined by SOUTER, GINSBURG, and BREYER, JJ., dissenting, expressed the view that (1) while there might have been a slight flaw in the Court of Appeals' brief explanation as to why the invalid commutation instruction was not harmless, the Court of Appeals' ruling was correct; and (2) whatever the shortcomings of the Court of Appeals' review, they were not so great as to warrant an expenditure of the Supreme Court's time and resources by granting certiorari.

IN RE MICHAEL KENNEDY, Petitioner

525 US 153, 142 L Ed 2d 573, 119 S Ct 635

[No. 98-6945]

Decided January 11, 1999.

Decision: Person who had been denied leave to proceed in forma pauperis on previous petition, denied such leave as to petition for extraordinary writ; order entered barring person's future in forma pauperis filings of petitions for certiorari or extraordinary writs.

SUMMARY

An individual sought leave to proceed in forma pauperis in the United States Supreme Court under Supreme Court Rule 39 with respect to an extraordinary writ. The individual had filed, in the Supreme Court, 11 previous petitions for either certiorari or extraordinary writs, including a petition with respect to which the court, earlier during the current term, had denied the person leave to proceed in forma pauperis by invoking Supreme Court Rule 39.8, which authorizes the court to deny such leave with respect to frivolous petitions. All of the previous petitions had been deemed frivolous by the court and had been denied without recorded dissent.

In a per curiam opinion expressing the view of REHNQUIST, Ch. J., and O'CONNOR, SCALIA, KENNEDY, SOUTER, THOMAS, GINSBURG, and BREYER, JJ., the Supreme Court (1) indicating that the instant petition was frivolous, invoked Rule 39.8 to denied the individual's request for leave to proceed in forma pauperis on the instant petition, and (2) directed the Clerk of the Supreme Court not to accept any further petitions for certiorari or for extraordinary writs in noncriminal matters from the individual unless he complied with Supreme Court Rules 33.1 and 38.

STEVENS, J., dissented for the reasons expressed in a previous Supreme Court case involving some similar issues.

EL AL ISRAEL AIRLINES, LTD., Petitioner

v

TSUI YUAN TSENG

525 US 155, 142 L Ed 2d 576, 119 S Ct 662

[No. 97-475]

Argued November 10, 1998.
Decided January 12, 1999.

Decision: Warsaw Convention held to preclude passenger from maintaining action for personal injury damages under local law (such as case's New York tort law) when claim did not satisfy Convention's conditions for carrier's liability for international air transportation.

SUMMARY

With respect to international air transportation, Article 17 of the Warsaw Convention (49 Stat 3000 et seq., later amended) provided that a carrier would be liable for damage sustained in the event of the death or wounding of a passenger or any other "bodily injury" suffered by a passenger, if the "accident" which caused the damage so sustained took place on board the aircraft or in the course of any of the operations of embarking or disembarking. In addition, Article 24 of the Convention, prior to its amendment by Montreal Protocol No. 4 (effective in the United States March 4, 1999), provided that "cases covered by article 17" could "only be brought subject to the conditions and limits set out in this [C]onvention." However, Article 25 of the Convention, prior to its amendment by Montreal Protocol No. 4, rendered the Convention's limits on liability inapplicable if the damage was caused by the carrier's "willful misconduct." In 1993, a passenger was subjected to an intrusive security search at an airport in New York state before she boarded an air carrier's flight to Israel. The passenger (1) filed suit against the carrier in a New York state court; (2) included a personal injury claim for damages based on the search episode; (3) pleaded matters such as assault and false imprisonment; and (4) alleged only psychic or psychosomatic injuries (the passenger later testified, for example, that she had been emotionally traumatized and disturbed after the search). The carrier removed the case to the United States District Court for the Southern District of New York, which in pertinent part dismissed the personal injury claim, as the District Court expressed the view that (1) the claim was not compensable under Article 17, for (a) the passenger had sustained no bodily injury during the search, (b) the Convention did not permit recovery for psychic or psychosomatic injury unaccompanied by bodily injury, and (c) there was an absence of willful misconduct within the meaning of Article 25; and (2) the passenger could not pursue her claim under state law, for Article 24 shielded the carrier from liability for personal injuries not compensable under Article 17 (919 F Supp 155, 1996 US Dist LEXIS 3060). On appeal, the United States Court of Appeals for the Second Circuit, in reversing in pertinent part and in ordering a remand, expressed the view that (1) the carrier could not be held liable under Article 17 on the personal injury claim, as there had been no accident and the passenger had not suffered bodily injury; but (2) the Convention did not preclude the passenger from pursuing her claim under state law, for Article 24 precluded resort to local law only where the incident was covered by Article 17 in the sense that there had been an accident, either on the plane or in the course of embarking or disembarking, that led to bodily injury (122 F3d 99, 1997 US App LEXIS 14870).

On certiorari, the United States Supreme Court reversed. In an opinion by O'CONNOR, J., joined by REHNQUIST, Ch. J., and SCALIA, KENNEDY, SOUTER, THOMAS, GINSBURG, and BREYER, JJ., it was held that (1) with respect to international air transportation not involving willful misconduct within the meaning of Article 25, the Convention precluded a passenger from maintaining an action against a carrier for personal injury damages under local law (such as the case at hand's New York tort law) when the passenger's claim did not satisfy the Convention's conditions for liability for a personal injury suffered on board an aircraft or in the course of any of the operations of embarking or disembarking, as among other matters, the revision of Article 24 by Montreal Protocol No. 4 merely clarified, and did not alter, the Convention's rule of exclusivity; (2) even if the Supreme Court accepted for the purpose of deciding the case at hand that no accident had occurred within the meaning of Article 17, the core question concerning the Convention's exclusivity remained, for (a) the passenger could not gain compensation under Article 17 for her solely psychic or psychosomatic injuries, and (b) the question whether the Convention precluded an action under local law when a passenger's claim failed to satisfy Article 17's conditions for liability did not turn on which of those conditions—concerning accident and bodily injury—the claim failed to satisfy; and (3) the passenger had not preserved any argument putting Article 25 at issue in the Supreme Court.

STEVENS, J., dissenting, expressed the view that prior to the Convention's amendment by Montreal Protocol No. 4, the Convention, in cases not involving willful misconduct within the meaning of Article 25, (1) pre-empted a victim's remedies under local law for claims concerning all personal injuries—whether physical or psychological—that arose out of an accident within the meaning of Article 17; but (2) did not pre-empt a victim's remedies under local law for claims of personal injury that did not arise out of such an accident.

COUNSEL

Diane W. Wilson argued the cause for petitioner.

Jonathan E. Nuechtherlein argued the cause for the United States, as amicus curiae, by special leave of court.

Robert H. Silk argued the cause for respondent.

VICTORIA BUCKLEY, Secretary of State of Colorado,
Petitioner

v

AMERICAN CONSTITUTIONAL LAW FOUNDA-
TION, INC., et al.

525 US 182, 142 L Ed 2d 599, 119 S Ct 636

[No. 97-930]

Argued October 14, 1998.
Decided January 12, 1999.

Decision: Colorado statutory provisions requiring initiative petition circulators to be registered voters
and wear name badges—and requiring initiative
proponents to make various reports about
circulators—held to violate First Amendment.

SUMMARY

A public interest organization that supported direct
democracy—joined by several individual participants in
Colorado's process under which citizens were allowed
to make laws directly through initiatives placed on
election ballots—brought suit in the United States
District Court for the District of Colorado against
Colorado's secretary of state to challenge some of the
state's statutory provisions governing the ballot-
initiative process. Under some of these challenged
provisions, which were alleged to violate the freedom of
speech guarantee of the Federal Constitution's First
Amendment, (1) a circulator of an initiative petition
was required to (a) be a registered voter, and (b) wear
an identification badge bearing the circulator's name
while soliciting signatures; and (2) proponents of an

33

initiative were required to report the names and addresses of all paid circulators and the amount paid to each circulator. After a bench trial, the District Court—among other matters—upheld the registration requirement but struck down the name badge requirement and portions of the disclosure requirements (870 F Supp 995, 1994 US Dist LEXIS 17134). The United States Court of Appeals for the Tenth Circuit, in affirming in part and reversing in part, concluded that the registration and name badge requirements, as well as the requirements to report the names and addresses of all paid circulators and the amount paid to each circulator, invalidly infringed on circulators' First Amendment rights (120 F3d 1092, 1997 US App LEXIS 20902).

On certiorari, the United States Supreme Court affirmed. In an opinion by GINSBURG, J., joined by STEVENS, SCALIA, KENNEDY, and SOUTER, JJ., it was held that each of the requirements at issue was invalid under the First Amendment as significantly inhibiting political speech without being warranted by alleged state interests, in that (1) the registration requirement imposed a speech burden—limiting (a) the number of voices to convey the initiative proponents' message, and (b) the size of the proponents' audience—that was not justified by the state's interest in policing lawbreakers among petition circulators by insuring that circulators were amenable to subpoena; (2) the name badge requirement (a) discouraged participation in the petition circulation process, and (b) was not needed to enable the identification and apprehension of petition circulators who engaged in misconduct; and (3) the reporting requirements at issue (a) forced paid circulators to surrender the anonymity enjoyed by volunteer circulators, and (b) were no more than tenuously related to the state's substantial interests in preventing fraud and informing the public concerning the financial resources available to initiative proponents.

THOMAS, J., concurring in the judgment, expressed the view that (1) each of the requirements at issue violated the Constitution's First and Fourteenth Amendments, (2) the proper standard to apply in evaluating the requirements was strict scrutiny, and (3) the Supreme Court's opinion had applied different reasoning.

O'CONNOR, J., joined by BREYER, J., concurring in the judgment in part and dissenting in part, expressed the view that (1) the Supreme Court had correctly held that the name badge requirement ought to be subject to—and failed—strict scrutiny, but (2) the registration and disclosure requirements ought to have been upheld as reasonable regulations of the electoral process.

REHNQUIST, Ch. J., dissenting, (1) expressed the view that (a) the registration and disclosure requirements did not violate the First Amendment, and (b) the Supreme Court's holding threatened to invalidate many historically established state regulations of the electoral process in general; but (2) agreed that the name badge requirement was unconstitutional.

COUNSEL

Gale Norton argued the cause for petitioner.
Neil D. O'Toole argued the cause for respondents.

CITY OF WEST COVINA, Petitioner

v

LAWRENCE PERKINS et al.

525 US 234, 142 L Ed 2d 636, 119 S Ct 678

[No. 97-1230]

Argued November 3, 1998.
Decided January 13, 1999.

Decision: Due process clause of Federal Constitution's Fourteenth Amendment held not to require notice to property owners of state law remedies for return of property lawfully seized but no longer needed for police investigation or criminal prosecution.

SUMMARY

In conducting a homicide investigation concerning a suspect who had been a boarder in a family's home, police officers of a California city, acting in accordance with the law and pursuant to a valid search warrant, searched the home when only the officers were present and seized personal property that belonged to the family. The officers left at the home a form specifying the fact of the search, the date of the search, the searching agency, the date of the warrant, the name and court of the judge who issued the warrant, the names of the persons to be contacted for further information, and an itemized list of the seized property. After failed attempts to obtain return of the property, which was no longer needed for police investigation or criminal prosecution, the family filed in a United States District Court a suit seeking the return of the property from the city. Eventually, the District Court, rejecting the family's assertion that the city had not given them adequate notice of the state law remedy for return of their property and the information needed to invoke the remedy, granted summary judgment for the city. On appeal, the United States Court of Appeals for the Ninth Circuit, reversing the grant of summary judgment, expressed the view that the due process clause of the Federal Constitution's Fourteenth Amendment required that the family be provided with (1) detailed notice of state procedures for the return of seized property, and (2) the information—including the search warrant number or a method for obtaining the number—necessary to invoke those procedures (113 F3d 1004).

On certiorari, the United States Supreme Court reversed and remanded. In an opinion by KENNEDY, J., joined by REHNQUIST, Ch. J., and STEVENS, O'CONNOR, SOUTER, GINSBURG, and BREYER, JJ., it was held that the Fourteenth Amendment's due process clause did not require notice of state law remedies for the return of the property seized by the city police officers, because (1) state law remedies, like those in the case at hand, were established by published and generally available state statutes and case law, (2) such a notice requirement lacked support in Supreme Court precedent, and (3) neither the Federal Government nor any state required their law enforcement officers to provide individualized notice of the procedures for seeking return of seized property.

THOMAS, J., joined by SCALIA, J., concurring in the judgment, (1) agreed that the Fourteenth Amendment's due process clause did not compel the city to provide the family with detailed notice of state law postdeprivation remedies, but (2) expressed the view that if the Constitution imposed a notice requirement on officers executing a search warrant, it did so because the failure to provide such notice rendered an otherwise lawful search unreasonable under the Constitution's Fourth Amendment.

COUNSEL

David D. Lawrence argued the cause for petitioner.

Jeffrey S. Sutton argued the cause for Ohio, et al., as amicus curiae, by special leave of court.

Patrick S. Smith argued the cause for respondents.

———————

JANE M. ROBERTS, Guardian for WANDA Y.
JOHNSON, Petitioner

v

GALEN OF VIRGINIA, INC., Formerly dba HU-
MANA HOSPITAL–UNIVERSITY OF LOUISVILLE,
dba UNIVERSITY OF LOUISVILLE HOSPITAL

525 US 249, 142 L Ed 2d 648, 119 S Ct 685

[No. 97-53]

Argued December 1, 1998.
Decided January 13, 1999.

Decision: Recovery for violation of Emergency Medical
Treatment and Active Labor Act provision (42
USCS § 1395dd(b)) held not to require proof that
hospital acted with improper motive in failing to
stabilize patient.

SUMMARY

An Emergency Medical Treatment and Active Labor
Act (EMTALA) provision (42 USCS § 1395dd(b)) requires a hospital or emergency room that receives a
patient who is suffering from an emergency medical
condition to stabilize the patient's condition before
transferring the patient to another medical facility.
After a patient who was taken to a hospital after being
run over by a truck was transferred to another facility,
allegedly before her medical condition was stabilized,
the patient's guardian filed against the hospital in a
Federal District Court under 42 USCS § 1395dd(d) an
action alleging that the hospital had violated
§ 1395dd(b). The District Court granted summary
judgment for the hospital. The United States Court of

Appeals for the Sixth Circuit, affirming the District Court judgment, expressed the view that in order to state a claim in an EMTALA suit alleging a violation of § 1395dd(b)'s stabilization requirement, a patient had to show that the hospital's inappropriate stabilization had resulted from an improper motive such as one involving the indigency, race, or sex of the patient (111 F3d 405).

On certiorari, the United States Supreme Court reversed and remanded. In a per curiam opinion expressing the unanimous view of the court, it was held that § 1395dd(b) contained no express or implied "improper motive" requirement, as (1) the text of § 1395dd(b) could not reasonably be read to require an improper motive, and (2) this fact was conceded by the hospital, which had noted in its brief that the "motive" test lacked support in any of the traditional sources of statutory construction.

COUNSEL

Joseph H. Mattingly, III argued the cause for petitioner.

James A. Feldman argued the cause for the United States, as amicus curiae, by special leave of court.

Carter G. Phillips argued the cause for respondent.

DEPARTMENT OF THE ARMY, Petitioner

v

BLUE FOX, INC.

525 US 255, 142 L Ed 2d 718, 119 S Ct 687

[No. 97-1642]

Argued December 1, 1998.
Decided January 20, 1999.

Decision: Section 10(a) of Administrative Procedure
Act (5 USCS § 702) held not to waive Federal
Government's sovereign immunity from subcontractor's claim for "equitable lien" on certain
funds allegedly held by Army with respect to Army
project.

SUMMARY

As a waiver of the sovereign immunity of the Federal
Government and its agencies from suit, § 10(a) of the
Administrative Procedure Act (APA) (5 USCS § 702)
authorizes federal judicial review of federal agency
action when an aggrieved party is seeking relief "other
than money damages." While the Miller Act (40 USCS
§§ 270a et seq.) provides that contractors for some
federal projects must post bonds that can protect
subcontractors, the United States Department of the
Army ultimately required no Miller Act bonds from the
prime contractor for an Army project to install a
telephone switching system at an Army depot in Oregon. A subcontractor on the project performed its
obligations to the prime contractor, but was not paid in
full by the prime contractor. After the Army had
disbursed some money to the prime contractor, the

41

Army terminated its contract with the prime contractor for various alleged defaults. The project was completed by a replacement contractor. Meanwhile, the subcontractor obtained a default judgment against the original prime contractor in an Indian tribal court. As the subcontractor asserted that it might not be able to collect from the original prime contractor or its officers, the subcontractor (1) filed suit in the United States District Court for the District of Oregon against defendants including the Army; (2) sought relief including (a) an "equitable lien" on certain funds allegedly held by the Army with respect to the project, and (b) an order directing the payment of these funds to the subcontractor; and (3) predicated jurisdiction on provisions including § 10(a). However, the District Court, in granting summary judgment against the subcontractor, expressed the view in pertinent part that (1) the APA's waiver of sovereign immunity did not extend to the subcontractor's equitable lien claim against the Army, and (2) thus, the District Court did not have jurisdiction over the claim (1996 US Dist LEXIS 8264). On appeal, the United States Court of Appeals for the Ninth Circuit, in reversing in pertinent part and in ordering a remand, expressed the view that the APA had waived the Army's immunity from the equitable lien claim (121 F3d 1357, 1997 US App LEXIS 22631).

On certiorari, the United States Supreme Court reversed and remanded. In an opinion by REHNQUIST, Ch. J., expressing the unanimous view of the court, it was held that § 10(a) did not waive the sovereign immunity of the Federal Government and its agencies from the equitable lien claim, because § 10(a) did not nullify the long-settled rule that sovereign immunity barred creditors from enforcing liens on Federal Government property, as among other matters, the sort of equitable lien sought by the subcontractor constituted

42

a claim for money damages that fell outside § 10(a)'s waiver of sovereign immunity, where the lien's goal was to seize or attach money in the hands of the government as compensation for the loss resulting from the default of the original prime contractor.

COUNSEL

Jeffrey Lamken argued the cause for petitioner.

Thomas F. Spaulding argued the cause for respondent.

VICKY M. LOPEZ, et al., Appellants

v

MONTEREY COUNTY et al.

525 US 266, 142 L Ed 2d 728, 119 S Ct 693

[No. 97-1396]

Argued November 2, 1998.
Decided January 20, 1999.

Decision: California county that was covered jurisdiction for purposes of § 5 of Voting Rights Act (42 USCS § 1973c) held obligated to seek federal preclearance under § 5 before giving effect to voting scheme changes mandated by noncovered state.

SUMMARY

In 1971, a California county was designated as a covered jurisdiction for purposes of § 5 of the Voting Rights Act of 1965 (42 USCS § 1973c), which requires a covered jurisdiction to obtain federal preclearance whenever the jurisdiction seeks to administer any departure from the voting scheme in place on November 1, 1968. Between 1972 and 1983, the county enacted a series of ordinances that consolidated the county's nine court districts into one countywide district served by judges whom county residents were to elect at large. In 1991, some Hispanic voters, alleging that the county had failed to fulfill a § 5 obligation to preclear these voting changes, filed suit in the United States District Court for the Northern District of California. The District Court ultimately (1) ruled that the county had to conduct an at-large countywide judicial election in

1996, and (2) enjoined future elections pending pre-clearance of a permanent plan (871 F Supp 1254). On appeal, the United States Supreme Court reversed the District Court's judgment and remanded the case for further proceedings, on the ground the District Court had erred in ordering the county to conduct the election under a plan that had not received federal approval pursuant to § 5 (519 US 9, 136 L Ed 2d 273, 117 S Ct 340). On remand, the District Court, in dismissing the complaint, accepted the argument—which the Supreme Court had declined to address—that (1) California had passed state legisla-tion requiring the very voting changes that had been challenged by the voters; and (2) the county did not have to seek federal preclearance before giving effect to these changes, as (a) California itself was not a covered jurisdiction under § 5, and (b) the county was merely implementing a California law without exercising any independent discretion.

On appeal, the Supreme Court reversed the District Court's judgment and remanded the case for further proceedings. In an opinion by O'CONNOR, J., joined by STEVENS, SCALIA, SOUTER, GINSBURG, and BREYER, JJ., it was held that (1) for purposes of § 5, a covered jurisdiction that is a state's political subdivision seeks to administer a voting change even where the jurisdiction exercises no discretion in giving effect to a change mandated by a noncovered state; (2) Congress has authority under the Federal Constitution's Fifteenth Amendment to require preclearance in such circum-stances; and (3) the county was thus obligated to seek preclearance under § 5 before giving effect to voting changes required by California law.

KENNEDY, J., joined by REHNQUIST, Ch. J., concurring in the judgment, expressed the view that (1) it was unnecessary for the Supreme Court to decide whether

45

§ 5's preclearance requirement applied to a covered county's nondiscretionary efforts to implement a voting change required by the law of a noncovered state, and (2) in the case at hand, the county was required to seek preclearance, because the state enactments requiring the voting changes at issue embodied the policy preferences and determinations of the county itself.

THOMAS, J., dissenting, expressed the view that (1) § 5 ought to have been read to require preclearance only of those voting changes that were the direct product of a covered jurisdiction's policy choices; and (2) in the case at hand, it was doubtful whether § 5 could be extended—consistent with the Constitution—to require preclearance of California's enactments.

COUNSEL

Joaquin G. Avila argued the cause for appellants.

Paul R. Q. Wolfson argued the cause for the United States, as amicus curiae, by special leave of court.

Daniel G. Stone argued the cause for appellees.

HUMANA INC., et al., Petitioners

v

MARY FORSYTH et al.

525 US 299, 142 L Ed 2d 753, 119 S Ct 710

[No. 97-303]

Argued November 30, 1998.
Decided January 20, 1999.

Decision: Insurance beneficiaries' recourse to RICO
(18 USCS §§ 1961 et seq.) held not blocked by
McCarran-Ferguson Act's § 2(b) (15 USCS
§ 1012(b)), as RICO's application did not impair
Nevada's insurance laws.

SUMMARY

The McCarran-Ferguson Act's § 2(b) (15 USCS
§ 1012(b)) provides that no federal statute shall be
construed to invalidate, impair, or supersede any state
law enacted for the purpose of regulating the business
of insurance, unless the federal statute specifically
relates to the business of insurance. Beneficiaries of
group health insurance policies issued by an insurer in
Nevada (1) brought an action against the insurer and a
hospital, and (2) included allegations that the insurer
and the hospital had engaged in a scheme—to gain
discounts for hospital services which the insurer did not
disclose and pass on to the beneficiaries—that violated,
through a pattern of fraudulent racketeering activity,
the Racketeer Influenced and Corrupt Organizations
Act (RICO) (18 USCS §§ 1961 et seq.), which provided
a private right of action and permitted treble damages
in 18 USCS § 1964(c). Nevada's insurance laws, among

other matters, provided a private right of action and permitted compensatory and punitive damages. The United States District Court for the District of Nevada, granting summary judgment for the insurer and the hospital, expressed the view that § 2(b) precluded application of RICO to the beneficiaries' complaint (827 F Supp 1498). The United States Court of Appeals for the Ninth Circuit, reversing in relevant part the District Court judgment, expressed the view that § 2(b) did not preclude application of RICO to the beneficiaries' complaint (114 F3d 1467).

On certiorari, the United States Supreme Court affirmed. In an opinion by GINSBURG, J., expressing the unanimous view of the court, it was held that § 2(b) did not preclude RICO's application to the alleged conduct of the insurer and the hospital, because even though RICO did not specifically relate to the business of insurance, (1) under the standard definitions of "invalidate" and "supersede," RICO's application to the beneficiaries' complaint would neither invalidate nor supersede Nevada law; and (2) RICO, in proscribing the same conduct as, but providing materially different remedies from, Nevada law, did not impair Nevada law under § 2(b), as RICO (a) advanced Nevada's interest in combating insurance fraud, and (b) did not frustrate any articulated Nevada policy or interfere with any Nevada administrative regime.

COUNSEL

James W. Colbert, III argued the cause for petitioners.

G. Robert Blakey argued the cause for respondents.

Lawrence G. Wallace argued the cause for the United States, as amicus curiae, by special leave of court.

———————

DEPARTMENT OF COMMERCE, et al., Appellants

v

UNITED STATES HOUSE OF REPRESENTATIVES et
al. (No. 98-404)

———

WILLIAM JEFFERSON CLINTON, President of the
United States, et al., Appellants

v

MATTHEW GLAVIN et al. (No. 98-564)

525 US 316, 142 L Ed 2d 797, 119 S Ct 765

[Nos. 98-404 and 98-564]

Argued November 30, 1998.
Decided January 25, 1999.

Decision: With respect to year 2000 decennial census,
Census Act (13 USCS §§ 1 et seq.) held to prohibit
two proposed uses of statistical sampling in calculating population for purposes of congressional
apportionment.

SUMMARY

The Federal Constitution's census clause (in Art I,
§ 2, cl 3) provides for the United States House of
Representatives to be apportioned among the states
according to an "actual Enumeration" of the population that is to be made every 10 years "in such Manner"
as Congress shall direct. Pursuant to the census clause,
Congress has enacted the Census Act (13 USCS §§ 1 et
seq.), which, as amended, (1) in 13 USCS § 141(a),
authorizes the Secretary of Commerce to "take a

decennial census of population . . . in such form and
content as [the Secretary] may determine, including
the use of sampling procedures and special surveys";
(2) in 13 USCS § 141(g), specifies that the term
"census of population," as used in § 141, "means a
census of population, housing, and matters relating to
population and housing"; and (3) in 13 USCS § 195,
provides that "[e]xcept for the determination of population for purposes of apportionment of Representatives in Congress among the several States, the Secretary shall, if [the Secretary] considers it feasible,
authorize the use of the statistical method known as
'sampling' in carrying out the provisions of" the Census Act. The proposals of the United States Census
Bureau—part of the Department of Commerce—for
use in the year 2000 decennial census included (1) a
form of statistical sampling in the Bureau's Nonre-
sponse Followup program (NRFU), in that (a) only 90
per cent of the housing units in a census tract would be
counted through individuals' responses to forms sent
by the Bureau or through Bureau followup visits, and
(b) a statistical technique would be employed to esti-
mate the characteristics of the remaining 10 per cent;
and (2) a second form of sampling that (a) was known
as Integrated Coverage Management (ICM), and (b)
would employ a statistical technique to adjust the
census results to account for "undercount" in the
initial enumeration. Two cases arose which involved
challenges, under the census clause and the Census
Act, to these two proposed uses of sampling. In the first
case, which began as a suit filed by four counties and
residents of 13 states against defendants including the
Department and the Bureau, the United States District
Court for the Eastern District of Virginia (1) held that
(a) the plaintiffs satisfied the standing requirements of
Article III of the Constitution, and (b) the Census Act

prohibited the two proposed uses of sampling to apportion Representatives; (2) denied a defense motion to
dismiss; (3) granted a motion by the plaintiffs for
summary judgment; and (4) permanently enjoined the
use of the challenged forms of sampling to determine
the population for purposes of congressional apportionment (19 F Supp 2d 543, 1998 US Dist LEXIS
15068). In the second case, which began as a suit by the
House against the Department and the Bureau, the
United States District Court for the District of Columbia (1) held that (a) the House had standing under
Article III, and (b) the Census Act did not permit the
proposed uses of sampling in counting the population
for apportionment; (2) declined to dismiss the case; (3)
granted a motion by the House for summary judgment;
and (4) issued an injunction preventing the Department and the Bureau from using the challenged forms
of sampling in the apportionment aspect of the 2000
census (11 F Supp 2d 76, 1998 US Dist LEXIS 13133).

On direct appeal, the United States Supreme
Court—having consolidated the two cases—affirmed
the judgment in the first case and dismissed the appeal
in the second case. In those portions of the opinion of
O'CONNOR, J., that constituted the opinion of the court
and were joined by REHNQUIST, Ch. J., and SCALIA,
KENNEDY, and THOMAS, JJ., and joined in part (as to
holding 1 below) by BREYER, J., it was held that (1) the
record supported the conclusion that several of the first
case's plaintiffs-appellees had met their burden of
proof regarding their Article III standing to bring the
suit, with respect to (a) a plaintiff-appellee who was a
resident of Indiana, which was expected to lose a House
seat under the Bureau's census plan, and (b) some
other plaintiffs-appellees, on the basis of the expected
effects of the proposed uses of sampling on intrastate
redistricting; (2) with respect to the year 2000 decen-

nial census, the Census Act prohibited the two proposed uses of sampling in calculating the population for purposes of congressional apportionment, as § 141(a)'s broad grant of sampling authority was informed by the narrower, more specific, and direct prohibition in § 195; (3) because of this conclusion, it was unnecessary to reach the constitutional question presented under the census clause; and (4) as the decision concerning the first case resolved the substantive issues presented in the second case, the second case no longer presented a substantial federal question. Also, O'CONNOR, J., in a portion joined by REHNQUIST, Ch. J., and KENNEDY, J., expressed the view that the statutory conclusion in holding 2 above found support in the debates and discussions surrounding Congress' 1976 revisions to the Census Act.

SCALIA, J., joined by THOMAS, J., and joined in part (as to point 2 below) by REHNQUIST, Ch. J., and KENNEDY, J., concurring in part, expressed the view that (1) he did not join the resort, by the opinion of O'CONNOR, J., to what was said, or not said, by individual legislators or committees of legislators; and (2) the statutory conclusion in holding 2 above was supported by (a) some additional arguments concerning textual interpretation, and (b) the doctrine of avoiding constitutional doubt with respect to the validity, under the census clause's requirement for an actual enumeration, of using statistical sampling techniques in an apportionment census.

BREYER, J., concurring in part and dissenting in part, (1) joined (a) the Supreme Court's holding 1 above, and (b) points 2 and 3 below of the dissent of STEVENS, J.; and (2) expressed the view that the Secretary's plan for the 2000 census was not barred by the Census Act, in that (a) as to ICM, § 195 did not bar the proposed use of sampling to supplement traditional enumeration methods, and (b) as to NRFU, the proposed use of sampling approached, but did not exceed, the limit of the Secretary's broad discretionary authority under § 141(a).

STEVENS, J., dissenting, expressed the view (1) joined by SOUTER and Ginsburg, JJ., that under the Census Act, as amended, § 141(a) granted the Secretary an unlimited authorization—which was not qualified by the limited mandate in § 195—to use sampling procedures when taking a decennial census, the census used to apportion the House; (2) joined by SOUTER, GINSBURG, and BREYER, JJ., that the census clause's reference to an actual enumeration did not preclude the use of sampling procedures to supplement data obtained through more traditional census methods; and (3) joined by BREYER, J., that (a) the Supreme Court's discussion of standing was correct with respect to the first case, (b) in addition, the House had standing in the second case to challenge the validity of the process that would determine the size of each state's congressional delegation, and (c) accordingly, the judgments in both cases ought to be reversed on the merits.

GINSBURG, J., joined by SOUTER, J., dissenting, expressed the view that she (1) agreed with the Supreme Court's conclusion that the Indiana resident had standing in the first case, (2) would not decide whether other appellees in the first case had standing, (3) agreed with the Supreme Court's conclusion that the appeal in the second case ought to be dismissed, and (4) with respect to the merits, joined points 1 and 2 above of the dissent of STEVENS, J.

COUNSEL

Seth P. Waxman argued the cause for all appellants.

Maureen E. Mahoney argued the cause for appellees in No. 98-404.

Michael A. Carvin argued the cause for appellees in No. 98-564.

AT&T CORPORATION, et al., Petitioners

v

IOWA UTILITIES BOARD et al. (No. 97-826)

AT&T CORPORATION, et al., Petitioners

v

CALIFORNIA et al.

———

MCI TELECOMMUNICATIONS CORPORATION,
Petitioner

v

IOWA UTILITIES BOARD et al. (No. 97-829)

MCI TELECOMMUNICATIONS CORPORATION,
Petitioner

v

CALIFORNIA et al.

———

ASSOCIATION FOR LOCAL TELECOMMUNICA-
TIONS SERVICES, et al., Petitioners

v

IOWA UTILITIES BOARD et al. (No. 97-830)

———

FEDERAL COMMUNICATIONS COMMISSION and
UNITED STATES, Petitioners

v

IOWA UTILITIES BOARD et al. (No. 97-831)

FEDERAL COMMUNICATIONS COMMISSION and
UNITED STATES, Petitioners

v

CALIFORNIA et al.

———

AMERITECH CORPORATION, et al., Petitioners

v

FEDERAL COMMUNICATIONS COMMISSION et al.
(No. 97-1075)

GTE MIDWEST, INCORPORATED, Petitioner

v

FEDERAL COMMUNICATIONS COMMISSION et al.
(No. 97-1087)

U S WEST, INC., Petitioner

v

FEDERAL COMMUNICATIONS COMMISSION et al.
(No. 97-1099)

SOUTHERN NEW ENGLAND TELEPHONE COM-
PANY, et al., Petitioners

v

FEDERAL COMMUNICATIONS COMMISSION et al.
(No. 97-1141)

525 US 366, 142 L Ed 2d 834, 119 S Ct 721

[Nos. 97-826, 97-829, 97-830, 97-831, 97-1075, 97-
1087, 97-1099, and 97-1141]

Argued October 13, 1998.
Decided January 25, 1999.

Decision: Federal Communications Commission (FCC)
held authorized to implement local-competition
provisions of Telecommunications Act of 1996 (47

USCS §§ 251 et seq.); FCC's implementing rules, with one exception, held consistent with 1996 Act.

SUMMARY

Prior to Congress' enactment of the Telecommunications Act of 1996 (PL 104-104, 110 Stat 56), states typically granted an exclusive franchise in each local telephone market to a local exchange carrier (LEC), which owned the various forms of equipment that constituted a local exchange network. The 1996 Act ended such state-granted monopolies and subjected incumbent LECs to various duties—including the obligation under 47 USCS § 251(c) to share networks with competitors—that were intended to facilitate market entry. Under § 251(c), a requesting carrier was permitted to obtain access to an incumbent's network by various means, such as (1) leasing elements of the incumbent's network "on an unbundled basis," or (2) interconnecting the requesting carrier's own facilities with the incumbent's network. After the Federal Communications Commission (FCC) issued rules implementing the 1996 Act's local-competition provisions, several incumbent LECs and state commissions challenged some of these rules by filing petitions for review which were consolidated in the United States Court of Appeals for the Eighth Circuit. The Court of Appeals concluded, among other matters, that (1) the FCC lacked jurisdiction to promulgate rules regarding (a) pricing (47 CFR §§ 51.503 and 51.505), (b) state review of pre-existing interconnection agreements between incumbent LECs and other carriers (47 CFR § 51.303), and (c) rural exemptions (47 CFR § 51.405); (2) with respect to the FCC's primary "unbundling" rule (47 CFR § 51.319), the FCC—in specifying the network elements available to requesting carriers—reasonably implemented the requirement of 47 USCS § 251(d)(2) that the FCC consider whether access to proprietary elements was "necessary" and whether lack of access to nonproprietary elements would "impair" an entrant's ability to provide local service; (3) the FCC's rule forbidding incumbent LECs to separate already-combined network elements before leasing them to competitors (47 CFR § 51.315(b)) had to be vacated as requiring access to those elements on a bundled rather than an unbundled—that is, physically separated—basis; and (4) the FCC's "pick and choose" rule (47 CFR § 51.809)—enabling a competing LEC to demand access to any individual interconnection, service, or network element arrangement on the same terms and conditions that the incumbent LEC gave anyone else in an agreement approved pursuant to 47 USCS § 252, but not obligating the competing LEC to accept the agreement's other provisions—had to be vacated as deterring the "voluntarily negotiated agreements" that the 1996 Act favored (120 F3d 753, 1997 US App LEXIS 18183). In a separate opinion, the Court of Appeals concluded that the FCC lacked jurisdiction to promulgate rules regarding dialing parity, that is, an arrangement enabling a new entrant's customers to make calls without having to dial an access code (47 CFR §§ 51.205-51.215) (124 F3d 934, 1997 US App LEXIS 22343).

On certiorari, the United States Supreme Court (1) reversed the Court of Appeals' first judgment in part and affirmed that judgment in part, (2) reversed the second judgment in part, and (3) remanded the cases for further proceedings. In an opinion by SCALIA, J., joined by STEVENS, KENNEDY, and GINSBURG, JJ., joined in part (except for holding 5 below) by SOUTER, J., and joined in part (except for holdings 1 and 2 below) by

59

REHNQUIST, Ch. J., and THOMAS and BREYER, JJ., it was held that (1) the FCC had rule-making authority under a provision of the Communications Act of 1934 (1934 Act) (47 USCS § 201(b)) to carry out the 1996 Act's local-competition provisions (47 USCS §§ 251 et seq.); (2) the FCC had jurisdiction to promulgate the rules regarding pricing, state review of pre-existing interconnection agreements, rural exemptions, and dialing parity; (3) the rule forbidding incumbents to separate already-combined network elements before leasing them to competitors was a reasonable interpretation of 47 USCS § 251(c)(3); (4) the "pick and choose" rule was a reasonable interpretation of 47 USCS § 252(i); and (5) the primary unbundling rule was invalid, since the FCC, in giving requesting LECs blanket access to network elements, had not adequately considered the "necessary" and "impair" standards set by § 251(d)(2).

SOUTER, J., concurring in part and dissenting in part, (1) agreed that the FCC had authority to implement and interpret the disputed provisions of the 1996 Act, and (2) expressed the view that the primary unbundling rule was based on a reasonable interpretation of § 251(d)(2).

THOMAS, J., joined by REHNQUIST, Ch. J., and BREYER, J., concurring in part and dissenting in part, (1) agreed with the Supreme Court's analysis of the unbundling and "pick and choose" rules, but (2) expressed the view that the FCC lacked jurisdiction to promulgate the regulations challenged on jurisdictional grounds, as such regulations contravened the division of authority set forth in the 1996 Act and disregarded a longstanding tradition of state authority over intrastate telecommunications.

BREYER, J., concurring in part and dissenting in part, expressed the view that the 1996 Act did not permit the FCC to promulgate the pricing and unbundling rules at issue.

O'CONNOR, J., did not participate.

COUNSEL

Seth P. Waxman argued the cause for federal petitioners and federal cross-respondents/petitioners.

Bruce J. Ennis, Jr., argued the cause for private petitioners.

Diane Munns for argued the cause for state commission respondents.

Laurence H. Tribe argued the cause for private respondents.

William P. Barr argued the cause for cross-petitioners/respondents.

David W. Carpenter for argued the cause for private cross-respondents/petitioners.

HUGHES AIRCRAFT COMPANY, et al., Petitioners

v

STANLEY I. JACOBSON et al.

525 US 432, 142 L Ed 2d 881, 119 S Ct 755

[No. 97-1287]

Argued November 2, 1998.
Decided January 25, 1999.

Decision: Employer's amendments to employee retirement plan to provide for early retirement program and noncontributory benefit structure held not to violate ERISA (29 USCS §§ 1001 et seq.).

SUMMARY

According to the complaint in the case at hand, an employer's defined benefit retirement plan that was contributory—in that the plan required mandatory contributions from all participating employees in addition to any contributions made by the employer—required employer contributions to the extent necessary to fund plan benefits but allowed the employer to suspend its contributions so long as doing so did not create an accumulated funding deficiency in the plan under the Employee Retirement Income Security Act of 1974 (ERISA), as amended (29 USCS §§ 1001 et seq.). The employer, which had suspended its plan contributions in light of an accumulated plan surplus, made two amendments to the plan. The first amendment established an early retirement program that provided significant additional retirement benefits to certain eligible active employees, while the second amendment provided that new participants could not contribute to the plan and thereby would receive fewer benefits and that pre-existing participants could continue to contribute or opt to be treated as new participants. Five retired plan beneficiaries brought a class action alleging that the two plan amendments by the employer violated ERISA. After the United States District Court for the Central District of California granted the employer's motion to dismiss the complaint for failure to state a claim, the United States Court of Appeals for the Ninth Circuit, reversing the District Court judgment, expressed the view that the retirees had alleged several causes of action claiming that the employer had (1) violated the prohibition in § 203(a) of ERISA (29 USCS § 1053(a)) against using employees' vested nonforfeitable benefits to meet the employer's obligations, (2) violated the anti-inurement provision of § 403(c)(1) of ERISA (29 USCS § 1103(c)(1)), (3) violated the employer's fiduciary duties under §§ 404 and 406(a)(1)(D) of ERISA (29 USCS §§ 1104 and 1106(a)(1)(D)), and (4) terminated the plan and therefore violated the requirement in § 4044(d)(3)(A) of ERISA (29 USCS § 1344(d)(3)(A)) that residual assets in a terminated plan be distributed to plan beneficiaries (105 F3d 1288, amended, 128 F3d 1305).

On certiorari, the United States Supreme Court reversed. In an opinion by THOMAS, J., expressing the unanimous view of the court, it was held that the employer's amendments to the retirement plan did not violate ERISA, because (1) as to the vested-benefits and anti-inurement claims, (a) the employer's creation of a noncontributory benefit structure did not affect the rights of pre-existing plan participants, and (b) the employer did not use the plan surplus for its own benefit; (2) the fiduciary duty claims were directly foreclosed by the Supreme Court's holding in a prior case that, without exception, retirement plan sponsors

63

who alter the terms of a plan do not fall into the category of fiduciaries; and (3) the employer's creation of a noncontributory benefit structure did not work an effective termination of the plan.

COUNSEL

Paul T. Cappuccio argued the cause for petitioners.

Lisa S. Blatt argued the cause for the United States, as amicus curiae, by special leave of court.

Seth Kupferberg argued the cause for respondents.

YOUR HOME VISITING NURSE SERVICES, INC.,
Petitioner

v

DONNA E. SHALALA, Secretary of Health and Human Services

525 US 449, 142 L Ed 2d 919, 119 S Ct 930

[No. 97-1489]

Argued December 2, 1998.
Decided February 23, 1999.

Decision: Medicare Provider Reimbursement Review Board and federal courts held to lack jurisdiction to review fiscal intermediary's refusal to reopen its decision on amount of reimbursement to provider for covered health services.

SUMMARY

A Medicare provider which seeks reimbursement, under the Social Security Act's Title XVIII (Medicare Act) (42 USCS §§ 1395 et seq.) from the Secretary of Health and Human Services for covered health services to Medicare beneficiaries, submits a yearly cost report to a fiscal intermediary—which generally is a private insurance company—that, acting as the Secretary's agent, analyzes the cost report and issues a Notice of Program Reimbursement (NPR) determining the reimbursement amount to which the provider is entitled for the year. A provider that is dissatisfied with an intermediary's final determination of a reimbursement amount can (1) under a Medicare Act provision (42 USCS § 1395oo(a)(1)(A)(i)), appeal within 180 days to an administrative review panel, the Provider Reimbursement Review Board, whose decision is subject to review in a Federal District Court, or (2) under 42 CFR § 405.1885, request the intermediary, within 3 years, to reopen the reimbursement determination. A home care health services provider that, with respect to the NPR from its intermediary for the year 1989, had not sought Board review within 180 days, asked within 3 years that the intermediary reopen the 1989 reimbursement determination on the asserted ground that new and material evidence demonstrated entitlement to additional reimbursement. After the intermediary denied the request and the Board, asserting that § 405.1885 divested it of jurisdiction to review the denial, dismissed the provider's appeal to the Board, the provider brought, in a District Court, an action seeking review of the Board's dismissal and of the intermediary's refusal to reopen. The District Court, in dismissing the provider's complaint in an unpublished opinion, expressed the view that the Board lacked jurisdiction to review the refusal to reopen and that neither the federal-question statute (28 USCS § 1331) nor the mandamus statute (28 USCS § 1361) gave the District Court jurisdiction to review the intermediary's refusal directly. The United States Court of Appeals for the Sixth Circuit affirmed (132 F3d 1135).

On certiorari, the United States Supreme Court affirmed. In an opinion by SCALIA, J., expressing the unanimous view of the court, it was held that (1) the Board lacked jurisdiction to review a fiscal intermediary's refusal to reopen a reimbursement determination, as the Secretary's reading of § 1395oo(a)(1)(A)(i) as not including a refusal to reopen was (a) reasonable and hence entitled to deference, and (b) not inconsistent with 42 USCS § 1395x(v)(1)(A)(ii), which required the Secretary to provide for the making of suitable retroactive adjustments to reimbursement determinations; and (2) the provider was not entitled to judicial review of the intermediary's refusal to reopen, as (a) judicial review under § 1331 was precluded by 42 USCS § 405(h)'s prohibition of actions under § 1331 to recover on any claim arising under the Medicare Act, (b) even if it were assumed that mandamus was available under the Medicare Act, the provider had not shown the existence of the clear nondiscretionary duty that was required for mandamus relief, and (c) the absence of new evidence that had not been before the intermediary at the time of its decision sufficed to defeat the provider's suggestion that it be granted relief under the Administrative Procedure Act's judicial review provision (5 USCS § 706).

COUNSEL

Diana L. Gustin argued the cause for petitioner.
Lisa S. Blatt argued the cause for respondent.

NATIONAL COLLEGIATE ATHLETIC ASSOCIA-
TION, Petitioner

v

R. M. SMITH

525 US 459, 142 L Ed 2d 929, 119 S Ct 924

[No. 98-84]

Argued January 20, 1999.
Decided February 23, 1999.

Decision: Dues payments received from members that received federal funds held not to suffice to make National Collegiate Athletic Association subject to sex discrimination suit under Title IX of Education Amendments of 1972, as amended (20 USCS §§ 1681 et seq.).

SUMMARY

Under Title IX of the Education Amendments of 1972, as amended (20 USCS §§ 1681 et seq.), 20 USCS § 1681(a) proscribes sex discrimination in "any education program or activity receiving Federal financial assistance." An individual (1) brought suit in the United States District Court for the Western District of Pennsylvania against a private, unincorporated, and nationwide athletic association of public and private colleges and universities; and (2) included a Title IX claim alleging that the association—through refusing to waive, on behalf of the individual during her post-graduate years, a bylaw restricting postbaccalaureate participation in intercollegiate athletics—had discriminated against her on the basis of sex by denying her permission to play intercollegiate volleyball at federally assisted institutions. However, the District Court, in granting a defense motion to dismiss, expressed the view that (1) the individual's Title IX claim had to be dismissed because of her failure to allege that the association was a recipient of federal funds; and (2) even if it were assumed that the association received dues from member schools which received federal funds, the association's connections with federal funding would be "too far attenuated" to subject it to the mandates of Title IX (978 F Supp 213, 1997 US Dist LEXIS 12220). The District Court then denied a motion by the individual for leave to amend her complaint. On appeal, the United States Court of Appeals for the Third Circuit, in reversing the refusal to allow an amendment of the complaint and in ordering a remand, expressed the view that an allegation in the individual's proposed amended complaint—that the association received dues from member institutions which received federal funds—would be sufficient, if proven, to bring the association within the scope of Title IX as a recipient of federal funds (139 F3d 180, 1998 US App LEXIS 4694).

On certiorari, the United States Supreme Court vacated and remanded. In an opinion by GINSBURG, J., expressing the unanimous view of the court, it was held that dues payments received from members that received federal funds would not suffice, without more, to make the association subject to suit under Title IX, for (1) a United States Department of Education regulation (34 CFR § 106.2(h)) accorded with the teaching of the Supreme Court's precedents that (a) entities that received federal assistance, whether directly or through an intermediary, were recipients within the meaning of Title IX, but (b) entities that only benefited economically from federal assistance were not; and (2) at most, the association's receipt of dues demonstrated that the

69

association indirectly benefited from the federal assistance allegedly afforded to the association's members.

COUNSEL

John G. Roberts, Jr. argued the cause for petitioner.

Carter G. Phillips argued the cause for respondent.

Edwin S. Kneedler argued the cause for the United States, as amicus curiae, by special leave of court.

JANET RENO, Attorney General, et al., Petitioners

v

AMERICAN-ARAB ANTI-DISCRIMINATION COM-
MITTEE et al.

525 US 471, 142 L Ed 2d 940, 119 S Ct 936

[No. 97-1252]

Argued November 4, 1998.
Decided February 24, 1999.

Decision: Provision of Illegal Immigration Reform and
Immigrant Responsibility Act of 1996 (8 USCS
§ 1252(g)) held to deprive federal courts of jurisdiction over aliens' selective-enforcement claim as
deportation defense.

SUMMARY

The Immigration and Naturalization Service (INS)
sought to deport eight resident aliens who belonged to
a group that the Federal Government characterized as
an international terrorist and communist organization.
In 1987, the aliens filed suit in the United States District
Court for the Central District of California against the
United States Attorney General, the INS, and various
immigration officials, in which suit it was alleged,
among other matters, that the INS was selectively
enforcing immigration laws against the aliens in violation of the Federal Constitution's First and Fifth
Amendments. Ultimately, the District Court (1) preliminarily enjoined deportation proceedings against six
of the aliens, on the ground that these aliens were likely
to prove that (a) the INS had selectively enforced
routine status requirements against those aliens, and

71

(b) the possibility of deportation, combined with the chill to First Amendment rights while the proceedings were pending, constituted irreparable injury; and (2) granted judgment to the federal parties, on other grounds, with respect to the two other aliens (883 F Supp 1365, 1995 US Dist LEXIS 3294). The United States Court of Appeals for the Ninth Circuit affirmed the District Court's judgment as to the six aliens and reversed as to the two others (70 F3d 1045, 1995 US App LEXIS 31415). On remand, the District Court (1) denied the Attorney General's request that the injunction as to the six aliens be dissolved, and (2) entered an injunction in favor of the two others. While the Attorney General's appeal of this decision was pending, Congress passed the Illegal Immigration Reform and Immigrant Responsibility Act of 1996 (IIRIRA) which, among other matters, repealed the old judicial-review scheme set forth in 8 USCS § 1105a and instituted a more restrictive scheme in 8 USCS § 1252. The Attorney General, filing motions in both the District Court and the Court of Appeals, argued that § 1252(g)—which barred judicial review of the Attorney General's decision to commence proceedings, adjudicate cases, or execute removal orders against any alien under the IIRIRA "except as provided in this section"—deprived those courts of jurisdiction over the selective-enforcement claim. The District Court denied the motion, and the Attorney General's appeal from that denial was consolidated with the appeal already pending. The Court of Appeals affirmed the existence of jurisdiction under § 1252 and affirmed the District Court's judgment on the merits (119 F3d 1367, 1997 US App LEXIS 17744, reh, en banc, den 132 F3d 531, 1997 US App LEXIS 36154).

On certiorari, the Supreme Court vacated the Court of Appeals' judgment and remanded with instructions for the Court of Appeals to vacate the District Court's judgment. In an opinion by SCALIA, J., joined by REHNQUIST, Ch. J., and O'CONNOR, KENNEDY, and THOMAS, JJ., and joined in part (as to holding 1 below) by GINSBURG and BREYER, JJ., it was held that (1) § 1252(g) deprived the federal courts of jurisdiction over the aliens' claims of selective enforcement, as (a) such a challenge to the Attorney General's decision to "commence proceedings" against the aliens fell squarely within § 1252(g), and (b) nothing elsewhere in § 1252 provided for such jurisdiction; (2) the aliens had no right under the Constitution to assert such claims; and (3) the doctrine of constitutional doubt thus did not require § 1252(g) to be interpreted in such fashion as to permit immediate review of the aliens' selective-enforcement claims.

GINSBURG, J., joined in part (as to points 1 and 2 below) by BREYER, J., concurring in part and concurring in the judgment, expressed the view that (1) § 1252(g) applied to the case at hand and deprived the federal courts of jurisdiction over the aliens' suit prior to a final order of removal, and (2) the First Amendment did not necessitate immediate judicial consideration of the aliens' selective-enforcement plea, but (3) it was an open question whether a First Amendment selective-enforcement claim would be cognizable upon judicial review of a final order.

STEVENS, J., concurring in the judgment, expressed the view that a fair reading of all relevant provisions in the IIRIRA made it clear that Congress had intended that (1) pursuant to 8 USCS § 306(c)(1), the prohibition of § 1252(g) as to collateral attacks on ongoing INS proceedings became effective immediately, and (2) pursuant to 8 USCS § 309(c)(1), the judicial review that remained available with respect to INS proceedings that were pending before the IIRIRA's effective date was restricted to a challenge to a final order of deportation.

SOUTER, J., dissenting, expressed the view that (1) §§ 306(c)(1) and 309(c)(1) were mutually exclusive as simultaneously denying and granting the right of judicial review to certain aliens who were in deportation proceedings prior to the IIRIRA's effective date; (2) the Supreme Court's interpretation of § 1252(g) in an attempt to avoid the contradiction was implausible; and (3) the principle of constitutional doubt ought to have been invoked so as to give prevalence to § 309(c)(1), which was the provision that preserved pre-existing judicial review and thus avoided a potential constitutional difficulty with respect to the vitality of selective-prosecution claims in the immigration context.

COUNSEL

Malcolm L. Stewart argued the cause for petitioners. David Cole argued the cause for respondents.

FRANCOIS HOLLOWAY, aka ABDU ALI, Petitioner

v

UNITED STATES

526 US —, 143 L Ed 2d 1, 119 S Ct 966

[No. 97-7164]

Argued November 9, 1998.
Decided March 2, 1999.

Decision: Phrase "intent to cause death or serious bodily harm" in carjacking statute (18 USCS § 2119) held to require proof of mere intent to kill or harm if necessary to effect carjacking, rather than proof of unconditional intent to kill or harm.

SUMMARY

The federal carjacking statute (18 USCS § 2119) prohibits the taking, with the intent to cause death or serious bodily harm, of a motor vehicle from another by force and violence or by intimidation. In each of the carjackings with which an accused was charged, the accused's alleged accomplice was found to have produced a gun and threatened to shoot the driver unless the driver handed over the car keys. The accomplice testified that although the accused and the accomplice had planned not to harm the drivers, the accomplice would have used the gun if any driver had given the accomplice a "hard time." The accused was convicted of several offenses related to stealing cars, including violation of § 2119, as the United States District Court for the Eastern District of New York denied the accused's postverdict motion for a new trial on the alleged basis that the jury erroneously had been instructed that the intent to kill or harm required under § 2119 could be conditioned on a driver's refusal to turn over a car (921 F Supp 155). The United States Court of Appeals for the Second Circuit, affirming the accused's convictions, expressed the view that the intent required under § 2119 included conditional intent (126 F3d 82).

On certiorari, the United States Supreme Court affirmed. In an opinion by STEVENS, J., joined by REHNQUIST, Ch. J., and O'CONNOR, KENNEDY, SOUTER, GINSBURG, and BREYER, JJ., it was held that a person who pointed a gun at a driver—having decided to pull the trigger if the driver did not comply with a demand for the car keys—had, at the relevant moment, the intent required for conviction under § 2119, as (1) the statute directed the factfinder's attention to an accused's state of mind at the precise moment the accused demanded or took control over the car by force and violence or by intimidation, (2) a natural reading of the statutory text was fully consistent with a congressional decision to cover both unconditional and conditional intent, and (3) interpreting the statute to include conditional intent did not render superfluous the statute's "by force and violence or by intimidation" element.

SCALIA, J., dissenting, expressed the view that (1) § 2119 unambiguously did not include conditional intent, as in customary usage "intent" never connoted a condition that the intending party hoped would not occur, and (2) even if ambiguity was assumed to existed, the rule of lenity would require the ambiguity to be resolved in the accused's favor.

THOMAS, J., dissenting, expressed the view that § 2119 could not be read to include conditional intent, as (1) neither § 2119 nor Title 18 of the United States Code, generally, defined intent to include conditional intent, and (2) it had not been demonstrated that the view that specific intent could be conditional was part of a well-established tradition.

COUNSEL

Kevin J. Keating argued the cause for petitioner.

Barbara D. Underwood argued the cause for respondent.

MANUEL DeJESUS PEGUERO, Petitioner

v

UNITED STATES

526 US —, 143 L Ed 2d 18, 119 S Ct 961

[No. 97-9217]

Argued January 11, 1999.
Decided March 2, 1999.

Decision: Federal District Court's failure to advise
defendant of right to appeal his sentence held not
to entitle defendant to postconviction relief, where
defendant knew of right and hence suffered no
prejudice.

SUMMARY

A defendant pleaded guilty to federal drug charges
and was sentenced by the United States District Court
for the Middle District of Pennsylvania. At sentencing,
the District Court failed to inform the defendant of his
right to appeal his sentence. In a later motion for
postconviction relief, the defendant alleged that such
failure violated the express terms of Rule 32(a)(2) of
the Federal Rules of Criminal Procedure, which provided that "[t]here shall be no duty on the court to
advise the defendant of any right of appeal after
sentence is imposed following a plea of guilty or nolo
contendere, except that the court shall advise the
defendant of any right to appeal the sentence" (Rule
32(a)(2), which was effective at the time of the defendant's sentencing, was later succeeded by Rule
32(c)(5), which likewise imposed on the District Court
the duty to advise the defendant at sentencing of any

right to appeal). The District Court (1) rejected the defendant's claim that any Rule 32 violation, without regard to prejudice, was enough to vacate a sentence, and (2) expressed the view that the defendant was not entitled to relief because he actually knew of his right to appeal when he was sentenced. The United States Court of Appeals for the Third Circuit affirmed, expressing the view that (1) the Rule 32(a)(2) violation was subject to harmless-error review, and (2) because the defendant was aware of his right to appeal, the rule's purpose had been served (order reported at 142 F3d 430, 1998 US App LEXIS 5222).

On certiorari, the United States Supreme Court affirmed. In an opinion by KENNEDY, J., expressing the unanimous view of the court, it was held that—although it was not disputed that the failure of the District Court to advise the defendant of his right to appeal his sentence was error in violation of Rule 32(a)(2)—such omission did not entitle the defendant to postconviction relief under 28 USCS § 2255, where the defendant knew of his right at the time of sentencing and hence suffered no prejudice from the omission.

O'CONNOR, J., joined by STEVENS, GINSBURG, and BREYER, JJ., concurring, expressed the view that (1) the defendant in this case was not prejudiced by the District Court's error in failing to advise him of his right to appeal his sentence because he knew about such right at the time of sentencing, but (2) with regard to another way in which such an error could be said not to have prejudiced a defendant—where a defendant might not be prejudiced because he had no meritorious grounds for appeal in any event—the defendant should not be required to demonstrate that he had meritorious grounds for an appeal when he was attempting to show that he was harmed by the District Court's error.

COUNSEL

Daniel L. Siegel argued the cause for petitioner.

Roy W. McLeese, III argued the cause for respondent.

ARIZONA DEPARTMENT OF REVENUE, Petitioner

v

BLAZE CONSTRUCTION COMPANY, INC.

526 US —, 143 L Ed 2d 27, 119 S Ct 957

[No. 97-1536]

Argued December 8, 1998.
Decided March 2, 1999.

Decision: Federal law held not to shield private federal
contractor from Arizona's transaction privilege tax
imposed with respect to work done by contractor
on Indian reservations in Arizona.

SUMMARY

The Bureau of Indian Affairs contracted with a
construction company to build, repair, and improve
roads on various Indian reservations in Arizona. Although the company was incorporated under the laws
of an Indian tribe and owned by a member of that tribe,
none of the work occurred on the reservation of the
contractor's own tribe. At the end of the contracting
period, Arizona's revenue department issued a tax
deficiency assessment against the company for failure
to pay Arizona's transaction privilege tax—a tax levied
on the gross receipts of companies doing business in
the state—on the proceeds from the construction contracts. The company protested the assessment and
prevailed at the end of administrative proceedings, but
on review, the Arizona Tax Court granted summary
judgment in the department's favor. The Court of
Appeals of Arizona, in reversing, expressed the view
that federal law pre-empted the application of the tax

81

to the company (190 Ariz 262, 947 P2d 836, 1997 Ariz App LEXIS 67). The Supreme Court of Arizona denied the department's petition for review.

On certiorari, the United States Supreme Court reversed the Court of Appeals' judgment and remanded the case for further proceedings. In an opinion by THOMAS, J., expressing the unanimous view of the court, it was held that (1) federal law did not shield the company from the transaction privilege tax, as (a) the company was the equivalent of a non-Indian for purposes of the case at hand, (b) the company was not an agency or instrumentality of the Federal Government, (c) the incidence of the tax fell on the company, not the Federal Government, (d) Congress had not expressly exempted the contracts from taxation, and (e) the tribes on whose reservations the work was performed had not assumed contracting responsibility under the Indian Self-Determination and Education Assistance Act (25 USCS §§ 450 et seq.); and (2) under such circumstances, the Supreme Court would not employ a balancing test—weighing the respective state, federal, and tribal interests—to infer from federal laws regulating the welfare of Indians a congressional intent to pre-empt the tax, as the need to avoid litigation and to insure efficient tax administration counseled in favor of a bright-line standard for taxation of federal contracts, regardless of whether the contracted-for activity took place on Indian reservations.

COUNSEL

Patrick Irvine argued the cause for petitioner.

Beth S. Brinkmann argued the cause for the United States, as amicus curiae, by special leave of court.

Bruce C. Smith argued the cause for respondent.

———————

AMERICAN MANUFACTURERS MUTUAL INSUR-
ANCE COMPANY, et al., Petitioners

v

DELORES SCOTT SULLIVAN et al.

526 US —, 143 L Ed 2d 130, 119 S Ct 977

[No. 97-2000]

Argued January 19, 1999.
Decided March 3, 1999.

Decision: Private insurer's decision, pursuant to Pennsylvania's workers' compensation statute, to withhold medical payments pending "utilization review" held not to be state action for due process
purposes; employees held not to have property
interest in payment of medical benefits.

SUMMARY

All employers subject to Pennsylvania's workers' compensation statute were required either (1) to obtain
workers' compensation insurance from a private insurer, (2) to obtain such insurance through the state
workers' insurance fund (SWIF), or (3) to seek permission from the state to self-insure. Also, once an employer became liable for an employee's work-related
injury—because liability either was not contested or was
no longer at issue—the employer or its insurer had to
pay for all "reasonable" and "necessary" medical treatment within 30 days of receiving a bill. However, in
1993, Pennsylvania amended its workers' compensation
system to create a "utilization review" procedure, under which, upon a request by an insurer within 30 days
of receiving such a bill, the reasonableness and neces-

sity of an employee's medical treatment would be initially reviewed by a private "utilization review organization" (URO) of health care providers before such a medical bill had to be paid. Some employees and employee organizations (1) filed a purported class action under 42 USCS § 1983 in the United States District Court for the Eastern District of Pennsylvania against defendants including various state officials, the director of the SWIF, and a number of private insurance companies; and (2) alleged that the state and private defendants, in withholding workers' compensation benefits under the utilization review procedure without predeprivation notice and an opportunity to be heard, acted under color of state law and deprived the plaintiffs of due process in violation of the Federal Constitution's Fourteenth Amendment. However, the District Court dismissed the private insurance companies from the lawsuit on the ground that they were not state actors (913 F Supp 895, 1996 US Dist LEXIS 610). Later, the District Court dismissed the state defendants as well, as the court expressed the view that—while the right to receive workers' compensation benefits was a constitutionally protected property interest—the state provisions concerning utilization review comported with due process (1996 US Dist LEXIS 16609). On appeal, the United States Court of Appeals for the Third Circuit (139 F3d 158, 1998 US App LEXIS 4488), in reversing and in ordering a remand, expressed the view that (1) the state provisions violated an employee's procedural due process rights by (a) failing to provide adequate notice that the employee's medical benefits might be suspended upon the invocation of utilization review, and (b) not granting the employee an opportunity to respond in writing before that termination took effect; and (2) private insurers were state actors when they elected to invoke the provisions to terminate or suspend an employee's constitutionally protected interest in receiving medical benefits (139 F3d 158, 1998 US App LEXIS 4488). In response, the state procedures were modified to provide for more extensive notice and an opportunity for employees to provide some input into URO decisions.

On certiorari, the United States Supreme Court reversed the Court of Appeals' judgment. In an opinion by REHNQUIST, Ch. J., joined by O'CONNOR, KENNEDY, and THOMAS, JJ., joined in part (as to holding 1 below) by SCALIA, SOUTER, and BREYER, JJ., and joined in part (as to holding 2 below) by GINSBURG, J., it was held that (1) a private insurer's decision, pursuant to Pennsylvania's workers' compensation statute, to withhold payment and seek utilization review of the reasonableness and necessity of a particular medical treatment for an employee's work-related injury (a) was not fairly attributable to the state, and (b) thus, did not satisfy the state-action requirement for finding a deprivation of due process under the Fourteenth Amendment; and (2) Pennsylvania's workers' compensation law did not confer upon employees a protected property interest, under the Fourteenth Amendment's due process clause, in the payment of medical benefits for the employees' work-related injuries—and thus, the plaintiffs failed in their due process claim—where the employees in question (a) had yet to make good on their claim that the particular medical treatment at issue was reasonable and necessary, and (b) did not contend that they had a property interest in their claims for payment, as distinct from the payments themselves.

GINSBURG, J., concurring in part and concurring in the judgment, (1) joined holding 2 above on the understanding that the Supreme Court rejected specifically, and only, the plaintiffs' demands for constant payment of each medical bill within 30 days of receipt, pending determination of the necessity or reasonableness of the medical treatment; and (2) expressed the view that (a) because holding 2 above disposed of the instant controversy with respect to all of the insurers involved, the Supreme Court ought to have declined to reach the state-action question of holding 1 above, and (b) the opinion of STEVENS, J., correctly concluded that—although Pennsylvania's original procedure for adjudicating employees' claims for medical care had been deficient—the dispute resolution process which the state later put in place met the Constitution's due process requirement of fair procedure.

BREYER, J., joined by SOUTER, J., concurring in part and concurring in the judgment, joined holding 1 above and expressed the view that—while holding 2 above correctly rejected the plaintiffs' facial attack on the state statute—there might be individual circumstances in which the receipt of earlier payments led an injured person (1) reasonably to expect their continuation, and (2) thus, to possess a constitutionally protected property interest.

STEVENS, J., concurring in part and dissenting in part, expressed the view that (1) the Constitution required that Pennsylvania's workers' compensation procedure for resolving disputes over the reasonableness or necessity of particular treatments for work-related injuries had to be fair, as (a) such disputes were resolved by decisionmakers who were state actors and who had to follow procedures established by state law, and (b) the resolution of such disputes determined the scope of property interests protected under the Fourteenth Amendment's due process clause, that is, the employees' right, under the state's law, to reasonable and necessary treatment of such injuries; and (2) while the Court of Appeals had correctly concluded that the

87

state's original procedure for resolving such disputes had been deficient, there was no constitutional defect in the procedures put in place after the Court of Appeals' decision, as it was not unfair, in and of itself, for a state to allow either a private or a publicly owned party to withhold payment of a state-created entitlement pending resolution of a dispute over its amount.

COUNSEL

Michael W. McConnell argued the cause for petitioners.

Malcolm L. Stewart argued the cause for the United States, as amicus curiae, by special leave of court.

Loralyn McKinley argued the cause for respondents.

CEDAR RAPIDS COMMUNITY SCHOOL DISTRICT,
Petitioner

v

GARRET F., a Minor by His Mother and Next Friend,
CHARLENE F.

526 US —, 143 L Ed 2d 154, 119 S Ct 992

[No. 96-1793]

Argued November 4, 1998.
Decided March 3, 1999.

Decision: Definition of "related services" in Individuals
with Disabilities Education Act provision (20 USCS
§ 1401(a)(17)) held to require public school district to provide nursing services necessary for
ventilator-assisted student during school hours.

SUMMARY

The Individuals with Disabilities Education Act
(IDEA) (20 USCS §§ 1400 et seq.) authorizes federal
financial assistance to states that agree to provide
disabled children with special education and related
services, where 20 USCS § 1401(a)(17) defines "related
services" to exclude medical services other than those
performed for diagnostic and evaluation purposes. The
mother of a ventilator-dependent student challenged,
under Iowa law and the IDEA, an Iowa public school
district's refusal to provide to the student the continuous one-on-one nursing services that the student required during school hours in order to remain in
school. After a state administrative law judge (ALJ)
concluded that the IDEA required the school district to
pay for the continuous nursing services, the school

district challenged the ALJ's decision in the United States District Court for the Northern District of Iowa. The District Court granted summary judgment against the school district, and the United States Court of Appeals for the Eighth Circuit, affirming the District Court judgment, determined that services that can be provided in school by a nurse or qualified layperson are not subject to § 1401(a)(17)'s medical services exclusion (106 F3d 822).

On certiorari, the United States Supreme Court affirmed. In an opinion by STEVENS, J., joined by REHNQUIST, Ch. J., and O'CONNOR, SCALIA, SOUTER, GINSBURG, and BREYER, JJ., it was held that § 1401(a)(17)'s definition of "related services" required the school district to provide the nursing services that were necessary for the student to remain in school, as the definition itself, the United States Supreme Court's decision in Irving Independent School Dist. v Tatro (1984) 468 US 883, 82 L Ed 2d 664, 104 S Ct 3371, requiring a school district to provide clean intermittent catheterization for a kidney patient, and the overall IDEA scheme all supported such a holding, where (1) the text of the "related services" definition broadly encompassed those support services that "may be required to assist a child with a disability to benefit from special education"; (2) the student's necessary in-school care (a) did not demand the training, knowledge, and judgment of a licensed physician, and (b) was no more medical than was the care sought in Tatro; (3) a rule limiting the medical services exclusion to physician services was unquestionably reasonable and generally workable; and (4) the IDEA required schools to hire specially trained personnel to meet disabled student needs.

THOMAS, J., joined by KENNEDY, J., dissenting, expressed the view that (1) because Tatro could not be squared with the IDEA's text, the court should not adhere to Tatro in the case at hand; and (2) even if Tatro was assumed to be correct in the first instance, the majority's extension of Tatro (a) was unwarranted, and (b) ignored the constitutionally mandated rules of construction applicable to legislation enacted pursuant to Congress' spending power.

COUNSEL

Susan L. Seitz argued the cause for petitioner.

Douglas R. Oelschlaeger argued the cause for respondent.

Beth S. Brinkmann argued the cause for the United States, as amicus curiae, by special leave of court.

NATIONAL FEDERATION OF FEDERAL EMPLOY-
EES, LOCAL 1309, Petitioner

v

DEPARTMENT OF THE INTERIOR et al. (No. 97-
1184)

———

FEDERAL LABOR RELATIONS AUTHORITY, Petitioner

v

DEPARTMENT OF THE INTERIOR et al. (No. 97-
1243)

526 US —, 143 L Ed 2d 171, 119 S Ct 1003

[Nos. 97-1184 and 97-1243]

Argued November 9, 1998.
Decided March 3, 1999.

Decision: Federal Service Labor-Management Relations
Statute (5 USCS §§ 7101 et seq.) held to delegate
to Federal Labor Relations Authority legal power
to determine whether federal agencies and unions
must engage in midterm bargaining.

SUMMARY

Under various provisions of the Federal Service
Labor-Management Relations Statute (FSLMRS) (5
USCS §§ 7101 et seq.), (1) federal agencies and the
unions that represent the agencies' employees are
required to meet and negotiate in good faith for the
purposes of arriving at a collective bargaining agreement (5 USCS § 7114(a)(4)), (2) "collective bargain-

ing agreement" is defined as an agreement entered into as a result of collective bargaining (5 USCS § 7103(a)(8)), and (3) "collective bargaining" is defined as involving the meeting of employer and employee representatives at reasonable times to consult and to bargain in a good-faith effort to reach agreement with respect to the conditions of employment, incorporating any collective bargaining agreement reached as a result of these negotiations in a written document (5 USCS § 7103(a)(12)). A union representing employees of a subagency of the United States Department of the Interior proposed including in the parties' basic labor contract a provision that would have obligated the Department, at the union's request, to negotiate midterm—that is, while the basic contract was in effect—on any negotiable matters not covered by the provisions of this basic contract. The Department, contending that the FSLMRS prohibited such a provision, refused to accept or bargain about the proposed clause. The FLRA, asserting that the FSLMRS had to be read to require midterm bargaining, (1) expressed the view that the Department's refusal to bargain amounted to an unfair labor practice under the FSLMRS, and (2) ordered the Department to bargain over the proposed clause. The Department petitioned the United States Court of Appeals for the Fourth Circuit for review of the order, while the FLRA, joined by the union as intervenor, cross-petitioned for enforcement of the order. The United States Court of Appeals for the Fourth Circuit, in granting review and denying enforcement, concluded that (1) the FSLMRS did not impose any midterm bargaining duty, and (2) the parties therefore ought not to be required to bargain endterm—that is, during the negotiations over adopting or renewing the basic contract—about including a

93

clause that would require bargaining midterm (132 F3d 157, 1997 US App LEXIS 30039).

On certiorari, the United States Supreme Court vacated and remanded. In an opinion by BREYER, J., joined by STEVENS, KENNEDY, SOUTER, and GINSBURG, JJ., it was held that (1) the FSLMRS delegated to the FLRA the legal power to determine whether, when, and where federal agencies and unions had to engage in midterm bargaining, because (a) the relevant language of the FSLMRS created ambiguity by using general language that might or might not have encompassed various forms of midterm bargaining, (b) such ambiguity was consistent with the conclusion that Congress had delegated to the FLRA the power to determine—within appropriate legal bounds—whether, when, where, and what sort of midterm bargaining was required; and (c) this conclusion was supported by (i) the FSLMRS' delegation of rulemaking, adjudicatory, and policymaking powers to the FLRA, and (ii) precedent recognizing the similarity of the FLRA's public-sector role and the National Labor Relations Board's private-sector role; and (2) the FSLMRS granted leeway, within ordinary legal limits, to the FLRA in determining whether federal agencies and unions had to bargain endterm about whether to include in the basic contract a clause that would require certain forms of midterm bargaining.

O'CONNOR, J., joined by REHNQUIST, Ch. J., and joined in part (as to point 1 below) by SCALIA and THOMAS, JJ., dissenting, expressed the view that (1) the FSLMRS was not ambiguous as to midterm bargaining, but rather excluded the duty to engage in such bargaining; and (2) even if the FSLMRS had been ambiguous with respect to the duty to bargain midterm, the Supreme Court ought not to have deferred to the FLRA's interpretation of the FSLMRS.

COUNSEL

David M. Smith argued the cause for petitioner in No. 97-1243.

Gregory O'Duden argued the cause for petitioner in No. 97-1184.

Irving L. Gornstein argued the cause for respondent in both cases.

THE FEDERAL REPUBLIC OF GERMANY et al., Petitioners

v

UNITED STATES et al.

526 US —, 143 L Ed 2d 192, 119 S Ct 1016

[No. 127, Orig. (A-736)]

Decided March 3, 1999.

Decision: Supreme Court's original jurisdiction not exercised to allow Germany's challenge to Arizona's scheduled execution of German citizen, given tardiness of Germany's pleas and jurisdictional barriers implicated.

SUMMARY

An accused, who was purportedly a citizen of the Federal Republic of Germany, was charged in Arizona with first-degree murder, attempted murder in the first degree, attempted armed robbery, and kidnapping. Following a jury trial, the accused was convicted on all charges and sentenced to death in 1984. The Federal Republic of Germany learned of the sentence in 1992. The accused's execution was ordered on January 15, 1999. On the day of the scheduled execution, the International Court of Justice, on its own motion and with no opportunity for the United States to respond, issued an order directing the United States to prevent Arizona's scheduled execution of the accused. Within 2 hours of the scheduled execution, the Federal Republic of Germany, invoking the United States Supreme Court's original jurisdiction, filed motions in the Supreme Court (1) for leave to file a bill of complaint, (2) for preliminary injunctions against the United States of America and Arizona's governor to enforce the order of the International Court of Justice, and (3) to dispense with printing requirements.

The Supreme Court denied the motions for leave to file a bill of complaint and for preliminary injunctions, but granted the motion to dispense with printing requirements. In a per curiam opinion expressing the view of REHNQUIST, Ch. J., and O'CONNOR, SCALIA, KENNEDY, and THOMAS, JJ., it was held that the Supreme Court would decline to exercise its original jurisdiction due to the tardiness of the pleas by Germany and due to the jurisdictional barriers which the pleas implicated (1) under both the sovereign immunity of the United States and under Art III, § 2, cl 2 of the Federal Constitution, with regard to the action against the United States; and (2) under both the Vienna Convention on Consular Relations (21 UST 77, TIAS No. 6820) and the Constitution's Eleventh Amendment, with regard to the action against the state of Arizona.

SOUTER, J., joined by GINSBURG, J., concurring, expressed the view that the decision to deny leave to file the bill of complaint ought not to rest on any Eleventh Amendment principle.

BREYER, J., joined by STEVENS, J., dissenting, expressed the view that the Supreme Court ought to grant a preliminary stay, because (1) the stay would give the Supreme Court time to consider the jurisdictional and international legal questions involved, and (2) there was a need for fuller briefing.

TERRY STEWART, Director, Arizona Department of
Corrections, et al., Petitioners

v

WALTER LaGRAND

526 US —, 143 L Ed 2d 196, 119 S Ct 1018

[No. A-735 (98-1412)]

Decided March 3, 1999.

Decision: For federal habeas corpus purposes, accused
held to have waived claim that execution by lethal
gas is unconstitutional; also, that claim and claim
of ineffective assistance of counsel held to have
been procedurally defaulted without excuse.

SUMMARY

An accused and his codefendant were each sentenced by an Arizona state court to death following
convictions on several charges including first-degree
murder. At that time, execution by lethal gas was the
only method available in the state. The state's highest
court affirmed the convictions and sentences, and the
United States Supreme Court denied certiorari. Subsequently, state law was changed to allow individuals
sentenced to death to choose execution by lethal gas or
by lethal injection. The accused filed a federal petition
for a writ of habeas corpus and claimed that execution
by lethal gas constituted cruel and unusual punishment
under the Eighth Amendment to the United States
Constitution. However, a Federal District Court found
the claim to have been procedurally defaulted by failing
to raise it either on direct appeal or in a petition for
state postconviction relief. On appeal, the United States

Court of Appeals for the Ninth Circuit did not reach
the issue of procedural default because it found the
claim was not ripe until and unless the accused chose
gas as his method of execution. Subsequently, however,
the Court of Appeals, ruling in the case of the codefendant, expressed the view that (1) while the codefendant's cruel and unusual punishment claim was procedurally barred, cause and prejudice existed so as to
excuse the default; and (2) the Eighth Amendment
protections may not be waived in the context of capital
punishment. The accused subsequently filed another
petition for habeas corpus, again raising the Eighth
Amendment claim, as well as a claim of ineffective
assistance of counsel. While the District Court again
denied relief, the Court of Appeals issued an order
enjoining the state from executing the accused by
means of lethal gas.

The Supreme Court granted a petition by the state
for a writ of certiorari, summarily reversed the Court of
Appeals' judgment, and vacated the injunctive order. In
a per curiam opinion expressing the view of REHN-
QUIST, Ch. J., and O'CONNOR, SCALIA, KENNEDY, and
THOMAS, JJ., it was held that (1) the accused had waived
his claim that execution by lethal gas is unconstitutional by selecting lethal gas as his method of execution
over the state's default method of execution, lethal
injection; (2) to hold otherwise—and to hold that
Eighth Amendment protections could not be waived in
the capital context—would create and apply a new
procedural rule in violation of Teague v Lane (1989)
489 US 288, 103 L Ed 2d 334, 109 S Ct 1060; (3) the
accused failed to show cause to overcome his procedural default in bringing the Eighth Amendment
claim; (4) the accused waived his claim of ineffective
assistance of counsel by representing to the District
Court, prior to filing his initial federal habeas corpus

petition, that there was no basis for such claims; (5) the ineffective assistance claim was procedurally defaulted pursuant to a state procedural rule; and (6) the accused failed to demonstrate cause or prejudice for his failure to raise the claim on direct review.

SOUTER, J., joined by GINSBURG and BREYER, JJ., concurring in part and concurring in the judgment, expressed the view that (1) holding 1 above was correct on the understanding that the accused made no claim that death by lethal injection would be cruel and unusual punishment under the Eighth Amendment, and (2) no issue of the applicability of Teague v Lane, supra, needed to be reached.

STEVENS, J., dissenting, expressed the view that (1) it was unclear whether an accused can consent to be executed by an unacceptably torturous method of execution, and (2) such an important question ought not to be decided without full briefing and argument.

BARBARA SCHWARZ, Petitioner

v

NATIONAL SECURITY AGENCY et al. (No. 98-7771)

———

BARBARA SCHWARZ, Petitioner

v

EXECUTIVE OFFICE OF THE PRESIDENT et al.
(No. 98-7782)

526 US —, 143 L Ed 2d 203, 119 S Ct 1109

[Nos. 98-7771 and 98-7782]

Decided March 8, 1999.

Decision: Person who had filed 35 frivolous certiorari petitions denied leave to proceed in forma pauperis as to latest petitions; order entered barring person's future in forma pauperis filings of noncriminal certiorari petitions.

SUMMARY

An individual sought leave to proceed in forma pauperis in the United States Supreme Court under Supreme Court Rule 39 with respect to two petitions for certiorari. The petitions were the 34th and 35th petitions for certiorari that the individual had filed with the court, and according to the court—which, on a single day earlier in the current Term, had denied the individual in forma pauperis status with respect to 4 of the 35 petitions by invoking Supreme Court Rule 39.8, which authorizes the court to deny such leave with respect to frivolous petitions—all 35 petitions were frivolous.

In a per curiam opinion expressing the view of REHNQUIST, Ch. J., and O'CONNOR, SCALIA, KENNEDY, SOUTER, THOMAS, GINSBURG, and BREYER, JJ., the Supreme Court (1) invoked Rule 39.8 to deny the individual's request for leave to proceed in forma pauperis on the two instant petitions, and (2) directed the Clerk of the Supreme Court not to accept any further petitions for certiorari in noncriminal matters from the individual unless she complied with Supreme Court Rules 33.1 and 38.

STEVENS, J., dissented for the reasons expressed in a previous Supreme Court case involving some similar issues.

————————

CENTRAL STATE UNIVERSITY, Petitioner

v

AMERICAN ASSOCIATION OF UNIVERSITY PRO-
FESSORS, CENTRAL STATE UNIVERSITY CHAP-
TER

526 US —, 143 L Ed 2d 227, 119 S Ct 1162

[No. 98-1071]

Decided March 22, 1999.

Decision: Ohio statute's exemption of state university
faculties' instructional workload standards from
collective bargaining held not to violate equal
protection clause of Federal Constitution's Fourteenth Amendment.

SUMMARY

In an effort to address the decline in the amount of
time that state university faculty members devoted to
teaching as opposed to research, Ohio enacted a statute
that (1) required state universities to develop standards
for faculty members' instructional workloads, and (2)
exempted such standards from collective bargaining.
After a particular state university adopted a workload
policy pursuant to the statute and notified the university faculty members' labor union that the university
would not bargain over the faculty workload issue, the
union brought in an Ohio state court an action alleging
that the statute created a class of public employees not
entitled to bargain regarding their workload and thus
violated the equal protection clauses of the Ohio and
Federal Constitutions. The Ohio Supreme Court, concluding that the state had failed to show any rational

basis for singling out university faculty members as the only public employees precluded from bargaining over their workload, held that the statute deprived the faculty members of equal protection of the laws (83 Ohio St 3d 229, 699 NE 2d 463).

Granting certiorari, the United States Supreme Court reversed and remanded. In a per curiam opinion expressing the views of REHNQUIST, Ch. J., and O'CONNOR, SCALIA, KENNEDY, SOUTER, THOMAS, GINS-BURG, and BREYER, JJ., it was held that the legislative classification created by the state statute did not violate the equal protection clause of the Federal Constitution's Fourteenth Amendment, as the classification passed the test, applicable to a classification neither involving fundamental rights nor proceeding along suspect lines, of a rational relationship between disparity of treatment and some legitimate governmental purpose, where the state legislature could properly have concluded that collective bargaining about the workload policy in the future would interfere with the legislative goal of having a uniform policy in place by a certain date.

GINSBURG, J., joined by BREYER, J., concurring, expressed the view that the Ohio Supreme Court was at liberty to resolve the matter under the Ohio Constitution.

STEVENS, J., dissenting, expressed the view that (1) the United States Supreme Court should deny the petition for certiorari, because the case has little, if any, national significance, and because the Ohio Supreme Court's purported misconstruction of the Fourteenth Amendment's equal protection clause would be harmless if the Ohio Supreme Court adhered to its previously announced interpretation of the Ohio Constitution, and (2) if the case warranted the United States Supreme Court's review, it should not be decided summarily.

———————

VINCENT F. RIVERA, Petitioner

v

FLORIDA DEPARTMENT OF CORRECTIONS

526 US —, 143 L Ed 2d 235, 119 S Ct 1166

[No. 98-7450]

Decided March 22, 1999.

Decision: Person who filed 13 frivolous petitions in Supreme Court denied leave to proceed in forma pauperis; order entered barring person's future in forma pauperis filings of noncriminal petitions for certiorari or extraordinary writs.

SUMMARY

An individual sought leave to proceed in forma pauperis in the United States Supreme Court under Supreme Court Rule 39 with respect to a petition for certiorari. According to the court, which twice earlier in the current Term had invoked Supreme Court Rule 39.8—which authorizes the court to deny leave to proceed in forma pauperis with respect to frivolous petitions—to deny the individual in forma pauperis status, (1) the instant petition was the individual's 13th frivolous filing in the court of a certiorari petition or a petition for an extraordinary writ, and (2) the individual had four additional frivolous filings currently pending before the court.

In a per curiam opinion expressing the view of REHNQUIST, Ch. J., and O'CONNOR, SCALIA, KENNEDY, SOUTER, THOMAS, GINSBURG, and BREYER, JJ., the Supreme Court (1) invoked Rule 39.8 to deny the individual's request for leave to proceed in forma pauperis on the instant petition, and (2) directed the Clerk of the Supreme Court not to accept any further petitions for certiorari or for extraordinary writs in noncriminal matters from the individual unless he complied with Supreme Court Rules 33.1 and 38.

STEVENS, J., dissented for the reasons expressed in a previous Supreme Court case involving some similar issues.

———————

KUMHO TIRE COMPANY, LTD., et al., Petitioners

v

PATRICK CARMICHAEL, etc., et al.

526 US —, 143 L Ed 2d 238, 119 S Ct 1167

[No. 97-1709]

Argued December 7, 1998.
Decided March 23, 1999.

Decision: Federal trial judge's gatekeeping obligation under Federal Rules of Evidence—to insure that expert witness' testimony rests on reliable foundation and is relevant to task at hand—held to apply to all expert testimony, not only scientific.

SUMMARY

In Daubert v Merrell Dow Pharmaceuticals, Inc. (1993) 509 US 579, 125 L Ed 2d 469, 113 S Ct 2786, a case involving the admissibility of scientific expert testimony, the United States Supreme Court held that (1) such testimony was admissible only if relevant and reliable; (2) the Federal Rules of Evidence (FRE) assigned to the trial judge the task of insuring that an expert's testimony rested on a reliable foundation and was relevant to the task at hand; and (3) some or all of certain specific factors—such as testing, peer review, error rates, and acceptability in the relevant scientific community—might possibly prove helpful in determining the reliability of a particular scientific theory or technique. In 1993, after a tire on a minivan blew out and the minivan overturned, one passenger died and the others were injured. The survivors and the decedent's representative, claiming that the failed tire had been defective, brought a diversity suit in the United States District Court for the Southern District of Alabama against the tire's maker and distributor. The plaintiffs rested their case in significant part upon the depositions of a mechanical engineer—an expert in tire failure analysis—who intended to testify that, in his expert opinion, a defect in the tire's manufacture or design caused the blowout. The expert's opinion was based upon (1) a visual and tactile inspection of the tire, and (2) the theory that in the absence of at least two of four specific physical symptoms indicating tire abuse, the tire failure of the sort that occurred in the case at hand was caused by a defect. The District Court—in granting a motion to exclude the expert's testimony as well as a motion for summary judgment against the plaintiffs—(1) agreed with the defendants that the District Court ought to act as a Daubert-type reliability "gatekeeper," even though the testimony at issue could be considered "technical" rather than "scientific"; (2) examined the expert's methodology in light of the reliability-related factors that Daubert had mentioned; and (3) concluded that all those factors argued against the reliability of the expert's methods (923 F Supp 1514, 1996 US Dist LEXIS 5706). On reconsideration, the District Court—although acknowledging that the Daubert factors ought to be applied flexibly and were simply illustrative—affirmed the earlier rulings on the ground that there were insufficient indications of the reliability of the expert's methodology of tire failure analysis. The United States Court of Appeals for the Eleventh Circuit, in reversing and remanding, expressed the view that the District Court had erred as a matter of law in applying the Daubert factors to the tire expert's testimony, as (1) Daubert was limited to the scientific context, and (2) the testimony in question relied on experience rather than the application of scientific principles (131 F3d 1433, 1997 US App LEXIS 35981).

On certiorari, the Supreme Court reversed. In an opinion by BREYER, J., joined by REHNQUIST, Ch. J., and O'CONNOR, SCALIA, KENNEDY, SOUTER, THOMAS, and GINSBURG, JJ., and joined (as to points 1 and 2 below) by STEVENS, J., it was held that (1) a federal trial judge's gatekeeping obligation under the FRE—to insure that an expert witness' testimony rests on a reliable foundation and is relevant to the task at hand—applies not only to testimony based on scientific knowledge, but rather to all expert testimony, that is, testimony based on technical and other specialized knowledge; (2) in determining the admissibility of an expert's testimony—including the testimony of an engineering expert—a federal trial judge may properly consider one or more of the specific Daubert factors, where doing so will help determine that testimony's reliability; and (3) in the case at hand, the District Court's decision not to admit the expert testimony in question was within the District Court's discretion.

SCALIA, J., joined by O'CONNOR and THOMAS, JJ., concurring, expressed the view that (1) a trial court's discretion in choosing the manner of testing expert reliability is not discretion to abandon the gatekeeping function or to perform that function inadequately; and (2) in a particular case, the failure to apply one or another of the Daubert factors may possibly be unreasonable and hence an abuse of discretion.

STEVENS, J., concurring in part and dissenting in part, (1) agreed that a federal trial judge may properly consider the Daubert factors in analyzing the admissibility of an engineering expert's testimony, and (2) expressed the view that the case ought to have been remanded to the Court of Appeals for a study of the record to determine whether the trial judge abused his discretion in excluding the expert testimony in question.

COUNSEL

Joseph H. Babington argued the cause for petitioners.

Jeffrey P. Minear argued the cause for the United States, as amicus curiae, by special leave of court.

Sidney W. Jackson argued the cause for respondents.

SOUTH CENTRAL BELL TELEPHONE COMPANY,
et al., Petitioners

v

ALABAMA et al.

526 US —, 143 L Ed 2d 258, 119 S Ct 1180

[No. 97-2045]

Argued January 19, 1999.
Decided March 23, 1999.

Decision: Alabama franchise tax held to discriminate
against interstate commerce in violation of Federal
Constitution's commerce clause; Alabama's claims
of res judicata and Eleventh Amendment immunity rejected.

SUMMARY

Alabama required each corporation doing business
in that state to pay a franchise tax based on the firm's
capital. The tax for a domestic firm was based on the
par value of the firm's stock, which the firm was able to
set at a level well below its book or market value. An
out-of-state firm was required to pay tax based on the
value of the actual amount of capital employed in the
state, with no similar leeway to control its tax base.
Several corporations sued state tax authorities and
sought a refund of the foreign franchise tax they had
paid on the ground that the tax allegedly discriminated
against foreign corporations in violation of provisions
of the Federal Constitution, including the commerce
clause (Art I, § 8, cl 3). The Alabama Supreme Court
rejected the claims, holding that the special burden
imposed on foreign corporations simply offset a differ-
112

ent burden imposed exclusively on domestic corporations by Alabama's domestic shares tax. Subsequently,
several other foreign corporations (1) went to trial in
the present suit against defendants including the state,
and (2) asserted similar constitutional claims, though
in respect to different tax years. A state trial court
agreed with the plaintiffs that the tax substantially
discriminated against foreign corporations, but nonetheless dismissed their claims as barred by res judicata
in light of the Alabama Supreme Court's decision in
the earlier case. The Alabama Supreme Court affirmed
(711 So 2d 1005).

On certiorari, the United States Supreme Court
reversed and remanded. In an opinion by BREYER, J.,
expressing the unanimous view of the court, it was held
that (1) the Supreme Court did not lack appellate
jurisdiction over the present case under the Federal
Constitution's Eleventh Amendment; (2) the refusal of
the Alabama Supreme Court to permit the plaintiffs in
the present case to raise their constitutional claims
because of res judicata or collateral estoppel was inconsistent with the due process guarantee of the Constitution's Fourteenth Amendment, and the plaintiffs in the
present case were not bound by the decision in the
earlier case, because (a) the two cases involved different plaintiffs and different tax years, (b) neither was a
class-action suit, and (c) there was no claim of privity or
some other special relationship between the two sets of
plaintiffs; (3) the state franchise tax discriminated
against interstate commerce in violation of the commerce clause, as among other matters, the state could
not justify the discrimination on the ground that the
foreign franchise tax was a complementary or compensatory tax that offset the tax burden which Alabama's
domestic shares tax imposed on domestic corporations;
and (4) the state's invitation to reconsider the United

States Supreme Court's negative commerce clause doctrine would not be entertained, where the state did not make it clear that it intended to make such an argument until the state filed its brief on the merits.

O'CONNOR, J., concurring, (1) agreed with the court's refusal to pass on the merits of the state's challenge to the court's negative commerce clause jurisprudence, and (2) expressed the view that nothing the state had done warranted reconsideration or abandonment of this jurisprudence.

THOMAS, J., concurring, expressed the view that the court properly declined to consider the state's challenge to the court's negative commerce clause jurisprudence.

COUNSEL

Mark L. Evans argued the cause for petitioners.
Charles J. Cooper argued the cause for respondents.

————

MINNESOTA, et al., Petitioners

v

MILLE LACS BAND OF CHIPPEWA INDIANS et al.

526 US —, 143 L Ed 2d 270, 119 S Ct 1187

[No. 97-1337]

Argued December 2, 1998.
Decided March 24, 1999.

Decision: Several Chippewa Indian bands held to retain
hunting, fishing, and gathering rights on land in
present-day Minnesota that they ceded to United
States in 1837 treaty.

SUMMARY

Several bands of Chippewa Indians, including the
Mille Lacs Band, entered into an 1837 treaty (7 Stat
536) in which (1) the bands ceded land in present-day
Minnesota to the United States, and (2) the United
States guaranteed the bands the usufructuary rights to
hunt, fish, and gather on the ceded land "during the
pleasure of the President of the United States." An
1850 executive order ordered the removal of Chippewa
Indians from the ceded land in question and revoked
the usufructuary rights that had been granted under
the 1837 treaty, and an 1855 treaty (10 Stat 1165) stated
that some Chippewa bands relinquished to the United
States "any and all right, title and interest, of whatso-
ever nature" in the land. Moreover, in 1858, Congress
enacted the enabling act under which Minnesota was
admitted as a state of the United States. In an action
brought in 1990 against the state of Minnesota by the
Mille Lacs Band of Chippewa Indians, seeking, among

other things, a declaratory judgment that the band
retained its usufructuary rights under the 1837 treaty
and an injunction to prevent the state's interference
with those rights, the United States District Court for
the District of Minnesota concluded that the Mille Lacs
Band retained its usufructuary rights under the 1837
treaty (861 F Supp 784). After the District Court
permitted several additional Chippewa bands to inter-
vene as plaintiffs in the Mille Lacs litigation and—in a
case in which the Fond du Lac Band of Chippewa
Indians sought a declaration that it retained its rights to
hunt, fish, and gather under the 1837 treaty and an
1854 treaty—held that the Fond du Lacs Band retained
its usufructuary rights, the District Court consolidated
the portions of the two cases that concerned the 1837
treaty, and the District Court issue a final order resolving several resource allocation and regulation issues
(952 F Supp 1362). The United States Court of Appeals
for the Eighth Circuit, affirming the District Court
judgments, expressed the view that (1) the 1850 executive order did not abrogate the bands' usufructuary
rights, (2) the 1855 treaty did not extinguish the Mille
Lacs Band's usufructuary privileges, and (3) Minnesota's admission as a state of the United States did not
extinguish any 1837 treaty rights (124 F3d 904).

On certiorari, the United States Supreme Court
affirmed. In an opinion by O'CONNOR, J., joined by
STEVENS, SOUTER, GINSBURG, and BREYER, JJ., it was
held that the Chippewa bands retained the usufructuary rights guaranteed to them under the 1837 treaty, as
(1) the 1850 executive order was ineffective to terminate the usufructuary rights, where (a) the state had
pointed to no statutory or constitutional authority for
the President's removal order, and (b) the part of the
executive order that revoked the usufructuary rights
was not severable from the invalid removal order; (2)

an analysis of the history, purpose, and negotiations of the 1855 treaty led to the conclusion that the Mille Lacs Band did not relinquish their 1837 treaty rights in the 1855 treaty; and (3) the 1858 admission of Minnesota into the United States did not terminate the usufructuary rights, where (a) there was no clear evidence that in the enabling act Congress intended to abrogate the usufructuary rights, and (b) because treaty rights were reconcilable with state sovereignty over natural resources, statehood by itself was insufficient to extinguish the usufructuary rights.

REHNQUIST, Ch. J., joined by SCALIA, KENNEDY, and THOMAS, JJ., dissenting, expressed the view that (1) the executive order constituted a valid revocation of the bands' hunting and fishing privileges, (2) the language of the 1855 treaty was so broad as to encompass the relinquishment of "all" interests in land possessed or claimed by the bands, including usufructuary rights, and (3) even if the executive order was invalid and the 1855 treaty did not cover the usufructuary rights, these rights were eliminated by the admission of Minnesota into the United States in 1858.

THOMAS, J., dissenting, expressed the view that (1) the court's prior cases did not dictate the conclusion, expressed in dicta, that the 1837 treaty curtailed Minnesota's regulatory authority over hunting, fishing, and gathering by the bands in the ceded lands, and (2) although such authority was not at issue in the instant case, in the appropriate case the court would have to explain whether reserved privileges limit states' ability to regulate Indians' off-reservation usufructuary activities in the same way as a treaty reserving rights.

COUNSEL

John L. Kirwin argued the cause for petitioners.

Randy V. Thompson argued the cause for respondents John W. Thompson, et al.

Marc D. Slonim argued the cause for respondents Mille Lacs Band of the Chippewa Indians, et al.

Barbara B. McDowell argued the cause for respondent United States.

NATHANIEL JONES, Petitioner

v

UNITED STATES

526 US —, 143 L Ed 2d 311, 119 S Ct 1215

[No. 97-6203]

Argued October 5, 1998.

Decided March 24, 1999.

Decision: Federal carjacking statute (18 USCS § 2119, later amended) held to define three separate offenses by specification of distinct elements, rather than to define single crime with choice of three maximum penalties.

SUMMARY

An accused was indicted on two federal counts, including a carjacking count. At that time, the federal carjacking statute (18 USCS § 2119, later amended) provided that a person possessing a firearm who "takes a motor vehicle . . . from the person or presence of another by force and violence or by intimidation, or attempts to do so, shall—(1) be fined under this title or imprisoned not more than 15 years, or both, (2) if serious bodily injury . . . results, be fined under this title or imprisoned not more than 25 years, or both, and (3) if death results, be fined under this title or imprisoned for any number of years up to life, or both." The indictment made no reference to § 2119's numbered subsections and charged none of the items mentioned in the latter two. At arraignment, a magistrate judge told the accused that he faced a maximum sentence of 15 years on the carjacking charge. Subsequently, the accused was convicted in the United States District Court for the Eastern District of California on both counts, pursuant to jury instructions which defined carjacking's elements solely by reference to § 2119's first paragraph, with no mention of serious bodily injury. When a presentence report recommended that the accused be sentenced to 25 years for carjacking—on the alleged basis of serious bodily injury to a victim—the accused objected and claimed that serious bodily injury was an element of an offense defined in part by 18 USCS § 2119(2), which had been neither pleaded in the indictment nor proven before the jury. However, the District Court (1) found that the allegation of serious bodily injury was supported by a preponderance of the evidence; and (2) sentenced the accused to a total of 30 years' imprisonment, including 25 years on the carjacking count. While the United States Court of Appeals for the Ninth Circuit vacated the sentencing decision in part on other grounds and remanded in part, the Court of Appeals expressed the view, as to carjacking, that (1) § 2119(2) did not set out an element of an independent offense, and (2) serious bodily injury was a factor which the District Court was free to consider in sentencing (60 F3d 547, 1995 US App LEXIS 16432). On remand, the District Court reduced the accused's sentence somewhat to a total of 25 years, including 20 years for carjacking. On appeal, the Court of Appeals affirmed (116 F3d 1487, reported in full 1997 US App LEXIS 16197).

On certiorari, the United States Supreme Court reversed and remanded. In an opinion by SOUTER, J., joined by STEVENS, SCALIA, THOMAS, and GINSBURG, JJ., it was held that at the time that the accused was charged, § 2119 defined three separate offenses by the specification of distinct elements, each of which had to be charged by indictment, proven beyond a reasonable doubt, and submitted to a jury for its verdict—rather than defining a single crime with a choice of three maximum penalties, two of which would have been dependent on sentencing factors exempt from the requirements of charge and jury verdict—as (1) the three-offenses reading was the better reading of § 2119; and (2) any interpretive uncertainty would be resolved in favor of the three-offenses reading in order to avoid serious questions about § 2119's constitutionality, where a series of Supreme Court decisions in the preceding quarter century suggested—although the decisions did not establish—the principle that under the due process clause of the Federal Constitution's Fifth Amendment and under the notice and jury trial guarantees of the Constitution's Sixth Amendment, any fact (other than prior conviction) that increased the maximum penalty for a crime had to be charged in an indictment, submitted to a jury, and proven beyond a reasonable doubt.

STEVENS, J., concurring, expressed the view that (1) it is unconstitutional for a legislature to remove from the jury the assessment of facts that increase the prescribed ranges of penalties to which a criminal defendant is exposed, (2) such facts must be established by proof beyond a reasonable doubt, and (3) a proper understanding of this principle would encompass facts that increased the minimum as well as the maximum permissible sentence, as well as facts that had to be established before a defendant could be put to death.

SCALIA, J., concurring, expressed the view that it was necessary to resolve all ambiguities in federal criminal statutes in such fashion as to avoid violation of the principle that it is unconstitutional to remove from the

jury the assessment of facts that alter the congressionally prescribed range of penalties to which a defendant
is exposed.

KENNEDY, J., joined by REHNQUIST, Ch. J., and
O'CONNOR and BREYER, JJ., dissenting, expressed the
view that (1) § 2119 contained in its first paragraph a
complete definition of the offense, with all of the
elements of the crime which Congress intended to
codify; and (2) the Supreme Court, in adopting a
contrary and strained reading according to which the
single statutory section prohibited three distinct offenses, misread § 2119 and sought to create constitutional
doubt where there was none.

COUNSEL

Quin Denvir argued the cause for petitioner.
Edward C. DuMont argued the cause for respondent.

RONALD DEAN LOWE, Petitioner

v

MARCUS POGUE et al. (No. 98-7591)

———

RONALD DEAN LOWE, Petitioner

v

OKLAHOMA DEPARTMENT OF CORRECTIONS
(No. 98-7952)

———

RONALD DEAN LOWE, Petitioner

v

FEDERAL BUREAU OF INVESTIGATION (No. 98-
8073)

———

RONALD DEAN LOWE, Petitioner

v

HELEN WOODALL et al. (No. 98-8082)

526 US —, 143 L Ed 2d 384, 119 S Ct 1238

[Nos. 98-7591, 98-7952, 98-8073, and 98-8082]

Decided March 29, 1999.

Decision: Person who filed more than 31 frivolous petitions in Supreme Court denied leave to proceed in forma pauperis as to 4 instant certiorari petitions; order entered barring person's future in forma pauperis filings of noncriminal petitions for certiorari or extraordinary writs.

SUMMARY

An individual sought leave to proceed in forma pauperis in the United States Supreme Court under Supreme Court Rule 39 with respect to four petitions for certiorari. According to the court, which earlier in the current Term had invoked Supreme Court Rule 39.8—which authorizes the court to deny leave to proceed in forma pauperis with respect to frivolous petitions—to deny the individual in forma pauperis status with respect to 4 other petitions, (1) the instant petitions brought the individual's total number of frivolous filing in the court to 31, and (2) the individual had several additional frivolous filings currently pending before the court.

In a per curiam opinion expressing the view of REHNQUIST, Ch. J., and O'CONNOR, SCALIA, KENNEDY, SOUTER, THOMAS, GINSBURG, and BREYER, JJ., the Supreme Court (1) invoked Rule 39.8 to deny the individual's request for leave to proceed in forma pauperis on the instant petitions, and (2) directed the Clerk of the Supreme Court not to accept any further petitions for certiorari or for extraordinary writs in noncriminal matters from the individual unless he complied with Supreme Court Rules 33.1 and 38.

STEVENS, J., dissented for the reasons expressed in a previous Supreme Court case involving some similar issues.

UNITED STATES, Petitioner

v

JACINTO RODRIGUEZ-MORENO

526 US —, 143 L Ed 2d 388, 119 S Ct 1239

[No. 97-1139]

Argued December 7, 1998.
Decided March 30, 1999.

Decision: Venue in prosecution under 18 USCS § 924(c)(1) for using or carrying firearm during and in relation to crime of violence held to be proper in any federal judicial district where crime of violence was committed.

SUMMARY

After a drug dealer stole cocaine from a drug distributor during a drug transaction in Texas, the distributor, an accused, and others, in seeking to find the dealer, drove from Texas to New Jersey to New York to Maryland while holding captive the middleman in the transaction. In Maryland, the accused took possession of a gun and threatened to kill the middleman. The middleman escaped, and the accused eventually was charged in the United States District Court for the District of New Jersey with, among other offenses, conspiracy to kidnap, kidnapping, and violating 18 USCS § 924(c)(1) (later amended), which prohibited using and carrying a firearm in relation to any crime of violence. After the District Court denied the accused's motion to dismiss the § 924(c)(1) charge on the asserted basis that venue for trial of that charge was proper in only Maryland, which was the only federal judicial district in which the government had proved that the accused had used the gun, the accused was found guilty on both kidnapping charges and on the 924(c)(1) charge. The United States Court of Appeals for the Third Circuit, in reversing the § 924(c)(1) conviction, applied what it called the "verb test" in concluding that venue for a 924(c)(1) charge was proper in only a district in which a defendant used or carried a firearm, and thus was improper in New Jersey in this case, even though venue was proper there for the kidnapping charges (121 F3d 841).

On certiorari, the United States Supreme Court reversed. In an opinion by THOMAS, J., joined by REHNQUIST, Ch. J., and O'CONNOR, KENNEDY, SOUTER, GINSBURG, and BREYER, JJ., it was held that venue in a prosecution under § 924(c)(1) was proper in any federal judicial district where the underlying crime of violence was committed, and therefore, venue was proper in New Jersey for prosecution of the § 924(c)(1) charge against the accused, because (1) the kidnapping, to which the § 924(c)(1) offense was attached, was committed in all of the places in which any part of the kidnapping took place, (2) 18 USCS § 3237(a) provided that a continuing offense can be tried in any district in which such offense was begun, continued, or completed, and (3) where venue was appropriate for the underlying crime of violence, so too it was for the § 924(c)(1) offense.

SCALIA, J., joined by STEVENS, J., dissenting, expressed the view that (1) the crime defined in § 924(c)(1) could be committed only where the defendant both engaged in the acts making up the predicate offense and used or carried a gun, and (2) because the accused's use of the gun occurred only in Maryland, venue lay only there.

COUNSEL

Paul R. Q. Wolfson argued the cause for petitioner.
John P. McDonald argued the cause for respondent.

DAVID CONN and CAROL NAJERA, Petitioners

v

PAUL L. GABBERT

526 US —, 143 L Ed 2d 399, 119 S Ct 1292

[No. 97-1802]

Argued February 23, 1999.
Decided April 5, 1999.

Decision: Two county prosecutors held not to have violated attorney's Fourteenth Amendment right to practice his profession when prosecutors arranged for attorney to be searched at same time that his client was testifying before grand jury.

SUMMARY

Two California county prosecutors were involved in arranging for the search, pursuant to a warrant, of an attorney in a private room while one of his clients was testifying before a county grand jury. The prosecutors had learned that the attorney's client might have received a letter which might have instructed the client to testify falsely and which the client might have given to the attorney. The search produced two pages of a three-page letter to the client. The client was unable to speak with the attorney during the search. The attorney (1) brought suit in a Federal District Court under 42 USCS § 1983 against the prosecutors and some others, and (2) included a claim that the prosecutors, in executing the search warrant at the same time that the client was testifying before the grand jury, violated the attorney's alleged right, under the Federal Constitution's Fourteenth Amendment, to practice his profession without unreasonable government interference. However, the District Court granted a motion by the prosecutors for summary judgment in the basis of qualified immunity. On appeal, the United States Court of Appeals for the Ninth Circuit—in reversing in pertinent part and in ordering a remand—expressed the view that the prosecutors were not entitled to qualified immunity on the Fourteenth Amendment claim, as (1) the attorney's right to practice his profession without undue and unreasonable government interference was "clearly established" at the time of the search, (2) the "plain and intended" result of the prosecutors' actions was to prevent the attorney from consulting with the client during the client's grand jury appearance, and (3) these actions were not objectively reasonable (131 F3d 793, 1997 US App LEXIS 34195).

On certiorari, the United States Supreme Court reversed. In an opinion by REHNQUIST, Ch. J., joined by O'CONNOR, SCALIA, KENNEDY, SOUTER, THOMAS, GINSBURG, and BREYER JJ., it was held that the prosecutors did not violate the attorney's Fourteenth Amendment right to practice his profession when the prosecutors arranged for the attorney to be searched at the same time that his client was testifying before the grand jury, regardless of whether the search warrant's execution was calculated to annoy or even to prevent consultation with the client, because (1) the Fourteenth Amendment's liberty right to choose and follow one's calling is not infringed by the inevitable interruptions of one's daily routine as a result of legal process which all may experience from time to time; (2) the attorney had no standing to raise the alleged infringement of his client's rights; and (3) while the attorney had standing to complain of the allegedly unreasonable timing of the warrant's execution to prevent him from advising his client, (a) this complaint in essence argued that the prosecutors searched the attorney in an unreasonable manner, and (b) challenges to the reasonableness of a search by government agents fell under the Constitution's Fourth Amendment, not the Fourteenth Amendment.

STEVENS, J., concurring in the judgment, expressed the view that (1) the prosecutors' conduct did not deprive the attorney of liberty or property in violation of the Fourteenth Amendment, as there was (a) no evidence that his income, reputation, clientele, or professional qualifications were adversely affected by the search, and (b) no real evidence or allegation that his client was substantially prejudiced by what occurred; and (2) this Fourteenth Amendment conclusion ought to be reached independently of the question whether the prosecutors might have violated the Fourth Amendment.

COUNSEL

Kevin C. Brazile argued the cause for petitioners.

Michael J. Lightfoot argued the cause for respondent.

WYOMING, Petitioner

v

SANDRA HOUGHTON

526 US —, 143 L Ed 2d 408, 119 S Ct 1297

[No. 98-184]

Argued January 12, 1999.
Decided April 5, 1999.

Decision: Police officers with probable cause to conduct warrantless search of car for contraband held not to violate Fourth Amendment by searching passenger's personal belongings in car that are capable of concealing contraband.

SUMMARY

During a Wyoming Highway Patrol officer's stop of an automobile, all three occupants of which were in the front seat, for speeding and driving with a faulty brake light, the driver admitted that he used a hypodermic syringe—that the officer had noticed in the driver's shirt pocket—to take drugs. In light of this admission, the officer searched the passenger compartment for contraband, and on the back seat, he found a purse, which a passenger claimed as hers. The officer (1) removed a wallet from the purse, (2) learned that the passenger had falsely identified herself, and (3) continued his search of the purse. After the officer's search of the purse revealed methamphetamine and drug paraphernalia, and after the officer found fresh needle-track marks on the passenger's arms, the passenger was arrested and was charged under state law with possession of methamphetamine. A state trial court denied

131

the passenger's motion to suppress all evidence obtained from the purse as the fruit of a violation of the prohibition, under the Federal Constitution's Fourth Amendment, of unreasonable searches, and the passenger was convicted as charged. The Wyoming Supreme Court, in reversing the conviction, concluded that the search of the purse violated the Fourth Amendment because (1) the officer knew or should have known that the purse did not belong to the driver, and (2) there was no probable cause to search the passengers' personal effects and no reason to believe that contraband had been placed within the purse (956 P2d 363).

On certiorari, the United States Supreme Court reversed. In an opinion by SCALIA, J., joined by REHNQUIST, Ch. J., and O'CONNOR, KENNEDY, THOMAS, and BREYER, JJ., it was held that police officers with probable cause to conduct a warrantless search of a car for contraband do not violate the Fourth Amendment by searching a passenger's personal belongings in the car that are capable of concealing contraband, because (1) neither United States v Ross (1982) 456 US 798, 72 L Ed 2d 572, 102 S Ct 2157—which held that if probable cause justifies the warrantless search of a lawfully stopped vehicle, it justifies the search of every part of the vehicle and its contents that may conceal the object of the search—nor the historical evidence it relied upon admits of a distinction among packages or containers based on ownership, and (2) the balancing of the relative interests weighs decidedly in favor of allowing searches of a passenger's belongings, as with respect to car searches, (a) a passenger's privacy expectations are considerably diminished, and (b) the governmental interests at stake are substantial.

BREYER, J., concurring, expressed the view that the rule being described by the court (1) applies only to (a) automobile searches, and (b) containers found within automobiles; and (2) does not extend to the search of a person found in that automobile.

STEVENS, J., joined by SOUTER and GINSBURG, JJ., dissenting, expressed the view that (1) regardless of whether the Fourth Amendment required a warrant to search the passenger's purse, the officer had to have probable cause to believe that the purse contained contraband, which the Wyoming Supreme Court concluded he did not, and (2) the state's legitimate interest in effective law enforcement did not outweigh the privacy concerns at issue.

COUNSEL

Paul S. Rehurek argued the cause for petitioner.

Barbara B. McDowell argued the cause for the United States, as amicus curiae, by special leave of court.

Donna D. Domonkos argued the cause for respondent.

AMANDA MITCHELL, Petitioner

v

UNITED STATES

526 US —, 143 L Ed 2d 424, 119 S Ct 1307

[No. 97-7541]

Argued December 9, 1998.
Decided April 5, 1999.

Decision: Guilty plea in federal case held not to be waiver of right to invoke privilege against self-incrimination in sentencing phase; also, drawing by sentencer of adverse inference from accused's failure to testify held to violate Fifth Amendment.

SUMMARY

An accused pleaded guilty to federal charges of conspiring to distribute 5 or more kilograms of cocaine and of distributing cocaine, but reserved the right to contest at sentencing the drug quantity attributable under the conspiracy count. Before accepting the plea, the Federal District Court judge (1) made the inquiries required by Rule 11 of the Federal Rules of Criminal Procedure; (2) told the accused that she faced a mandatory minimum of 1 year in prison for distributing cocaine, but a 10-year minimum for conspiracy if the government could show the required 5 kilograms; and (3) explained that, by pleading guilty, she would be waiving her right at trial to remain silent. The judge put the accused under oath and asked her "Did you do that?" The accused indicated that she had done some of the proffered conduct and confirmed her guilty plea. At her sentencing hearing, three codefendants testified that she had sold $1^{1}/_{2}$ to 2 ounces of cocaine twice a week for $1^{1}/_{2}$ years, and another person testified that petitioner had sold her 2 ounces of cocaine. The accused put on no evidence and argued that the only reliable evidence showed that she had sold only 2 ounces of cocaine. The District Court (1) ruled that as a consequence of accused's guilty plea, she had no right, at the sentencing hearing, to remain silent about her crime's details; (2) found that the codefendants' testimony put her over the 5-kilogram threshold, thus mandating the 10-year minimum; and (3) noted that her failure to testify was a factor in persuading the court to rely on the codefendants' testimony. The United States Court of Appeals for the Third Circuit affirmed (122 F3d 185).

On certiorari, the United States Supreme Court reversed and remanded. In an opinion by KENNEDY, J., joined by STEVENS, SOUTER, GINSBURG, and BREYER, JJ., it was held that (1) in the federal criminal system, a guilty plea was not a waiver of an accused's privilege against self-incrimination under the Federal Constitution's Fifth Amendment, as (a) the accused's testimony under oath in a plea colloquy did not waive her right to invoke the privilege against self-incrimination, (b) Rule 11 did not prevent the accused from relying upon the privilege at sentencing, and (c) under the Fifth Amendment, incrimination was not complete until a sentence was fixed and the judgment of conviction became final; and (2) in determining facts about the crime which bore upon the severity of the sentence, the trial court could not, under the Fifth Amendment, draw an adverse inference from the accused's silence in exercising her privilege against self-incrimination, where (a) a sentencing hearing was part of the criminal case, and

(b) the concerns mandating the rule against negative inferences at trial applied with equal force at sentencing.

SCALIA, J., joined by REHNQUIST, Ch. J., and O'CONNOR and THOMAS, JJ., dissenting, expressed the view that (1) the Supreme Court properly held that the accused did not waive her privilege against self-incrimination by entering a guilty plea, but (2) the accused did not have the right, under the Fifth Amendment, to have the sentencer abstain from making the adverse inferences that reasonably flowed from her failure to testify.

THOMAS, J., dissenting, expressed the view that (1) the Fifth Amendment does not prohibit a sentencer from drawing an adverse inference from an accused's failure to testify, and (2) the Supreme Court should be willing to reconsider, in the appropriate case, its precedents regarding the rule against negative inferences.

COUNSEL

Steven A. Morley argued the cause for petitioner.

Michael R. Dreeben argued the cause for respondent.

MURPHY BROTHERS, INC., Petitioner

v

MICHETTI PIPE STRINGING, INC.

526 US —, 143 L Ed 2d 448, 119 S Ct 1322

[No. 97-1909]

Argued March 1, 1999.
Decided April 5, 1999.

Decision: Under 28 USCS § 1446(b), defendant's time
to remove case held triggered by service of summons and complaint—or receipt of complaint
after and apart from service of summons—and not
by receipt of complaint without any formal service.

SUMMARY

On January 26, 1996, a Canadian company filed a
complaint against an Illinois corporation in an Alabama state court with regard to an alleged breach of
contract and fraud. The plaintiff did not serve the
defendant at that time, but 3 days later the plaintiff's
counsel faxed a so-called courtesy copy of the file-
stamped complaint to one of the defendant's officers.
On February 12, 1996, the plaintiff officially served the
defendant under local law by certified mail. On March
13, 1996—30 days after service but 44 days after receiving the faxed copy of the complaint—the defendant
removed the case under 28 USCS § 1441 to the United
States District Court for the Northern District of Alabama. The plaintiff moved to remand the case to the
state court on the ground that the removal had been
untimely under 28 USCS § 1446(b), which provides, in
relevant part, that a notice of removal must be filed

137

within 30 days after the receipt by the defendant, through service or otherwise, of a copy of the complaint—or within 30 days after the service of summons upon the defendant if the complaint has then been filed in the state court and is not required to be served on the defendant—whichever period is shorter. The District Court denied the remand motion on the ground that the 30-day removal period had not commenced until the defendant had been officially served with a summons. On interlocutory appeal, the United States Court of Appeals for the Eleventh Circuit—in reversing, remanding, and instructing the District Court to remand the action to state court—reasoned that the words "receipt . . . or otherwise" in § 1446(b) indicated that the defendant's receipt of a faxed copy of the filed complaint had sufficed to commence the 30-day removal period (125 F3d 1396, 1997 US App LEXIS 29128).

On certiorari, the United States Supreme Court reversed and remanded. In an opinion by GINSBURG, J., joined by STEVENS, O'CONNOR, KENNEDY, SOUTER, and BREYER, JJ., it was held that under § 1446(b), a named defendant's time to remove is triggered by simultaneous service of the summons and complaint—or receipt of the complaint, through service or otherwise, after and apart from service of the summons—and not by mere receipt of the complaint unattended by any formal service, for (1) such an interpretation of § 1446(b) (a) adheres to tradition, (b) makes sense of the phrase "or otherwise," and (c) assures defendants adequate time to decide whether to remove an action; (2) Rule 81(c) of the Federal Rules of Civil Procedure, which uses the identical "receipt through service or otherwise" language in specifying a 20-day time period that a defendant has to answer the complaint once the case has been removed, has sensibly has been interpreted to afford the defendant at least 20 days after service of process to respond; and (3) a so-called "receipt rule"—starting the time to remove on receipt of a copy of the complaint, however informally, despite the absence of any formal service—could operate with unfairness to individuals and entities in foreign nations.

REHNQUIST, Ch. J., joined by SCALIA and THOMAS, JJ., dissenting, expressed the view that the receipt of the facsimile complaint triggered the 30-day removal period under the plain language of § 1446(b), which ought to have controlled.

COUNSEL

Deborah A. Smith argued the cause for petitioner.
J. David Pugh argued the cause for respondent.

UNUM LIFE INSURANCE COMPANY OF AMERICA,
Petitioner

v

JOHN E. WARD

526 US —, 143 L Ed 2d 462, 119 S Ct 1380

[No. 97-1868]

Argued February 24, 1999.
Decided April 20, 1999.

Decision: California's notice-prejudice rule held saved
from pre-emption by Employee Retirement In-
come Security Act of 1974 (ERISA) (29 USCS
§§ 1001 et seq.); however, California's agency rule
held not to escape ERISA's pre-emption clause.

SUMMARY

An insurance company issued a long-term group
disability policy to an employer as an insured welfare
benefit plan governed by the Employee Retirement
Income Security Act of 1974 (ERISA) (29 USCS §§ 1001
et seq.). The policy provided that proofs of claim had to
be furnished to the insurance company, at the latest, 1
year and 180 days after the onset of a disability. An
employee (1) became permanently disabled on May 5,
1992; (2) informed the employer of his disability in late
February or early March 1993; and (3) completed an
application for benefits under the ERISA-governed
plan and forwarded it to the employer in April 1994.
The employer forwarded the application to the insurance company, which received proof of the employee's
claim on April 11, 1994. This notice was late under the
terms of the policy. The insurance company advised the

employee that his claim was denied as untimely. In September 1994, the employee filed suit in a Federal District Court against the employer's plan under § 502(a) of ERISA (29 USCS § 1132(a)) to recover the disability benefits provided by the plan. The insurance company appeared as a defendant and answered on behalf of itself and the plan. The employee argued that (1) under California's common-law agency rule, a California employer that administers an insured group health plan should be deemed to act as the agent of the insurance company; and (2) therefore, the notice of permanent disability to the employer sufficed to supply timely notice to the insurance company. However, the District Court rendered summary judgment in the insurance company's favor, as the court expressed the view that the agency rule was (1) pre-empted under § 514(a) of ERISA (29 USCS § 1144(a)) as a law which related to ERISA plans, and (2) not saved from pre-emption as a law that regulated insurance within the compass of the saving clause, § 514(b)(2)(A), of ERISA (29 USCS § 1144(b)(2)(A)). The United States Court of Appeals for the Ninth Circuit, in reversing and ordering a remand, expressed the view that (1) California's notice-prejudice rule—under which an insurer could not avoid liability where a proof of claim was untimely unless the insurer showed it suffered actual prejudice from the delay—was saved from ERISA pre-emption as a law that regulated insurance; and (2) California's agency rule did not relate to employee benefit plans and therefore was not pre-empted by reason of ERISA (135 F3d 1276).

On certiorari, the United States Supreme Court affirmed in part, reversed in part, and remanded. In an opinion by GINSBURG, J., expressing the unanimous view of the court, it was held that (1) the notice-prejudice rule was a "law . . . which regulates insurance," and was therefore saved from pre-emption by § 514(b)(2)(A), where the rule (a) regulated insurance as a matter of common sense, (b) served as an integral part of the policy relationship between the insurer and the insured, and (c) was limited to entities within the insurance industry; and (2) the agency rule related to an employee benefit plan such that the rule was subject to ERISA's pre-emption clause, as such a rule—in forcing an employer to assume a role, with attendant legal duties and consequences, that it had not undertaken voluntarily—had a marked effect on administration of the plan.

COUNSEL

William J. Kayatta, Jr. argued the cause for petitioner.

Edwin S. Kneedler argued the cause for the United States, as amicus curiae, by special leave of court.

Jeffrey I. Erlich argued the cause for respondent.

UNITED STATES, Petitioner

v

HAGGAR APPAREL COMPANY

526 US —, 143 L Ed 2d 480, 119 S Ct 1392

[No. 97-2044]

Argued January 11, 1999.
Decided April 21, 1999.

Decision: Customs classification regulation held (1)
subject to analysis under rule of Chevron U. S. A. v
Natural Resources Defense Council, and (2) required to be given judicial deference if regulation
is reasonable interpretation of ambiguous statutory provision.

SUMMARY

Subheading 9802.00.80 of the Harmonized Tariff
Schedule of the United States (HTSUS) (19 USCS
§ 1202) provided importers a partial exemption from
duties otherwise imposed for articles which (1) were
assembled abroad, but (2) were not advanced in value
or improved in condition abroad, except by operations
incidental to the assembly process. A regulation issued
by the United States Customs Service provided that (1)
chemical treatment of components or assembled articles to impart new characteristics were operations not
considered incidental to the assembly, and (2) among
examples of such operations was "permapressing" (19
CFR § 10.16(c)(4)). An importer had customs duties
imposed upon garments which it shipped to the United
States from an assembly plant it controlled in Mexico.
While in Mexico, the garments were subjected to one of

several different methods of permapressing to maintain creases and avoid wrinkles. The Customs Service denied a duty exemption under § 10.16(c)(4). The importer brought suit for refund in the Court of International Trade, which did not treat the regulation as controlling and ruled in the importer's favor. The United States Court of Appeals for the Federal Circuit (1) declined to analyze the regulation, under the rule of Chevron U. S. A. v Natural Resources Defense Council (1984) 467 US 837, 81 L Ed 2d 694, 104 S Ct 2778, to determine whether the regulation was required to be given judicial deference, and (2) affirmed (127 F3d 1460).

On certiorari, the United States Supreme Court vacated the judgment of the Court of Appeals and remanded the case. In an opinion by KENNEDY, J., expressing the unanimous view of the court as to holdings (1) and (2) below, and joined by REHNQUIST, Ch. J., and O'CONNOR, SCALIA, SOUTER, THOMAS, and BREYER, JJ., as to holding (3) below, it was held that (1) the regulation was subject to analysis under Chevron U. S. A. v Natural Resources Defense Council, supra, as (a) the regulation was not limited in application to customs officers, but governed the adjudication of the importer's suit for refund, (b) the Court of International Trade was not empowered by statutory provision to interpret the tariff statute without giving deference to regulations, and (c) the historical practice in customs cases did not indicate that judicial deference would thwart congressional intent; (2) if the regulation was a reasonable interpretation and implementation of an ambiguous statutory provision, it was required to be given judicial deference in the Court of International Trade; and (3) the Supreme Court declined to consider the question whether the regulation met the conditions for judicial deference as a reasonable interpretation of a statutory phrase, as such a question was best addressed in the first instance to the Court of Appeals or to the Court of International Trade.

STEVENS, J., joined by GINSBURG, J., concurring in part and dissenting in part, expressed the view that the Supreme Court should have (1) decided the reasonableness of the regulation, and (2) held that (a) the regulation was a reasonable elaboration of the statute, and (b) the denial of the duty allowance was consistent with the regulation and well within the scope of the Customs Service's congressionally delegated authority.

COUNSEL

Kent L. Jones argued the cause for petitioner.
Carter G. Phillips argued the cause for respondent.

UNITED STATES, Petitioner

v

SUN-DIAMOND GROWERS OF CALIFORNIA

526 US —, 143 L Ed 2d 576, 119 S Ct 1402

[No. 98-131]

Argued March 2, 1999.
Decided April 27, 1999.

Decision: Conviction under illegal gratuity statute (18 USCS § 201(c)(1)(A)) held to require link between thing of value conferred upon public official and specific official act for or because of which thing was given.

SUMMARY

The illegal gratuity statute (18 USCS § 201(c)(1)(A)) makes it a criminal offense for anyone to give anything of value to a public official "for or because of any official act performed or to be performed" by such official. An agricultural trade association was charged, among other things, with violating § 201(c)(1)(A) by giving tickets, luggage, meals, and other gratuities worth more than $5,000 to the United States Secretary of Agriculture. The indictment, while mentioning certain matters as to which the association allegedly had an interest in favorable decisions by the Secretary at the time that the association made the gifts, did not allege a specific connection between those matters and the gratuities. The association therefore moved to dismiss that charge. The United States District Court for the District of Columbia (1) denied the motion (941 F Supp 1262); and (2) included, in the court's instruc-

tion to the jury concerning the scope of
§ 201(c)(1)(A), statements that (a) it was sufficient if
the association provided the Secretary with unautho-
rized compensation simply because he held public
office, and (b) the government did not need to prove
that "the alleged gratuity was linked to a specific or
identifiable official act or any act at all." The United
States Court of Appeals for the District of Columbia
Circuit, however, reversed the association's subsequent
conviction on the illegal gratuity charge and remanded
the case for a new trial on that charge, as the court
ruled that the District Court's instructions had invited
the jury to convict on materially less evidence than the
statute demanded (138 F3d 961).

On certiorari, the United States Supreme Court
affirmed. In an opinion by SCALIA, J., expressing the
unanimous view of the court, it was held that in order
to establish a violation of § 201(c)(1)(A), the government had to prove a link between a thing of value
conferred upon a public official and a specific official
act for or because of which the thing was given.

COUNSEL

Robert W. Ray argued the cause for petitioner.
Eric W. Bloom argued the cause for respondent.

———

IMMIGRATION AND NATURALIZATION SERVICE,
Petitioner

v

JUAN ANIBAL AGUIRRE-AGUIRRE

526 US —, 143 L Ed 2d 590, 119 S Ct 1439

[No. 97-1754]

Argued March 3, 1999.
Decided May 3, 1999.

Decision: Federal Court of Appeals held to have failed
to accord required deference to Board of Immigration Appeals' interpretation of 8 USCS
§ 1253(h) with respect to alien's entitlement to
withholding of deportation.

SUMMARY

Provisions of the Immigration and Nationality Act
(INA) (8 USCS §§ 1101 et seq.) (later amended)
provided that (1) the United States Attorney General
shall not have deported or returned any alien to a
country if the Attorney General determined that such
alien's life or freedom would have been threatened in
such country on account of political opinion (8 USCS
§ 1253(h)(1)), however (2) such withholding of deportation was not available if the Attorney General found
that an alien committed a "serious nonpolitical crime"
before arriving in the United States (8 USCS
§ 1253(h)(2)(C)). An alien, a citizen of Guatemala,
requested withholding of his deportation by the Immigration and Naturalization Service. The alien
testified—in Spanish through an interpreter—at an
administrative hearing that in protesting various gov-

ernment policies and actions in Guatemala, he had burned buses, assaulted passengers, and vandalized and destroyed private property. An immigration judge granted the alien's request, but the Board of Immigration Appeals (BIA) found that his were serious nonpolitical crimes and vacated the order. The BIA (1) applied the weighing test it had developed in an earlier decision, and (2) concluded that the common-law or criminal character of the alien's acts outweighed their political nature. The United States Court of Appeals for the Ninth Circuit, in ordering a remand, found that the BIA should have (1) balanced the alien's admitted offenses against the threat of persecution; (2) considered whether his acts were grossly disproportionate to their alleged objective and were atrocious, especially with reference to Court of Appeals precedent; and (3) considered the political necessity and success of the alien's methods (121 F3d 521).

On certiorari, the United States Supreme Court reversed and remanded. In an opinion by KENNEDY, J., expressing the unanimous view of the court, it was held that in requiring the BIA to supplement its weighing test for determining the alien's entitlement to withholding of deportation under the INA, the Court of Appeals failed to accord to the BIA's interpretation of the statute the deference required under the rule of Chevron U. S. A. Inc. v Natural Resources Defense Council (1984) 467 US 837, 81 L Ed 2d 694, 104 S Ct 2778, as (1) the questions confronted by the Court of Appeals implicated an agency's construction of the statute which it administered, (2) Chevron deference applied to the statutory scheme of the INA, and (3) the reason given by the Court of Appeals for ordering a remand—that the BIA should have considered the three additional factors—did not withstand scrutiny under Chevron principles.

COUNSEL

Patricia A. Millett argued the cause for petitioner.

Nadine K. Wettstein argued the cause for respondent.

BANK OF AMERICA NATIONAL TRUST AND SAV-
INGS ASSOCIATION, Petitioner

v

203 NORTH LaSALLE STREET PARTNERSHIP

526 US —, 143 L Ed 2d 607, 119 S Ct 1411

[No. 97-1418]

Argued November 2, 1998.
Decided May 3, 1999.

Decision: Under 11 USCS § 1129(b)(2)(B)(ii), debt-
or's prebankruptcy equity holders held to be disqualified from contributing new capital and receiving ownership interests in reorganized entity
under nonconsensual reorganization plan giving
holders exclusive ownership opportunity.

SUMMARY

In order for confirmation of a plan for reorganization of a bankrupt entity to be imposed under the 11
USCS § 1129(b) "cramdown" process over the objection of an impaired class of unsecured creditors whose
claims will not be paid in full under the plan, 11 USCS
§ 1129(b)(2)(B)(ii) imposes an absolute priority rule
that bars the holder of any claim or interest that is
junior to a class of impaired unsecured creditors from
receiving or retaining under the plan on account of
such junior claim or interest any property, when any
member of the senior class objects to such a plan
arrangement. A real estate limited partnership filed a
voluntary petition for relief under Chapter 11 of the
Bankruptcy Code (11 USCS §§ 1101 et seq.) and proposed a reorganization plan under which certain for-

151

mer partners of the partnership would contribute new capital in exchange for the entire ownership of the reorganized partnership. After a bank whose outstanding loan balance due from the original partnership would not be paid in full under the plan, which bank was the sole member of an impaired class of unsecured creditors, objected to the plan, and thereby blocked consensual confirmation of the plan under 11 USCS § 1129(a)(8), the United States Bankruptcy Court for the Northern District of Illinois confirmed the plan (190 BR 567). The Bankruptcy Court's judgment was affirmed by the United States District Court for the Northern District of Illinois (195 BR 692), whose judgment was affirmed by the United States Court of Appeals for the Seventh Circuit, which expressed the view that the phrase "on account of" in § 1129(b)(2)(B)(ii) permitted recognition of a "new value corollary" under which a debtor's old equity holders who retained a property interest in the debtor after reorganization did not do so on account of prior equitable ownership of the debtor, if they contributed new capital that was reasonably equivalent to the property's value and was necessary for successful reorganization of the restructured enterprise (126 F3d 955).

On certiorari, the United States Supreme Court reversed and remanded. In an opinion by SOUTER, J., joined by REHNQUIST, Ch. J., and O'CONNOR, KENNEDY, GINSBURG, and BREYER, JJ., it was held, without deciding whether the statute included a new value corollary, that the reorganization plan proposed by the original partnership could not be confirmed, because old equity holders were disqualified from participating in such a "new value" transaction by the terms of § 1129(b)(2)(B)(ii), as (1) the better reading of § 1129(b)(2)(B)(ii) recognized that a causal relationship between holding the prior claim or interest and receiving or retaining property was what activated the absolute priority rule, where "on account of" was meant to mean "because of" at other places in the Bankruptcy Code (11 USCS §§ 101 et seq.), (2) the partners' exclusive opportunity to obtain equity in the reorganized partnership should be treated as an item of property in its own right, and (3) the exclusiveness of the opportunity, with its protection against the market's scrutiny of the purchase price, rendered the partners' right a property interest extended on account of the old equity position.

THOMAS, J., joined by SCALIA, J., concurring in the judgment, (1) agreed that the reorganization plan could not be confirmed, but (2) expressed the view that the reasons that the plan could not be confirmed were (a) the bank did not receive, under the plan, property equal to the amount of the bank's unsecured deficiency claim, and (b) the partners received at least one form of property—the exclusive opportunity to obtain equity in the reorganized partnership—on account of their equity interest in the original partnership.

STEVENS, J., dissenting, expressed the view that (1) under § 1129(b)(2)(B)(ii), the holder of a junior claim or interest does not receive property on account of such a claim when the holder's participation in a reorganization plan is based on adequate new value; and (2) the court's objections to the plan in question were unsupported by either the text of § 1129(b)(2)(B)(ii) or the record in the case, for if the new capital that a junior claimant invests has a value equivalent to or greater than the claimant's interest in the reorganized venture, then the claimant's participation is (a) based on the fair price being paid, and (b) not on account of the claimant's old claim or equity.

COUNSEL

Roy T. Englert, Jr. argued the cause for petitioner.

Patricia A. Millett argued the cause for the United States, as amicus curiae, by special leave of court.

Richard M. Bendix, Jr. argued the cause for respondent.

EL PASO NATURAL GAS COMPANY, et al., Petitioners

v

LAURA NEZTSOSIE, et al.

526 US —, 143 L Ed 2d 635, 119 S Ct 1430

[No. 98-6]

Argued March 2, 1999.
Decided May 3, 1999.

Decision: Tribal court exhaustion doctrine held not to require Federal District Court to let tribal court decide whether tribe members' causes of action against uranium mine operators were claims under Price-Anderson Act (42 USCS § 2210).

SUMMARY

The Price-Anderson Act, in pertinent part, (1) grants Federal District Courts original and removal jurisdiction over all public liability actions arising out of nuclear incidents (42 USCS § 2210(n)(2)), (2) makes such a public liability action a federal action (42 USCS § 2014(hh)), and (3) defines nuclear incidents as occurrences that cause various forms of harm arising from hazardous properties of nuclear material (42 USCS § 2014(q)). Some members of the Navajo Nation filed tort suits under tribal law in the District Court of the Navajo Nation—a tribal court—against some uranium mine operators for damages allegedly suffered as a result of mining operations. The mine operators, filing suit in the United States District Court for the District of Arizona, sought to enjoin the plaintiffs from pursuing their claims in the tribal court. The Federal

District Court, citing the judicially created doctrine of tribal court exhaustion—which requires a Federal District Court to stay its hand while a tribal court determines its own jurisdiction—(1) denied preliminary injunctions except to the extent that the plaintiffs sought relief in the tribal court under the Price-Anderson Act, (2) declined to decide whether the Price-Anderson Act applied to the plaintiffs' claims, and (3) left such determinations to the tribal court in the first instance. On the mine operators' consolidated appeals, the United States Court of Appeals for the Ninth Circuit (1) affirmed the Federal District Court's decisions (a) not to enjoin the plaintiffs from pursuing non-Price-Anderson Act claims, and (b) to allow the tribal court to decide in the first instance whether the plaintiffs' claims fell within the ambit of the Price-Anderson Act; (2) addressed, on the Court of Appeals' own motion, the partial injunctions against the plaintiffs on the ground that important comity considerations were involved; and (3) reversed as to the injunctions on the ground that the Price-Anderson Act did not expressly bar the tribal court from determining the tribal court's own jurisdiction over Price-Anderson Act claims (136 F3d 610, 1998 US App LEXIS 1858).

On certiorari, the United States Supreme Court (1) vacated the Court of Appeals' judgment, and (2) remanded the case with instructions to remand to the Federal District Court for further proceedings. In an opinion by SOUTER, J., expressing the unanimous view of the court, it was held that (1) those portions of the Federal District Court's orders that enjoined the tribe members from pursuing Price-Anderson Act claims were not properly before the Court of Appeals; and (2) the tribal court exhaustion doctrine did not require the Federal District Court to abstain from deciding whether the tribe members' causes of action were, as a matter of

156

law, claims under the Price-Anderson Act, for (a) in the Price-Anderson Act's pre-emption provision (§ 2014(hh)), Congress expressed an unmistakable preference for a federal forum, at the behest of the defending party, both for litigating a Price-Anderson Act claim on the merits and for determining whether a claim falls under the Price-Anderson Act when removal is contested, (b) the apparent reasons for the congressional policy of immediate access to a federal forum were as much applicable to tribal court litigation as to state court litigation, and (c) the force of these congressional concerns sapped of any plausibility various arguable justifications for applying tribal court exhaustion.

COUNSEL

James R. Atwood argued the cause for petitioners.

Jonathan E. Nuechterlein argued the cause for the United States, as amicus curiae, by special leave of court.

H. Bartow Farr, III argued the cause for respondents.

RITA L. SAENZ, Director, California Department of
Social Services, et al., Petitioners

v

BRENDA ROE and ANNA DOE, on Behalf of Themselves and All Others Similarly Situated

526 US —, 143 L Ed 2d 689, 119 S Ct 1518

[No. 98-97]

Argued January 13, 1999.
Decided May 27, 1999.

Decision: California durational residency statute limiting new residents' welfare benefits to amount
receivable in state of former residence held (1) to
violate Fourteenth Amendment right to travel, and
(2) not to be resuscitated by 42 USCS § 604(c),
purporting to authorize such benefit limits.

SUMMARY

California, which has welfare benefit levels that are
lower than the levels in 5 states but higher than the
levels in 44 states and the District of Columbia, enacted
in 1992 a statute that limited the amount of welfare
benefits for a family that had resided in California for
less than 12 months to the amount that would have
been received by the family from the state of the
family's prior residence. Subsequently, Congress enacted a Personal Responsibility and Work Opportunity
Reconciliation Act of 1996 (PRWORA) provision, 42
USCS § 604(c), that expressly authorized such durational residency requirements. A class action challenging the federal constitutionality of California's durational residency requirement and the PRWORA's

authorization of the requirement was filed in the United States District Court for the Eastern District of California. After the District Court preliminarily enjoined the implementation of the California statute, the United States Court of Appeals for the Ninth Circuit, agreeing with the District Court that the class members might suffer irreparable harm if the California statute became operative, affirmed the issuance of the injunction without reaching the merits of the case (134 F3d 1400).

On certiorari, the United States Supreme Court affirmed. In an opinion by STEVENS, J., joined by O'CONNOR, SCALIA, KENNEDY, SOUTER, GINSBURG, and BREYER, JJ., it was held that (1) the state statute violated the interstate travel right, protected under the citizenship clause contained in § 1 of the Federal Constitution's Fourteenth Amendment, of a newly arrived citizen of a state to the same privileges and immunities enjoyed by other citizens of the state, because (a) the citizenship clause does not allow for degrees of citizenship based on length of residence and does not tolerate a hierarchy of 45 subclasses of similarly situated citizens based on the location of their prior residence, and (b) the state's legitimate interest in saving money provided no justification for its decision to discriminate among equally eligible citizens; and (2) congressional approval, in § 604(c), of such durational residency requirements as the requirement in question did not resuscitate the constitutionality of the state statute, as Congress has no affirmative power to authorize the states to violate the Fourteenth Amendment and is implicitly prohibited from passing legislation that purports to validate any such violation.

REHNQUIST, Ch. J., joined by THOMAS, J., dissenting, expressed the view that (1) the state statute was a reasonable measure falling under the head of a good-faith residency requirement, (2) the right to travel and the right to become a citizen of a new state are distinct, their relationship is not reciprocal, and one is not a component of the other, and (3) the durational residency requirement was a permissible exercise of the state's power to assure that services provided for its residents were enjoyed only by residents.

THOMAS, J., joined by REHNQUIST, Ch. J., dissenting, expressed the view that the court (1) had attributed a meaning to the Fourteenth Amendment's privileges and immunities clause that likely was unintended when the Amendment was enacted and ratified, and (2) should have looked to history to ascertain the original meaning of the clause.

COUNSEL

Theodore Garelis argued the cause for petitioners.

Seth P. Waxman argued the cause for the United States, as amicus curiae, by special leave of court.

Mark D. Rosenbaum argued the cause for respondents.

WILLIAM J. CLINTON, President of the United
States, et al., Petitioners

v

JAMES T. GOLDSMITH

526 US —, 143 L Ed 2d 720, 119 S Ct 1538

[No. 98-347]

Argued March 22, 1999.
Decided May 17, 1999.

Decision: United States Court of Appeals for Armed
Forces held to lack jurisdiction, under All Writs
Act, to enjoin various federal officials from dropping major, who had been convicted by court-
martial, from rolls of United States Air Force.

SUMMARY

The All Writs Act (28 USCS § 1651(a)) authorizes
federal courts to issue all writs necessary or appropriate
in aid of their respective jurisdictions. A United States
Air Force major (1) allegedly disobeyed an order (a) to
inform his sex partners that he was HIV-positive, and
(b) to take measures to block any transfer of bodily
fluids during sexual relations; (2) was convicted by a
general court-martial on several charges; and (3) was
sentenced, in 1994, to 6 years' confinement and to a
forfeiture of some of his salary, but not to dismissal
from the service. In 1995, the Air Force Court of
Criminal Appeals affirmed the major's conviction and
sentence. When he sought no review of that decision in
the United States Court of Appeals for the Armed
Forces (CAAF), his conviction and sentence became
final. In 1996, Congress, by some changes codified at 10

USCS §§ 1161(b)(2) and 1167, expanded the President's authority by empowering the President to drop from the rolls of the Armed Forces any officer who had (1) been sentenced by a court-martial to more than 6 months' confinement, and (2) served at least 6 months. The Air Force, in reliance on this statutory authorization, notified the major that it was taking action to drop him from the rolls. Eventually, the major (1) filed with the CAAF a combined document that included a petition for extraordinary relief, and (2) asserted that the Air Force's proposed action would violate the Federal Constitution's Art I, § 9, cl 3 prohibition against ex post facto laws and the Constitution's Fifth Amendment prohibition against double jeopardy. The CAAF (1) granted the petition, and (2) relied on the All Writs Act in enjoining the President and various other executive branch officials from dropping the major from the rolls of the Air Force (48 MJ 84).

On certiorari, the United States Supreme Court reversed. In an opinion by SOUTER, J., expressing the unanimous view of the court, it was held that the CAAF lacked jurisdiction, under the All Writs Act, to issue the injunction in question, because (1) the injunction was not "in aid of" the CAAF's strictly circumscribed jurisdiction, under 10 USCS § 867, to review court-martial findings and sentences; and (2) even if the CAAF might have had some seriously arguable basis for jurisdiction, the injunction was neither "necessary" nor "appropriate," in light of the alternative federal administrative and judicial remedies available, under other federal statutes, to a service member demanding to be kept on the rolls.

COUNSEL

Michael R. Dreeben argued the cause for petitioners.

John M. Economidy argued the cause for respondent.

JAMES B. HUNT JR., Governor of North Carolina, et al., Appellants

v

MARTIN CROMARTIE et al.

526 US —, 143 L Ed 2d 731, 119 S Ct 1545

[No. 98-85]

Argued January 20, 1999.
Decided May 17, 1999.

Decision: Plaintiffs held not entitled to summary judgment on claim that North Carolina congressional district was racial gerrymander that violated equal protection, because North Carolina's motivation in drawing district was in dispute.

SUMMARY

In response to a decision of the United States Supreme Court—which held that an unusually shaped North Carolina congressional district was the product of unconstitutional racial gerrymandering—North Carolina enacted a new congressional districting plan. The plan altered the previously invalidated district in several respects, including (1) reducing the percentage of blacks in the district such that blacks no longer constituted a majority, (2) splitting fewer counties, and (3) reducing the distance between the district's farthest points. The redrawn district, however, retained its unusual snakelike shape. Some individuals, believing that the redrawn district was also unconstitutional, filed suit in the United States District Court for the Eastern District of North Carolina against several state officials to enjoin elections under the new plan. The parties filed competing motions for summary judgment and supporting materials, and the District Court heard argument on the pending motions. Before discovery, and without an evidentiary hearing, the District Court granted the individuals summary judgment and entered the injunction (order reported at 34 F Supp 2d 1029). The court concluded that (1) the district was redrawn to collect precincts with high racial identification rather than political identification, and (2) therefore had violated the equal protection clause of the Federal Constitution's Fourteenth Amendment.

On direct appeal, the United States Supreme Court reversed. In an opinion by THOMAS, J., joined by REHNQUIST, Ch. J., and O'CONNOR, SCALIA, and KENNEDY, JJ., it was held that the plaintiffs were not entitled to summary judgment, because the state legislature's motivation in drawing the district was a factual question and was in dispute, where (1) the plan was race-neutral on its face; (2) the plaintiffs were (a) required to prove that race was the predominant factor motivating the legislature's districting decision, and (b) obliged to show that the state subordinated traditional race-neutral districting principles to racial considerations; (3) while the plaintiffs' evidence tended to support an inference that the state drew its district lines with an impermissible racial motive, the state (a) asserted that the legislature intended to make a strong Democratic district, and (b) supported that contention; and (4) evidence that blacks constituted even a supermajority in one congressional district while amounting to less than a plurality in a neighboring district would not, by itself, suffice to prove that a jurisdiction was motivated by race in drawing its district lines when the evidence also showed a high correlation between race and party preference.

STEVENS, J., joined by SOUTER, GINSBURG, and BREYER, JJ., concurring in the judgment, expressed the view that two undisputed matters of fact—that (1) bizarre configuration is the traditional hallmark of the political gerrymander, and (2) a great many registered Democrats in the South do not always vote for Democratic candidates in federal elections—should be emphasized.

COUNSEL

Walter E. Dellinger argued the cause for appellants.

James A. Feldman argued the cause for the United States, as amicus curiae, by special leave of court.

Robinson O. Everett argued the cause for appellees.

FLORIDA, Petitioner

v

TYVESSEL TYVORUS WHITE

526 US —, 143 L Ed 2d 748, 119 S Ct 1555

[No. 98-223]

Argued March 23, 1999.
Decided May 17, 1999.

Decision: Federal Constitution's Fourth Amendment
held not to require police to obtain warrant before
seizing automobile from public place when police
have probable cause to believe that automobile is
forfeitable contraband.

SUMMARY

Florida police officers, while arresting an individual
on unrelated charges, seized his automobile from his
employer's parking lot without a warrant, on the
ground that (1) the individual had previously been
observed using the vehicle to deliver narcotics, and (2)
the vehicle was therefore allegedly subject to forfeiture
under the state's contraband forfeiture statute. During
a subsequent inventory search, the police found narcotics in the vehicle. The individual was charged with
possession of a controlled substance on the basis of that
discovery. At his trial on the possession charge, the
individual moved to suppress the narcotics from evidence on the theory that they were the fruits of the
warrantless seizure of the vehicle, which allegedly violated the Federal Constitution's Fourth Amendment. A
Florida trial court denied that motion after the jury
returned a guilty verdict. The First District Court of

Appeal of Florida affirmed (680 So 2d 550). However, the Supreme Court of Florida (1) expressed the view that absent exigent circumstances, the Fourth Amendment required police to obtain a warrant prior to seizing property which had been used in violation of the state statute; and (2) therefore, quashed the District Court's opinion and remanded the case (710 So 2d 949).

On certiorari, the United States Supreme Court reversed and remanded. In an opinion by THOMAS, J., joined by REHNQUIST, Ch. J., and O'CONNOR, SCALIA, KENNEDY, SOUTER, and BREYER, JJ., it was held that (1) the Fourth Amendment does not require police to obtain a warrant before seizing an automobile from a public place when the police have probable cause to believe that the vehicle itself is forfeitable contraband, and (2) therefore, the Fourth Amendment did not require a warrant under the circumstances of the case at hand.

SOUTER, J., joined by BREYER, J., concurred, expressing the view that the court's decision ought not to be read as a general endorsement of warrantless searches of anything a state chose to call contraband, regardless of whether the property was in public when seized.

STEVENS, J., joined by GINSBURG, J., dissented, expressing the view that (1) warrantless searches are presumptively invalid under the Fourth Amendment; and (2) there was no legitimate basis for an exception to that rule where (a) the seizure was based on a belief that the vehicle might have been used in the past to assist illegal activity, and (b) the vehicle's owner was already in custody.

COUNSEL

Carolyn M. Snurkowski argued the cause for petitioner.

Malcolm L. Stewart argued the cause for the United States, as amicus curiae, by special leave of court.

David P. Gauldin argued the cause for respondent.

RUHRGAS AG, Petitioner

v

MARATHON OIL COMPANY, et al.

526 US —, 143 L Ed 2d 760, 119 S Ct 1563

[No. 98-470]

Argued March 22, 1999.
Decided May 17, 1999.

Decision: Federal District Court held not to have abused discretion in addressing question of personal jurisdiction in removed case without first addressing question of subject matter jurisdiction.

SUMMARY

Two United States corporations with their principal place of business in Texas—together with a Norwegian company owned by those corporations—sued a German gas company in Texas state court on state-law claims including fraud and tortious interference with prospective business relations. The plaintiffs alleged, among other matters, that the defendant had diminished the value of a gas-production license that at one time had been held by the Norwegian company. The defendant, in removing the case to the United States District Court for the Southern District of Texas, (1) asserted (a) diversity jurisdiction under 28 USCS § 1332, on the theory that the Norwegian company had been fraudulently joined as a plaintiff in order to defeat diversity, (b) federal question jurisdiction under 28 USCS § 1331, on the ground that the plaintiffs' claims raised questions of international relations, and (c) jurisdiction under 9 USCS § 205, authorizing removal of cases relating to international arbitration agreements; and (2) moved to dismiss the complaint for lack of personal jurisdiction. The plaintiffs moved to remand the case to the state court for lack of federal subject matter jurisdiction. The District Court —without first addressing the question of subject matter jurisdiction—dismissed the case on the ground that the defendant's contacts with Texas were insufficient to support personal jurisdiction, absent evidence that the defendant had engaged in any tortious conduct in Texas or maintained systematic and continuous contacts with Texas. A panel of the United States Court of Appeals for the Fifth Circuit, in vacating and remanding on appeal, (1) concluded that respect for the proper balance of federalism impelled the Court of Appeals to turn first to the issue presented as to subject matter jurisdiction, and (2) examined and rejected each of the defendant's asserted bases of federal subject matter jurisdiction (115 F3d 315, 1997 US App LEXIS 13676, cert den 522 US 967, 139 L Ed 2d 316, 118 S Ct 413). On rehearing en banc, the Court of Appeals (1) expressed the view that in removed cases, District Courts must (a) decide issues of subject matter jurisdiction first, and (b) reach issues of personal jurisdiction only if subject matter jurisdiction is found to exist; and (2) vacated the panel's decision and remanded the case to the District Court for consideration of the subject matter jurisdiction issues presented (145 F3d 211, 1998 US App LEXIS 13358).

On certiorari, the United States Supreme Court reversed and remanded. In an opinion by GINSBURG, J., expressing the unanimous view of the court, it was held that (1) in cases removed from state court to federal court, there are circumstances in which the federal court appropriately accords priority to an inquiry as to personal jurisdiction rather than an inquiry as to subject matter jurisdiction; and (2) the federal court does not abuse its discretion by turning directly to personal jurisdiction, where—as in the case at hand—(a) there is a straightforward personal jurisdiction issue that presents no complex question of state law, and (b) the alleged defect in subject matter jurisdiction raises a difficult and novel question.

COUNSEL

Charles Alan Wright argued the cause for petitioner.

Clifton T. Hutchinson argued the cause for respondents.

———————

CHARLES H. WILSON, et ux., et al., Petitioners

v

HARRY LAYNE, Deputy United States Marshal, et al.

526 US —, 143 L Ed 2d 818, 119 S Ct 1692

[No. 98-83]

Argued March 24, 1999.
Decided May 24, 1999.

Decision: Media representatives' accompanying federal and county officers during 1992 attempt to execute arrest warrants in home held to violate Fourth Amendment, but officers held entitled to qualified immunity from damages liability under Bivens decision and under 42 USCS § 1983.

SUMMARY

On April 16, 1992, a team of police officers from the United States Marshals Service and from a Maryland county engaged in a "media ride-along," in which a print reporter and a photographer for a newspaper accompanied the officers during an attempt to execute, in a private home at a Maryland address, three arrest warrants for a suspect who was listed by a police computer as likely to be armed and to resist arrest. The execution was not successful, as among other matters (1) contrary to data in the police computer, the home in question was actually that of the suspect's parents; (2) the officers, when confronted by the suspect's father—who angrily demanded that they state their business—believed him to be the suspect and subdued him; (3) this confrontation was observed by (a) the suspect's mother, and (b) apparently, the print reporter; (4) the photographer took numerous pictures (although these were not subsequently published in the newspaper); and (5) the officers eventually departed after learning that the suspect was not in the home. Later, plaintiffs including the two parents (1) brought suit in a Federal District Court; (2) included claims for money damages against (a) the federal officers under Bivens v Six Unknown Named Agents of Federal Bureau of Narcotics (1971) 403 US 388, 29 L Ed 2d 619, 91 S Ct 1999, and (b) the county officers under 42 USCS § 1983; and (3) contended that the officers' actions in bringing representatives of the media to observe and record the attempted execution of the warrants violated the parents' rights under the Federal Constitution's Fourth Amendment. The District Court denied a motion by the officers for summary judgment on the basis of qualified immunity. On interlocutory appeal, the United States Court of Appeals for the Fourth Circuit eventually reversed in an en banc ruling, as the court (1) declined to decide whether the officers' actions violated the Fourth Amendment, and (2) upheld the defense of qualified immunity under the court's view that the right allegedly violated by the officers was not clearly established at the time of the 1992 incident (141 F3d 111, 1998 US App LEXIS 6863).

On certiorari, the United States Supreme Court affirmed. In an opinion by REHNQUIST, Ch. J., expressing the unanimous view of the court as to holding 1 below and joined by O'CONNOR, SCALIA, KENNEDY, SOUTER, THOMAS, GINSBURG, and BREYER, JJ., as to holding 2 below, it was held that (1) the media ridealong in question violated the Fourth Amendment, as (a) it is a violation of the Fourth Amendment for police to bring media representatives or other third parties into a home during the execution of a warrant when the presence of the third parties in the home is not in aid of the execution of the warrant, and (b) among other factors concerning the case at hand, (i) it was conceded that the newspaper's representatives did not engage in the execution of the warrants or assist the officers in their task, (ii) the possibility of good public relations, standing alone, was not enough to justify a ride-along intrusion into a home, and (iii) even the need for accurate reporting on police issues in general bore no direct relation to the constitutional justification for the police intrusion in question; but (2) the federal and county officers were entitled to the defense of qualified immunity from damages liability, under the Bivens decision and under § 1983, to the parents for the violation, because the Fourth Amendment right in question was not clearly established on the date of the ride-along, where among other matters, in April 1992, there were no judicial opinions holding that the practice of media ride-alongs became unlawful when a home was entered.

STEVENS, J., concurring in part and dissenting in part, (1) agreed that it violates the Fourth Amendment for police to bring media representatives or other third parties into a private dwelling during the execution of a warrant unless (a) the homeowner has consented, or (b) the presence of the third parties is in aid of the execution of the warrant; but (2) expressed the view that the defense of qualified immunity should not be available in the case at hand, because a homeowner's right to protection against this type of trespass was clearly established long before April 16, 1992.

COUNSEL

Richard K. Willard argued the cause for petitioners.

Richard A. Cordray argued the cause for federal respondents.

Lawrence P. Fletcher-Hill argued the cause for state respondents.

AURELIA DAVIS, as next friend of LaSHONDA D.,
PETITIONER

v

MONROE COUNTY BOARD OF EDUCATION et al.

526 US —, 143 L Ed 2d 839, 119 S Ct 1661

[No. 97-843]

Argued January 12, 1999.
Decided May 24, 1999.

Decision: Private action held to lie against public school
board for Title IX sex discrimination if board acted
with deliberate indifference to acts of student-on-
student sexual harassment which were sufficiently
severe, pervasive, and objectively offensive.

SUMMARY

A student was allegedly the victim of a prolonged
pattern of sexual harassment by one of her fifth-grade
classmates at a public school in a Georgia county. The
student's mother brought suit on behalf of her daughter in the United States District Court for the Middle
District of Georgia against defendants including the
county board of education, which was a recipient of
federal education funds. Among the mother's claims
was a claim for monetary and injunctive relief under
Title IX of the Education Amendments of 1972 (20
USCS §§ 1681 et seq.), which claim alleged that the
school board's deliberate indifference to the classmate's persistent sexual advances created an intimidat-
ing, hostile, offensive, and abusive school environment.
According to the complaint, the harassment was reported to school authorities, but no disciplinary action

was taken in response nor was any effort made to separate the classmate from the student. The District Court dismissed the Title IX claim on the ground that student-on-student harassment provided no ground for a private cause of action under the statute (862 F Supp 363). A panel of the United States Court of Appeals for the Eleventh Circuit reversed (74 F3d 1186). However, the Court of Appeals (1) granted the school board's motion for rehearing en banc (91 F3d 1418), and (2) subsequently affirmed the District Court's dismissal (120 F3d 1390).

On certiorari, the United States Supreme Court reversed and remanded. In an opinion by O'CONNOR, J., joined by STEVENS, SOUTER, GINSBURG, and BREYER, JJ., it was held that (1) under Title IX, a private damages action may lie against a public school board in cases of student-on-student harassment, but only where (a) the school board acted with deliberate indifference to known acts of harassment in the school board's programs or activities, and (b) the harassment was so severe, pervasive, and objectively offensive that it effectively barred the victim's access to an educational opportunity or benefit; and (2) it was error to dismiss the Title IX claim in the case at hand, because it could not be said beyond doubt that the mother could prove no set of facts in her case in support of her claim which would entitle her to relief.

KENNEDY, J., joined by REHNQUIST, Ch. J., and SCALIA and THOMAS, JJ., dissenting, expressed the view that Title IX did not give states unambiguous notice that accepting federal funds meant ceding to the Federal Government power over the day-to-day disciplinary decisions of schools.

COUNSEL

Verna L. Williams argued the cause for petitioner.

Barbara D. Underwood argued the cause for the United States, as amicus curiae, by special leave of court.

W. Warren Plowden, Jr. argued the cause for respondents.

CITY OF MONTEREY, Petitioner

v

DEL MONTE DUNES AT MONTEREY, LTD., and
MONTEREY-DEL MONTE DUNES CORPORATION

526 US —, 143 L Ed 2d 882, 119 S Ct 1624

[No. 97-1235]

Argued October 7, 1998.
Decided May 24, 1999.

Decision: Pursuant to Seventh Amendment, Federal
District Court held to have properly submitted to
jury question of California city's liability on landowner's 42 USCS § 1983 claim of uncompensated
regulatory taking in violation of Fifth Amendment.

SUMMARY

After a California city repeatedly denied various
proposals by a landowner and its predecessor in interest
to develop a 37.6-acre parcel located in the city—each
time imposing more rigorous demands on the
developers—the landowner (1) filed suit against the
city in the United States District Court for the Northern
District of California; and (2) among other claims,
asserted a claim under 42 USCS § 1983 that the city's
denial of the final development proposal was an uncompensated regulatory taking in violation of the takings clause of the Federal Constitution's Fifth Amendment. Eventually, the District Court submitted claims
including the takings claim to a jury. With respect to
the takings claim, the District Court's jury instructions,
the essence of which were proposed by the city, directed
the jury that (1) it should find for the landowner if the

jury found that (a) the landowner had been denied all economically viable use of its property, or (b) the city's decision to reject the landowner's final development proposal did not substantially advance a legitimate public purpose; and (2) the various purposes asserted by the city were legitimate public interests. The results of the jury's deliberations included (1) a general verdict for the landowner on its takings claim, and (2) a damages award of $1.45 million. The District Court denied motions by the city for a new trial or for judgment as a matter of law. On appeal, the United States Court of Appeals for the Ninth Circuit, in affirming, expressed the view that (1) the District Court did not err in allowing the § 1983 takings claim to be tried before a jury; (2) the District Court properly submitted to the jury the issues whether (a) the land-owner was deprived of all economically viable use of the property, and (b) the city's actions substantially advanced a legitimate public purpose; (3) even if the city had a legitimate interest in denying the landowner's development application, the city's action had to be roughly proportional to furthering that interest; and (4) in light of the evidence proffered by the landowner, the city was incorrect in arguing that no rational juror could have concluded that the city's denial lacked a sufficient nexus with the city's stated objectives (95 F3d 1422, 1996 US App LEXIS 24118).

On certiorari, the United States Supreme Court affirmed. In that portion of the opinion of KENNEDY, J., that constituted the opinion of the court, it was held—expressing the unanimous view of the court as to holding 1 below and joined by REHNQUIST, Ch. J., and STEVENS, SCALIA, and THOMAS, JJ., as to holdings 2-6 below—that (1) while the rough-proportionality test was inapposite to a denial-of-development case such as the one at hand, the fact that the Court of Appeals discussed the rough-proportionality test was irrelevant to the Supreme Court's disposition of the case; (2) the Court of Appeals, in holding that the jury could have found that the city's denial of the landowner's final development proposal was not reasonably related to legitimate public interests, did not improperly adopt a rule of takings law that allowed wholesale interference by a judge or jury with municipal land-use policies, laws, or routine regulatory decisions; (3) § 1983 did not confer a statutory right to a jury trial; (4) a § 1983 suit seeking legal relief was an action at law to which the Constitution's Seventh Amendment guarantee of the right to a jury trial applied; (5) under this test, the landowner's § 1983 takings claim was an action at law for purposes of the Seventh Amendment guarantee; and (6) accordingly, it was proper for the District Court to submit to the jury the question of the city's liability on the takings claim, for (a) the issue whether the landowner was deprived of all economically viable use of the landowner's property was a predominantly factual question that was for the jury, and (b) it was proper to submit to the jury the narrow and factbound question in the case at hand as to whether, when viewed in light of the context and protracted history of the development application process, the city's decision to reject a particular development plan bore a reasonable relationship to the city's proffered justifications. Also, KENNEDY, J., joined by REHNQUIST, Ch. J., and STEVENS and THOMAS, JJ., expressed the view that even when the landowner's takings claim was analyzed not simply as a § 1983 action, but as a § 1983 action seeking redress for an uncompensated taking, the claim remained an action at law for purposes of the Seventh Amendment jury right.

SCALIA, J., concurring in part and concurring in the judgment, expressed the view that (1) all § 1983 actions must be treated alike insofar as the Seventh Amendment right to a jury trial is concerned, (2) that right exists when monetary damages are sought, and (3) the issues submitted to the jury in the case at hand were properly sent there.

SOUTER, J., joined by O'CONNOR, GINSBURG, and BREYER, JJ., concurring in part and dissenting in part, (1) agreed that (a) the rough-proportionality test should not be extended as a standard for reviewing land-use regulation generally, and (b) § 1983 did not provide a statutory right to a jury trial; but (2) expressed the view that (a) the landowner did not have a right to a jury trial, under the Seventh Amendment, on the landowner's regulatory taking—or inverse condemnation—claim under § 1983, and (b) the District Court thus erred in submitting this claim to the jury.

COUNSEL

George A. Yuhas argued the cause for petitioner.

Edwin S. Kneedler argued the cause for the United States, as amicus curiae, by special leave of court.

Michael M. Berger argued the cause for respondents.

CALIFORNIA DENTAL ASSOCIATION, Petitioner

v

FEDERAL TRADE COMMISSION

526 US —, 143 L Ed 2d 935, 119 S Ct 1604

[No. 97-1625]

Argued January 13, 1999.
Decided May 24, 1999.

Decision: FTC jurisdiction held to extend to nonprofit dental association that provided substantial economic benefits to its for-profit members; FTC's "quick look" held to be insufficient to justify finding that association's advertising restrictions on members were anticompetitive.

SUMMARY

A nonprofit dental association to which approximately three-quarters of the dentists practicing in California belonged (1) provided insurance and financing arrangements to members, and (2) engaged, on behalf of members, in lobbying, litigation, marketing, and public relations. Members were prohibited, under the association's code of ethics, from engaging in false or misleading advertising, and the association had issued advisory opinions and guidelines concerning advertising. The Federal Trade Commission (FTC) brought a complaint alleging that the association had applied its guidelines so as to unreasonably restrict two types of truthful and nondeceptive advertising—price advertising, particularly as to discounted fees, and advertising related to the quality of dental services—in violation of § 5 of the Federal Trade Commission Act (15 USCS

§ 45), which, in 15 USCS § 45(a)(1), prohibits unfair competition and deceptive acts or practices. An administrative law judge (ALJ) (1) held the FTC to have jurisdiction under the Act (15 USCS §§ 41 et seq.)—which in 15 USCS § 45(a)(2) gives the FTC authority over corporations and in 15 USCS § 44 defines "corporation" to include any incorporated or unincorporated association that is organized to carry on business for its own profit or that of its members—over the association; and (2) found a violation of § 5. The FTC, in affirming, under an abbreviated rule-of-reason analysis, the ALJ's judgment, held that the association's advertising restrictions violated provisions including § 5. The United States Court of Appeals for the Ninth Circuit, in affirming the FTC's judgment, sustained the FTC's assertion of jurisdiction over the association and concluded that the FTC had properly applied an abbreviated or "quick look" rule-of-reason analysis in the instant case (128 F3d 720).

On certiorari, the United States Supreme Court vacated and remanded. In an opinion by SOUTER, J, expressing the unanimous view of the court with respect to holding 1 below, and joined by REHNQUIST, Ch. J., and O'CONNOR, SCALIA, and THOMAS, JJ., with respect to holdings 2 and 3 below, it was held that (1) FTC jurisdiction under the Act extended to the association, because (a) the economic benefits provided by the association fell within the object of enhancing the members' profits, (b) nonprofit entities organized on behalf of for-profit members had the same capacity and derivatively, at least, the same incentives as for-profit organizations to engage in unfair competition, and (c) the legislative history, like the text of the Act, was devoid of any hint at an exemption for professional associations as such; (2) the Court of Appeals had erred in deciding that a "quick look" by the FTC was

185

sufficient for finding that the restrictions were anticompetitive, as any anticompetitive effects of the restraints were far from intuitively obvious; and (3) thus, a fuller consideration of the issues was called for on remand.

BREYER, J., joined by STEVENS, KENNEDY, and GINSBURG, JJ., concurring in part and dissenting in part, (1) agreed that the FTC had jurisdiction over the association; but (2) expressed the view that a traditional application of the rule of reason to the facts as found by the FTC required affirming the FTC decision, where (a) to restrain truthful advertising about lower prices was likely to restrict competition in respect to price, and (b) the restrictions on the advertising of service quality also had serious anticompetitive tendencies.

COUNSEL

Peter M. Sfikas argued the cause for petitioner.

Lawrence G. Wallace argued the cause for respondent.

––––––––––––

CAROLYN C. CLEVELAND, Petitioner

v

POLICY MANAGEMENT SYSTEMS CORPORATION
et al.

526 US —, 143 L Ed 2d 966, 119 S Ct 1597

[No. 97-1008]

Argued February 24, 1999.
Decided May 24, 1999.

Decision: Pursuit and receipt of Social Security Disability Insurance benefits held not to estop—and not to erect strong presumption against success of—employment discrimination claim under Americans with Disabilities Act (42 USCS §§ 12101 et seq.).

SUMMARY

The Social Security Disability Insurance (SSDI) program provides benefits to persons with disabilities so severe that, as set forth in § 223(a) of the Social Security Act (42 USCS § 423(d)(2)(A)), the persons are "unable to do [their] previous work" or to "engage in any other kind of substantial gainful work." Also, § 102(a) of the Americans with Disabilities Act (ADA) (42 USCS § 12112(a)) prohibits employment discrimination against a "qualified individual with a disability," a term defined in § 101(8) of the ADA (42 USCS § 12111(8)) as covering any person who has a disability but is nonetheless able to "perform the essential functions" of the job in question, including persons who can do so only with "reasonable accommodation." A corporate employee who had had a stroke applied for SSDI

187

benefits, then returned to work when her condition improved, only to be fired by the corporation 3 months later. Her SSDI application was initially denied, but was granted retroactively after the employee had filed an action alleging that the corporation had violated § 102(a) by refusing to reasonably accommodate her disability. A Federal District Court granted summary judgment in favor of the corporation on the theory that (1) the employee, by applying for and receiving SSDI benefits, had conceded that she was totally disabled; and (2) this concession estopped her from proving that she could perform the essential functions of her job as required by the ADA. The United States Court of Appeals for the Fifth Circuit, affirming the grant of summary judgment, (1) noted that such SSDI applications and ADA claims might conceivably be consistent under certain unusual circumstances, (2) expressed the view that application for or receipt of SSDI benefits created a rebuttable presumption that such an applicant was estopped from claiming to be a qualified individual with a disability under § 101(8), and (3) ruled that the employee had failed to raise a genuine issue of material fact rebutting that presumption in the case at hand (120 F3d 513).

On certiorari, the United States Supreme Court reversed and remanded. In an opinion by BREYER, J., expressing the unanimous view of the court, it was held that (1) the pursuit and receipt of SSDI benefits does not automatically estop the recipient from pursuing an ADA claim of employment discrimination and does not erect a strong presumption against the recipient's success under the ADA, for SSDI and ADA claims do not inherently conflict to the point where a special negative presumption is warranted; (2) however, an ADA plaintiff who has also sought and obtained SSDI benefits (a) cannot simply ignore the plaintiff's SSDI contention of inability to work, and (b) in order to survive a defense motion for summary judgment, must provide a sufficient explanation why that contention is consistent with the plaintiff's ADA assertion that the plaintiff could perform the essential functions of the job; and (3) in the case at hand—where the plaintiff employee had attempted to explain the discrepancy by referring to (a) SSDI's not taking into account reasonable workplace accommodations, and (b) the different times at which her SSDI and ADA claims were made—the parties should have an opportunity to present or contest these explanations before the trial court.

COUNSEL

John E. Wall, Jr. argued the cause for petitioner.

Matthew D. Roberts argued the cause for the United States, as amicus curiae, by special leave of court.

Stephen G. Morrison argued the cause for respondent.

RODNEY C. HANLON, JOEL SCRAFFORD, KRIS A.
McLEAN, RICHARD C. BRANZELL, and ROBERT
PRIEKSAT, Petitioners

v

PAUL W. BERGER et ux.

526 US —, 143 L Ed 2d 978, 119 S Ct 1706

[No. 97-1927]

Argued May 24, 1999.
Decided May 24, 1999.

Decision: Complaint asserting that media representatives accompanied federal officials during 1993
execution of search warrant at ranch held to allege
Fourth Amendment violation, but officials held
entitled to qualified immunity from damages liability under Bivens decision.

SUMMARY

Two residents of a Montana ranch filed a Federal
District Court suit which asserted claims against some
federal officials—special agents of the United States
Fish and Wildlife Service and an assistant United States
attorney—for damages under Bivens v Six Unknown
Named Agents of Federal Bureau of Narcotics (1971)
403 US 388, 29 L Ed 2d 619, 91 S Ct 1999. The
residents' complaint included allegations to the effect
that the officials had violated the residents' rights
under the Federal Constitution's Fourth Amendment,
in that allegedly (1) in 1993, a magistrate judge had
issued a warrant authorizing the search of the ranch
with appurtenant structures, excluding the residence,
for evidence of the taking of wildlife in violation of

federal laws; (2) about a week later, a multiple-vehicle caravan consisting of government agents and a crew of photographers and reporters from a cable news network had proceeded to a point near the ranch; (3) the agents had executed the warrant; (4) the agents later explained that over the course of the day, "the officers" had searched the ranch and its outbuildings pursuant to the authority conferred by the warrant; and (5) the agents further explained that the media crew had accompanied and observed the officers and had recorded the officers' conduct in executing the warrant. However, the District Court, in granting summary judgment in favor of the federal officials, ruled that the officials were entitled to qualified immunity, as the court expressed the view that at the time of the alleged incident, there was no clearly established law protecting individuals from the commercial recording of a search of their premises. On appeal, the United States Court of Appeals for the Ninth Circuit, in reversing in pertinent part and in ordering a remand, expressed the view that—viewing the evidence in the light most favorable to the residents for purposes of decision—(1) the search of the ranch violated the Fourth Amendment, and (2) the federal officials were not entitled to qualified immunity (129 F3d 505, 1997 US App LEXIS 31848).

On certiorari, the United States Supreme Court vacated and remanded. In a per curiam opinion expressing the view of REHNQUIST, Ch. J., and O'CONNOR, SCALIA, KENNEDY, SOUTER, THOMAS, GINSBURG, and BREYER, JJ., it was held that (1) the detailed allegations in the residents' complaint alleged a violation of the Fourth Amendment, under the court's decision in Wilson v Layne (1999) 526 US ——, 143 L Ed 2d 818, 119 S Ct 1692 (decided on the same day as the case at hand), that the police violate the Fourth Amendment

191

rights of homeowners when the police allow media representatives to accompany the police during the execution of a warrant in the owners' home; but (2) the federal officials in the case at hand were entitled to the defense of qualified immunity, as (a) the court's holding in Wilson v Layne made it clear that the Fourth Amendment right in question was not clearly established in 1992, and (b) the parties in the case at hand had not called the court's attention to any decisions which would have made the state of the law any clearer a year later.

STEVENS, J., concurring in part and dissenting in part, (1) noted that his dissent in Wilson v Layne expressed the view that the constitutional rule recognized in the Wilson case had been clearly established long before 1992, and (2) therefore, dissented from the court's disposition of the case at hand on qualified immunity grounds.

COUNSEL

Richard A. Cordray argued the cause for petitioners.
Henry H. Rossbacher argued the cause for respondents.

RICHARD M. CROSS, Petitioner

v

PELICAN BAY STATE PRISON et al. (No. 98-8486)

———

RICHARD M. CROSS, Petitioner

v

RICHARD WIEKING, Clerk, United States District
Court for the Northern District of California (No.
98-8487)

526 US —, 143 L Ed 2d 982, 119 S Ct 1596

[Nos. 98-8486 and 98-8487]

Decided May 24, 1999.

Decision: Person who filed 12 frivolous petitions in
Supreme Court denied leave to proceed in forma
pauperis; order entered barring person's future in
forma pauperis filings of noncriminal certiorari
petitions.

SUMMARY

An individual sought leave to proceed in forma
pauperis in the United States Supreme Court under
Supreme Court Rule 39 with respect to two petitions.
According to the court, which on a single day earlier in
the current Term, had invoked Supreme Court Rule
39.8—which authorizes the court to deny leave to
proceed in forma pauperis with respect to frivolous
petitions—to deny the individual in forma pauperis
status with respect to four petitions, (1) the two instant
petitions were the individual's 11th and 12th frivolous

filings in the court, and (2) the individual had four additional frivolous filings pending before the court.

In a per curiam opinion expressing the view of REHNQUIST, Ch. J., and O'CONNOR, SCALIA, KENNEDY, SOUTER, THOMAS, GINSBURG, and BREYER, JJ., the Supreme Court (1) invoked Rule 39.8 to deny the individual's request for leave to proceed in forma pauperis on the two instant petitions, and (2) directed the Clerk of the Supreme Court not to accept any further petitions for certiorari in noncriminal matters from the individual unless he complied with Supreme Court Rules 33.1 and 38.

STEVENS, J., dissenting, expressed the view that the court uses more of its resources by preparing, entering, and policing orders barring future in forma pauperis filings than it would by simply denying the frivolous petitions that are filed.

EDDIE RICHARDSON, Petitioner

v

UNITED STATES

526 US —, 143 L Ed 2d 985, 119 S Ct 1707

[No. 97-8629]

Argued February 22, 1999.
Decided June 1, 1999.

Decision: Jury in continuing criminal enterprise case under 21 USCS § 848 held required to agree unanimously not only that accused committed continuing series of violations, but also which specific violations made up continuing series.

SUMMARY

A federal criminal statute forbade any person from engaging in a "continuing criminal enterprise" (21 USCS § 848(a)) and defined continuing criminal enterprise as involving a violation of the drug statutes where such violation was part of a "continuing series of violations" (21 USCS § 848(c)). An accused was charged under this statute. At trial, in Federal District Court, the government presented evidence designed to show that the accused had (1) organized a street gang which distributed heroin, crack cocaine, and powder cocaine over a period of several years, and (2) run the gang, managed the sales, and obtained substantial income from those unlawful activities. The trial court judge rejected a proposal by the accused to instruct the jury that it must unanimously agree on which specific acts constituted the alleged series of violations. Instead, the judge instructed the jurors that they must unanimously agree that the defendant committed at least three federal narcotics offenses, but did not have to unanimously agree as to the particular offenses. The jury convicted the accused, and on appeal the United States Court of Appeals for the Seventh Circuit upheld the trial judge's jury instruction (130 F3d 765).

On certiorari, the United States Supreme Court vacated the judgment of the Court of Appeals and remanded the case for further proceedings. In an opinion by BREYER, J., joined by REHNQUIST, Ch. J., and STEVENS, SCALIA, SOUTER, and THOMAS, JJ., it was held that under 21 USCS § 848, a federal jury must unanimously agree not only that the defendant committed a continuing series of violations but also that the defendant committed each of the individual violations necessary to make up that continuing series, as (1) an interpretation of the statute that each violation is a separate element is supported by considerations of (a) the statutory language, (b) history and tradition regarding jury unanimity, and (c) potential unfairness; (2) a jury in a federal criminal case can not convict unless it unanimously finds that the government has proven each element of a crime; and (3) arguments for an interpretation that each violation is a means making up a single element are not sufficiently powerful to overcome the considerations of language, tradition, and potential unfairness.

KENNEDY, J., joined by O'CONNOR and GINSBURG, JJ., dissenting, expressed the view that (1) Congress intended the "continuing series of violations" to be one of the defining characteristics of a continuing criminal enterprise and therefore to be a single element of the offense, subject to fulfillment in various ways, (2) there is no problem under the due process clause of the Federal Constitution's Fifth Amendment with interpreting the continuing series requirement as a single element of the crime, and (3) in the absence of any reason to think Congress' definition of the offense was irrational, unfair under fundamental principles, or an illicit attempt to avoid the constitutional requirement of jury unanimity, there is no constitutional barrier to requiring jury unanimity on the existence of a continuing series of violations without requiring unanimity as to the underlying predicate offenses.

COUNSEL

William A. Barnett, Jr. argued the cause for petitioner.

Irving L. Gornstein argued the cause for respondent.

———————

WILLIAM D. O' SULLIVAN, Petitioner

v

DARREN BOERCKEL

526 US —, 144 L Ed 2d 1, 119 S Ct 1728

[No. 97-2048]

Argued March 30, 1999.
Decided June 7, 1999.

Decision: Illinois state prisoner who sought federal
habeas corpus relief held not to have exhausted
state remedies, as required by 28 USCS § 2254, as
to claims that were not raised in prisoner's petition
for discretionary review in Illinois' highest court.

SUMMARY

Under Illinois' two-tiered appellate process, (1) most
criminal appeals are heard first by the Appellate Court
of Illinois, (2) a party may generally petition the Illinois
Supreme Court for leave to appeal a decision of the
Appellate Court, and (3) the granting of such a petition
is a matter of judicial discretion. An Illinois state
prisoner who had been convicted of rape and other
offenses appealed his convictions to the Appellate
Court, which affirmed his convictions and sentences
(68 Ill App 3d 103, 385 NE2d 815). The prisoner filed
a petition for leave to appeal to the Illinois Supreme
Court. This petition, in which the prisoner raised three
issues, was denied. The United States Supreme Court
denied the prisoner's subsequent petition for a writ of

certiorari (447 US 911, 64 L Ed 2d 861, 100 S Ct 2998).
In 1994, the prisoner filed a petition for a writ of habeas
corpus under 28 USCS § 2254 in the United States
District Court for the Central District of Illinois. This
petition, as amended in 1995, asked for relief on six
grounds. The District Court, which ultimately denied
the habeas corpus petition, concluded that the prisoner
had procedurally defaulted three of these claims, because (1) the three claims had not been included in the
petition for leave to appeal to the Illinois Supreme
Court, and (2) the time period in which the prisoner
could have raised the three claims to the Illinois
Supreme Court had passed. The United States Court of
Appeals for the Seventh Circuit, in reversing and
remanding on appeal, expressed the view that (1) the
prisoner, by including the three claims in his direct
appeal to the Appellate Court, had exhausted his state
remedies as required under § 2254, which did not
require him to include all of his claims in a petition for
leave to appeal to the Illinois Supreme Court; and (2)
there was thus no need to reach the question whether
the Illinois Supreme Court would have found the three
claims procedurally barred because of the timing requirement (135 F3d 1194, 1998 US App LEXIS 1768).

On certiorari, the United States Supreme Court
reversed. In an opinion by O'CONNOR, J., joined by
REHNQUIST, Ch. J., and SCALIA, KENNEDY, SOUTER, and
THOMAS, JJ., it was held that (1) in order to satisfy the
rule of 28 USCS § 2254(c) that a state prisoner who
petitions for federal habeas corpus relief shall not be
deemed to have exhausted state court remedies if the
prisoner has the right under state law to raise, by any
available procedure, the question presented, the prisoner's claims must be presented to the state's court of
last resort in a petition for discretionary review, where
such review is part of the state's ordinary appellate

review procedure; (2) in the case at hand, comity dictated that the prisoner use Illinois' two-tiered appellate procedures before presenting claims to a federal court; and (3) with respect to the three claims that had not been included in the petition for discretionary review in the Illinois Supreme Court, (a) those claims had not been properly presented to the state courts, and (b) the prisoner had procedurally defaulted those claims.

SOUTER, J., concurring, expressed the view that the United States Supreme Court had left open the possibility that under § 2254, a state prisoner seeking federal habeas corpus relief was free to skip a state's appellate procedure—even where a state court had occasionally employed such a procedure to provide relief—so long as the state had (1) identified the procedure as outside the standard review process, and (2) plainly said that the procedure need not be sought for the purpose of exhaustion.

STEVENS, J., joined by GINSBURG and BREYER, JJ., dissenting, expressed the view that (1) the United States Supreme Court had improperly confused the rule of exhaustion of state remedies with the procedural default rule; (2) the case at hand did not raise an exhaustion issue; and (3) the prisoner had not defaulted the three claims that he had failed to present to the Illinois Supreme Court, for Illinois prisoners were not required to present their claims in discretionary review petitions before raising such claims in federal court.

BREYER, J., joined by STEVENS and GINSBURG, JJ., dissenting, expressed the view that (1) the United States Supreme Court's holding created a kind of rebuttable presumption that a state prisoner must raise a given claim in a petition for discretionary review in state court prior to raising that claim on federal habeas corpus review; but (2) instead, it should be presumed—on the basis of Illinois's own rules and related statistics and in the absence of any clear legal expression to the contrary—that Illinois does not mind if a state prisoner does not ask the Illinois Supreme Court for discretionary review prior to seeking habeas corpus relief in federal court.

COUNSEL

William L. Browers argued the cause for petitioner.
David B. Mote argued the cause for respondent.

———————

AMOCO PRODUCTION COMPANY, on Behalf of
Itself and the Class it Represents, Petitioner

v

SOUTHERN UTE INDIAN TRIBE et al.

526 US —, 144 L Ed 2d 22, 119 S Ct 1719

[No. 98-830]

Argued April 19, 1999.
Decided June 7, 1999.

Decision: Coalbed methane (CBM) gas held not encompassed by term "coal" as used in Coal Lands
Acts of 1909 (30 USCS § 81) and 1910 (30 USCS
§§ 83-85), reserving coal rights in lands patented
under Acts.

SUMMARY

Under the Coal Lands Acts of 1909 (30 USCS § 81)
and 1910 (30 USCS §§ 83-85), all land patents issued
pursuant to the Acts reserved to the United States all
rights to the coal contained in the subject properties. In
order to encourage the development of coalbed methane (CBM) gas as an energy source, (1) the United
States Department of the Interior issued a 1981 opinion
concluding that the reservation of coal under the Acts
did not encompass CBM gas, and (2) energy companies
relying on that opinion entered into leases with land-
owners holding title under the Acts to produce CBM
gas. An Indian tribe, which had received equitable title
to the United States' coal rights in patented lands that
had formerly been part of the tribe's reservation, (1)
filed an action in the United States District Court for
the District of Colorado against the royalty owners and

producers under the gas leases covering those lands and against various federal agencies; and (2) sought a declaration that the reservation of coal under the Acts included the CBM gas, which therefore belonged to the tribe. The District Court, holding that the plain meaning of the term "coal" was limited to the solid rock substance and did not include the CBM gas, granted summary judgment for the defendants (874 F Supp 1142). However, the United States Court of Appeals for the Tenth Circuit, upon rehearing en banc, agreed with a decision by a panel of the Court of Appeals (119 F3d 816), and held, reversing the District Court's decision, that (1) the Acts' use of the term "coal" was ambiguous, (2) ambiguities in land grants must be resolved in favor of the sovereign, and (3) the Acts' reservation of coal therefore included the CBM gas (151 F3d 1251).

On certiorari, the United States Supreme Court reversed. In an opinion by KENNEDY, J., joined by REHNQUIST, Ch. J., and STEVENS, O'CONNOR, SCALIA, SOUTER, and THOMAS, JJ., it was held that the reservation of "coal" in the Acts did not encompass CBM gas, since the common conception of coal at the time the Acts were passed was limited to the solid rock substance.

GINSBURG, J., dissented, expressing the view that (1) at the time the Acts were passed, Congress would have assumed that the coal owner had dominion over and responsibility for the CBM gas, which was then regarded as a liability; (2) it was not clear that Congress understood that dominion would shift if CBM gas became an asset; and (3) therefore, the canon that ambiguities in land grants are construed in favor of the sovereign should be applied.

BREYER, J., did not participate.

COUNSEL

Carter G. Phillips argued the cause for petitioner.

Thomas J. Davidson argued the cause for Wyoming, as amicus curiae, by special leave of court.

Thomas H. Shipps argued the cause for respondent Southern Ute Indian Tribe.

Jeffrey P. Minear argued the cause for respondent United States.

ELLIS E. NEDER, Jr., Petitioner

v

UNITED STATES

527 US —, 144 L Ed 2d 35, 119 S Ct 1827

[No. 97-1985]

Argued February 23, 1999.
Decided June 10, 1999.

Decision: Federal District Court's refusal, with respect
to criminal charges of tax fraud, to submit materiality issue to jury held to be harmless error;
materiality of falsehood held to be element of
offenses under federal mail, wire, and bank fraud
statutes.

SUMMARY

A federal indictment charged an accused with,
among other matters, various counts of (1) mail fraud
in violation of 18 USCS § 1341, which included a
prohibition against the use of the mails with respect to
any scheme or artifice to defraud; (2) wire fraud in
violation of 18 USCS § 1343, which included a prohibition against the use of interstate wire facilities with
respect to any scheme or artifice to defraud; (3) bank
fraud in violation of 18 USCS § 1344, which included a
prohibition against any scheme or artifice to defraud a
financial institution; and (4) tax fraud through filing a
false income tax return in violation of 26 USCS
§ 7206(1), which included a prohibition against filing a
return which the filer did "not believe to be true and
correct as to every material matter." Over the accused's
objections, a Federal District Court (1) instructed the

jury that with respect to tax fraud, the jury did not need to consider the materiality of any false statements; (2) gave a similar instruction concerning bank fraud; and (3) did not include, in the jury instructions concerning mail and wire fraud, materiality as an element of those two offenses. The jury convicted the accused on counts including the mail, wire, bank, and tax fraud counts. On appeal, the United States Court of Appeals for the Eleventh Circuit, in affirming, expressed the view that (1) while the District Court erred in failing to submit the materiality element of the tax fraud offense to the jury, this error was (a) subject to harmless-error analysis, and (b) harmless, in that materiality was not in dispute; and (2) the District Court did not err in failing to submit the materiality issue to the jury with respect to the mail, wire, and bank fraud counts, as materiality was not an element of those offenses (136 F3d 1459, 1998 US App LEXIS 5102).

On certiorari, the United States Supreme Court affirmed the Court of Appeals' judgment respecting the tax fraud counts, reversed the Court of Appeals' judgment on the remaining counts, and remanded the case for further proceedings. In an opinion by REHN-QUIST, Ch. J., expressing the unanimous view of the court as to holding 3 below and joined by O'CONNOR, KENNEDY, THOMAS, and BREYER, JJ., as to holdings 1 and 2 below, it was held that (1) with respect to the tax fraud counts, the District Court's refusal to submit the issue of materiality to the jury, which refusal was not disputed by the Federal Government to have been error, was subject to harmless-error analysis under Rule 52(a) of the Federal Rules of Criminal Procedure, for among other factors, (a) the error in question—a jury instruction that omitted an element of the offense—differed markedly from the federal constitutional violations which the Supreme Court had found

to defy harmless-error review, and (b) the Federal
Constitution's Sixth Amendment guarantee of the right
to a jury trial did not require a reversal without any
consideration of the effect of the error upon the
verdict; (2) this refusal was harmless error under Rule
52(a), where, beyond a reasonable doubt, the omitted
element of materiality was uncontested and was supported by overwhelming evidence, such that the jury
verdict would have been the same absent the error; and
(3) materiality was an element of the "scheme or
artifice to defraud" prohibited by §§ 1341, 1343, and
1344, even though the statutes' text did not mention
materiality, where the government (a) did not dispute
that at the time of the original enactment of each
statute, actionable fraud had a well-settled meaning at
common law that required a misrepresentation or
concealment of material fact, and (b) had failed to
rebut the presumption that Congress intended to in-
corporate the common-law materiality requirement in
the three statutes.

STEVENS, J., concurring in part and concurring in the
judgment, expressed the view that (1) with respect to
the tax fraud counts, the trial judge's failure to give a
separate jury instruction on materiality was harmless
error because under the circumstances, the jury's verdict necessarily included a finding of materiality; and
(2) the Supreme Court correctly concluded that materiality was an element of the offenses defined in §§
1341, 1343, and 1344.

SCALIA, J., joined by SOUTER and GINSBURG, JJ.,
concurring in part and dissenting in part, joined holding 3 above, but expressed the view that depriving a
criminal defendant of the right, under Art III, § 2, cl 3
of the Constitution and under the Sixth Amendment,
to have the jury determine the defendant's guilt of the

crime charged—which necessarily meant the defendant's commission of every element of the crime charged—could never be harmless error when the defendant objected to the deprivation in a timely fashion.

COUNSEL

Javier H. Rubenstein argued the cause for petitioner.
Roy W. McLeese, III argued the cause for respondent.

CITY OF CHICAGO, Petitioner

v

JESUS MORALES et al.

527 US —, 144 L Ed 2d 67, 119 S Ct 1849

[No. 97-1121]

Argued December 9, 1998.
Decided June 10, 1999.

Decision: Chicago ordinance that prohibited loitering together in any public place by two or more people, of whom at least one was criminal street gang member, held to be impermissibly vague, in violation of Fourteenth Amendment's due process clause.

SUMMARY

The city of Chicago enacted a "gang congregation" ordinance that prohibited loitering together in any public place by two or more people, of whom at least one was a "criminal street gang member." The ordinance created a criminal offense that was punishable by a fine of up to $500, imprisonment for not more than 6 months, and a requirement to perform up to 120 hours of community service. Under the ordinance, which defined "loitering" as remaining in any one place with no apparent purpose, (1) a police officer who observed a person whom the officer reasonably believed to be a criminal street gang member loitering in a public place with one or more persons was required to order all of the persons to disperse, and (2) any person, regardless of whether the person was a gang member, who disobeyed such a dispersal order was guilty of violating the ordinance. The Chicago Police Department promulgated guidelines that purported to prevent arbitrary or discriminatory enforcement of the ordinance by confining arrest authority to designated officers, establishing detailed criteria for defining street gangs and membership in such gangs, and providing for designated but publicly undisclosed enforcement areas. After 2 trial judges upheld the federal constitutionality of the ordinance but 11 others held that it was invalid, the Illinois Appellate Court, in affirming the judgments in the cases in which the ordinance was held invalid and reversing the convictions in the other cases, determined that the ordinance violated the Federal Constitution and the state constitution. The Illinois Supreme Court, in affirming the Appellate Court judgment, expressed the view that the ordinance violated due process of law, in that the ordinance was impermissibly vague on its face and was an arbitrary restriction on personal liberties (177 Ill 2d 440, 687 NE 2d 53).

On certiorari, the United States Supreme Court affirmed. In those portions of an opinion by STEVENS, J., which constituted the opinion of the court and were joined by O'CONNOR, KENNEDY, SOUTER, GINSBURG and BREYER, JJ., it was held that the ordinance was impermissibly vague, in violation of the due process clause of the Federal Constitution's Fourteenth Amendment, because the broad sweep of the ordinance violated the requirement that a legislature establish minimal guidelines to govern law enforcement, where (1) the ordinance's mandatory language directed the police to issue a dispersal order without making any inquiry about the possible purposes of persons who stood or sat in the company of a gang member, (2) the ordinance required no harmful purpose and applied to nongang members as well as suspected gang members, (3) the most harmful gang loitering was motivated by an apparent purpose, and (4) the police guidelines did not sufficiently limit the discretion granted to the police in enforcing the ordinance. Also, STEVENS, J., joined by SOUTER and GINSBURG, JJ., expressed the view that (1) the freedom to loiter for innocent purposes is part of the liberty protected by the due process clause, (2) the ordinance was vague in the sense that it specified no standard of conduct, and (3) the ordinance afforded too little notice to citizens who wished to use the public streets.

O'CONNOR, J., joined by BREYER, J., concurring in part and concurring in the judgment, expressed the view that the ordinance was unconstitutionally vague, because it lacked sufficient minimal standards to guide law enforcement officers.

KENNEDY, J., concurring in part and concurring in the judgment, expressed the view that the fact that a citizen had to disobey an order to disperse before being guilty of violating the ordinance was not sufficient to eliminate doubts regarding the adequacy of notice under the ordinance.

BREYER, J., concurring in part and concurring in the judgment, expressed the view that the ordinance was unconstitutional, because it allowed a police officer too much discretion in every case, there being no way to distinguish in the ordinance's terms between one application of discretion and another.

SCALIA, J., dissenting, expressed the view that (1) the minor limitation upon the free state of nature that the ordinance imposed was a small price to pay for liberation of the streets of a city which had been afflicted with criminal street gangs, and (2) the court invalidated a perfectly reasonable measure by (a) ignoring rules

211

governing facial challenges, (b) elevating loitering to a constitutionally guaranteed right, and (c) discerning vagueness where, according to the court's usual standards, none existed.

THOMAS, J., joined by REHNQUIST, Ch. J., and SCALIA, J., dissenting, expressed the view that (1) the ordinance (a) was not vague in all of it applications, and (b) did not violate the due process clause; and (2) there is no fundamental right to loiter, as loitering has been consistently criminalized throughout the nation's history.

COUNSEL

Lawrence Rosenthal argued the cause for petitioner. Harvey Grossman argued the cause for respondents.

BENJAMIN LEE LILLY, Petitioner

v

VIRGINIA

527 US —, 144 L Ed 2d 117, 119 S Ct 1887

[No. 98-5881]

Argued March 29, 1999.
Decided June 10, 1999.

Decision: Accused's rights under confrontation clause
of Federal Constitution's Sixth Amendment held
violated by introduction at trial of accomplice's
confession which incriminated accused for murder.

SUMMARY

An accused and two alleged accomplices were arrested in Virginia in connection with several crimes,
including the theft of liquor and guns and an abduction and murder. Under police questioning, one accomplice admitted to having committed some of the
crimes, implicated the accused in other crimes, and
stated that the accused shot the murder victim. The
accused was tried in state court, separately from his
alleged accomplice. At the accused's trial, the government called the accomplice as a witness. The accomplice invoked his privilege against self-incrimination
under the Federal Constitution's Fifth Amendment,
and the government then offered to introduce into
evidence the statements the accomplice made to the
police after his arrest, arguing that the statements were
admissible as declarations of an unavailable witness
against penal interest. The accused objected on the

213

ground that the statements were not actually against the accomplice's penal interest, and that their admission would violate the confrontation clause of the Federal Constitution's Sixth Amendment. The trial judge overruled the objection and admitted the tape recordings and written transcripts of the statements in their entirety. The jury found the accused guilty of several crimes, including capital murder, as to which the trial judge followed the jury's recommendation of a death sentence. Virginia's highest court affirmed the accused's convictions and sentences, concluding (1) that the accomplice's statements fell within an exception to the Virginia hearsay rule as (a) they were declarations of an unavailable witness against penal interest, and (b) the statements' reliability was established by other evidence; and (2) under the United States Supreme Court's opinion in White v Illinois (1992) 502 US 346, 116 L Ed 2d 848, 112 S Ct 736—which held that where proffered hearsay has sufficient guarantees of reliability to come within a firmly rooted exception to the hearsay rule, the confrontation clause is satisfied—the trial court did not err in admitting the accomplice's statements into evidence, as admissibility into evidence of the statement against penal interest of an unavailable witness is a firmly rooted exception to the hearsay rule in Virginia.

On certiorari, the United States Supreme Court reversed and remanded. In those portions of an opinion by STEVENS, J., which constituted the opinion of the court and were joined by SCALIA, SOUTER, THOMAS, GINSBURG, and BREYER, JJ., as to holdings (1) and (3) below, and by SCALIA, SOUTER, GINSBURG, and BREYER, JJ., as to holding (2) below, it was held that (1) the accused's Sixth Amendment right to be confronted with the witnesses against him was violated by the admission into evidence of the nontestifying accomplice's confession; (2) although the accused focused on state hearsay law in his challenge, before Virginia's highest court, to the admission of the accomplice's statements, the Supreme Court had jurisdiction over the accused's confrontation clause claim, because (a) the accused argued that claim in his opening brief and reply brief to the Virginia's highest court, and (b) such arguments sufficed to raise the Sixth Amendment issue in that court; and (3) in remanding, the Supreme Court leaves it to the Virginia courts to consider in the first instance whether the Sixth Amendment error was harmless beyond a reasonable doubt. Also, STEVENS, J., joined by SOUTER, GINSBURG, and BREYER, JJ., expressed the view that (1) the central concern of the confrontation clause is to ensure the reliability of the evidence against a criminal defendant by subjecting it to rigorous testing in the context of an adversary proceeding before the trier of fact; (2) under the rule of Ohio v Roberts (1980) 448 US 56, 65 L Ed 2d 597, 100 S Ct 2531, the veracity of hearsay statements is sufficiently dependable to allow the untested admission of such statements against an accused when (a) the evidence falls within a firmly rooted hearsay exception, or (b) it contains particularized guarantees of trustworthiness such that adversarial testing would be expected to add little, if anything, to the statements' reliability; (3) an accomplice's confession that inculpates a criminal defendant is not within a firmly rooted exception to the hearsay rule as that concept has been defined in the Supreme Court's confrontation clause jurisprudence; and (4) the Supreme Court should not defer to the determination of Virginia's highest court that the accomplice's statements were reliable, as (a) courts should independently review whether the government's proffered guarantees of trustworthiness satisfy the confrontation clause, and (b) in this case the asserted guarantees of trustworthiness were unconvincing.

BREYER, J., concurring, expressed the view that while, in this case, the Supreme Court did not need to re-examine the way in which its cases have connected the confrontation clause and the hearsay rule, the court may leave the question open for another day.

SCALIA, J., concurring in part and concurring in the judgment, expressed the view that (1) the introduction of the tape recording of the alleged accomplice's statements was a paradigmatic confrontation clause violation, and (2) since the violation was clear, the case needed only be remanded for a harmless-error determination.

THOMAS, J., concurring in part and concurring in the judgment, expressed the view that (1) the confrontation clause extends to any witness who actually testifies at trial and is implicated by extrajudicial statements only insofar as they are contained in formalized testimonial material, (2) the confrontation clause does not impose a blanket ban on the government's use of accomplice statements that incriminate a defendant, and (3) as the lower courts did not analyze the confession under the second prong of the inquiry under Ohio v Roberts, supra, the Supreme Court should not address that issue in this case.

REHNQUIST, Ch. J., joined by O'CONNOR and KENNEDY, JJ., concurring in the judgment, expressed the view that (1) the portions of the accomplice's confession incriminating the accused were not declarations against penal interest and therefore did not fall within a firmly rooted hearsay exception; and (2) there is no reason for the Supreme Court to do more than reverse the decision of the Virginia court and remand the case for the state to demonstrate that the confession bears particularized guarantees of trustworthiness and, if any error is found, to determine whether that error is harmless, as (a) the lower courts did not analyze the confession under the second prong of the inquiry under Ohio v Roberts, supra, and (b) the Supreme Court should not address an issue upon which the lower courts did not pass.

COUNSEL

Ira S. Sacks argued the cause for petitioner.
Kathleen P. Baldwin argued the cause for respondent.

Q. TODD DICKINSON, Acting Commissioner of Patents and Trademarks, Petitioner

v

MARY E. ZURKO et al.

527 US —, 144 L Ed 2d 143, 119 S Ct 1816

[No. 98-377]

Argued March 24, 1999.
Decided June 10, 1999.

Decision: Court of Appeals for Federal Circuit held required to use framework of Administrative Procedure Act provision (5 USCS § 706), rather than "clear error" standard of review, when reviewing factfinding by Patent and Trademark Office.

SUMMARY

Under an Administrative Procedure Act (APA) provision (5 USCS § 706), a reviewing court is generally required to set aside a federal agency's factual findings (1) if they are found to be arbitrary, capricious, or an abuse of discretion; or (2) in certain circumstances involving review on the record of an agency hearing, if the findings are found to be unsupported by substantial evidence. However, there is a provision in 5 USCS § 559 that the APA does not limit or repeal additional requirements "recognized by law," which has been interpreted to mean so recognized at the time of the APA's original enactment in 1946. A patent examiner of the Patent and Trademark Office (PTO), in denying an application for a patent on a method of increasing computer security, concluded that the applicants' method was obvious in light of the prior art. A PTO review board, the Board of Patent Appeals and Interferences, upheld the examiner's decision. Under 35 USCS § 141, the applicants sought direct review in the United States Court of Appeals for the Federal Circuit (CAFC). A panel of the CAFC, in reversing, expressed the view that (1) the question as to what the prior art taught was one of fact, and (2) the PTO's finding on this matter was clearly erroneous (111 F3d 887, 1997 US App LEXIS 7150). On rehearing en banc, the CAFC (1) noted that since its genesis in 1982, the court had been using a standard, which was more searching than the standards in § 706, of reviewing PTO factfinding for clear error; (2) expressed the view that § 559 permitted—and the doctrine of stare decisis warranted—the court's continued application of the clear-error standard of review, as this standard was an additional requirement that was recognized prior to 1947; and (3) reversed the Board's decision for the reasons set out in the panel opinion (142 F3d 1447, 1998 US App LEXIS 8811).

On certiorari, the United States Supreme Court reversed and remanded. In an opinion by BREYER, J., joined by STEVENS, O'CONNOR, SCALIA, SOUTER, and THOMAS, JJ., it was held that when, under § 141, the CAFC directly reviewed findings of fact made by the PTO, the CAFC had to use the "court/agency" framework for review that was set forth in § 706—rather than the traditionally stricter "court/court" standard of reviewing for clear error, which standard was of the type set forth in Rule 52(a) of the Federal Rules of Civil Procedure for appellate court review of factual findings by a Federal District Court judge—as (1) the CAFC had to use the § 706 framework in the absence of an exception; and (2) the circumstances did not justify an exception, under § 559, on the basis of the common law at the time of the APA's adoption in 1946, for the 89 pre-APA cases cited, all of which involved review by the Court of Customs and Patent Appeals (a predecessor of the CAFC) of PTO administrative decisions which either had denied a patent or had awarded priority to one of several competing applicants, did not reflect a well-established stricter court/court standard for reviewing PTO factfinding.

REHNQUIST, Ch. J., joined by KENNEDY and GINSBURG, JJ., dissenting, expressed the view that at the time of the APA's enactment, judicial review of PTO factfinding under the stricter standard of clear error was an additional requirement recognized by law, within the meaning of § 559.

COUNSEL

Lawrence G. Wallace argued the cause for petitioner. Ernest Gellhorn argued the cause for respondents.

GREATER NEW ORLEANS BROADCASTING ASSO-
CIATION, INC., et al., Petitioners

v

UNITED STATES et al.

527 US —, 144 L Ed 2d 161, 119 S Ct 1923

[No. 98-387]

Argued April 27, 1999.
Decided June 14, 1999.

Decision: First Amendment held violated by 18 USCS
§ 1304 and 47 CFR § 73.1211, as applied to prohibit private casino gambling advertisements
broadcast by radio or television stations located in
state where such gambling was legal.

SUMMARY

Under 18 USCS § 1304 and an implementing Federal
Communications Commission (FCC) regulation (47
CFR § 73.1211), radio and television broadcasters were,
among other matters, prohibited from carrying advertising about privately operated commercial casino gambling, regardless of the location of the station or casino
in question. Some radio and television broadcasters in
the New Orleans metropolitan area—with broadcast
areas in Louisiana, Mississippi, and other
states—wished to broadcast promotional advertisements for gambling available at private, for-profit casi-
nos that were lawful in Louisiana and Mississippi. In an
action brought against the United States and the FCC
in the United States District Court for the Eastern
District of Louisiana, the broadcasters sought (1) a
declaration that § 1304 and § 73.1211, as applied to the

broadcasters, violated the Federal Constitution's First Amendment, and (2) an injunction preventing enforcement of § 1304 and § 73.1211 against the broadcasters. The District Court, in granting summary judgment in favor of the government, concluded that the restrictions at issue adequately advanced the government's substantial interests in (1) protecting the interests of nonlottery states, and (2) reducing participation in gambling and thereby minimizing associated social costs (866 F Supp 975, 1994 US Dist LEXIS 15728). The United States Court of Appeals for the Fifth Circuit, in affirming, reasoned in part that because gambling was an activity that could be banned altogether, advertising of gambling could lay no greater claim on constitutional protection than the underlying activity (69 F3d 1296, 1995 US App LEXIS 33420, reh, en banc, den 78 F3d 583, 1996 US App LEXIS 2206). On certiorari, the United States Supreme Court vacated the Court of Appeals' judgment and remanded the case for further consideration in light of 44 Liquormart, Inc. v Rhode Island (1996) 517 US 484, 134 L Ed 2d 711, 116 S Ct 1495, where the Supreme Court's plurality opinion had, among other matters, rejected the argument that the power to restrict speech about certain socially harmful activities was as broad as the power to prohibit such conduct (519 US 801, 136 L Ed 2d 3, 117 S Ct 39). On remand, the Court of Appeals—in affirming once again the District Court's judgment—concluded that § 1304's restriction on speech (1) sufficiently advanced the asserted governmental interests, and (2) was not broader than necessary to control participation in casino gambling (149 F3d 334, 1998 US App LEXIS 17608).

On certiorari, the Supreme Court reversed. In an opinion by STEVENS, J., joined by REHNQUIST, Ch. J., and O'CONNOR, SCALIA, KENNEDY, SOUTER, GINSBURG, and BREYER, JJ., it was held that § 1304 and § 73.1211, as applied to advertisements of private casino gambling that were broadcast by radio or television stations located in a state where such gambling was legal, violated the First Amendment, because (1) the content of the broadcasts in question was not misleading and concerned lawful activities; (2) although the governmental interests assertedly served by the restriction in question—(a) reducing the social costs associated with casino gambling, and (b) assisting states that prohibited casino gambling within their own borders—were substantial, the federal policy of discouraging casino gambling was equivocal, given Congress' unwillingness to adopt a single national policy that consistently endorsed either asserted interest; (3) the restriction in question did not directly and materially further either of these interests, for the operation of § 1304 and its attendant regulatory regime was pierced by exemptions and inconsistencies; and (4) § 1304 sacrificed an intolerable amount of truthful speech about lawful conduct when compared to all of the policies at stake and the social ills that such a ban might reasonably be hoped to eliminate.

REHNQUIST, Ch. J., concurring, (1) agreed that the First Amendment standard of review with respect to commercial speech regulation was not met in the case at hand; and (2) expressed the view that if Congress were to undertake substantive regulation of the gambling industry, rather than simply the manner in which the industry may broadcast advertisements, exemptions and inconsistencies such as those in § 1304 might well prove constitutionally tolerable.

THOMAS, J., concurring in the judgment, expressed the view that in cases such as the one at hand, in which the government's asserted interest is to keep legal users of a product or service ignorant in order to manipulate the users' choices in the marketplace, such an interest is per se illegitimate and can no more justify regulation of commercial speech than it can justify regulation of noncommercial speech.

COUNSEL

Bruce J. Ennis, Jr. argued the cause for petitioners.

Barbara D. Underwood argued the cause for respondents.

TERESA L. CUNNINGHAM, Petitioner

v

HAMILTON COUNTY, OHIO

527 US —, 144 L Ed 2d 184, 119 S Ct 1915

[No. 98-727]

Argued April 19, 1999.
Decided June 14, 1999.

Decision: Order imposing sanctions on attorney, pursuant to Rule 37(a)(4) of Federal Rules of Civil Procedure for failure to comply with discovery orders, held not to be final decision appealable under 28 USCS § 1291, even where attorney was no longer representing party in case.

SUMMARY

An attorney representing the administrator of the estate of an individual who had committed suicide while an inmate at a county justice center filed a federal civil rights action against the county in the United States District Court for the Southern District of Ohio. In the course of that litigation, the attorney failed to comply with various discovery orders issued by a Magistrate Judge. The Magistrate Judge granted the county's motion to sanction the attorney for such conduct pursuant to Rule 37(a)(4) of the Federal Rules of Civil Procedure, and fined the attorney $1,494, but specifically did not hold the attorney to be in contempt of court. The District Court affirmed the sanctions order and granted defense motions to disqualify the attorney as counsel, because the attorney was a material witness in the case. The attorney immediately appealed the

225

sanctions order to the United States Court of Appeals for the Sixth Circuit, which dismissed the appeal for lack of jurisdiction and held that the attorney must wait until final disposition of the underlying case before filing an appeal (144 F3d 418).

On certiorari, the United States Supreme Court affirmed. In an opinion by THOMAS, J., expressing the unanimous view of the court, it was held that an order imposing sanctions on an attorney pursuant to Rule 37(a)(4) was not a final decision appealable under 28 USCS § 1291, even where the attorney no longer represented a party in the case.

KENNEDY, J., concurred, expressing the view that an attorney ordered to pay sanctions was not without a remedy in every case, but could (1) petition for a writ of mandamus, if a sanction order imposed an exceptional hardship and the trial court refused to grant a stay; or (2) appeal immediately if a contempt order was entered and there was no congruence of interests between the contemnor and a party to the underlying litigation.

COUNSEL

Thomas C. Goldstein argued the cause for petitioner. John J. Arnold argued the cause for respondent.

————————

TOGO D. WEST, JR., Secretary of Veterans Affairs,
Petitioner

v

MICHAEL GIBSON

527 US —, 144 L Ed 2d 196, 119 S Ct 1906

[No. 98-238]

Argued April 26, 1999.
Decided June 14, 1999.

Decision: Equal Employment Opportunity Commission
held to possess legal authority to require federal
agencies to pay compensatory damages when they
discriminate in violation of Title VII of Civil Rights
Act of 1964.

SUMMARY

In 1972, Congress extended Title VII of the Civil
Rights Act of 1964 (42 USCS §§ 2000e et seq.) to
prohibit employment discrimination in the Federal
Government (42 USCS § 2000e-16a), to authorize the
Equal Employment Opportunity Commission (EEOC)
to enforce that prohibition through appropriate remedies, including reinstatement or hiring with or without
backpay (42 USCS § 2000e-16(b)), and to empower
courts to entertain an action by a complainant still
aggrieved after final agency action (42 USCS § 2000e-
16(c)). In 1991, Congress again amended Title VII in
the Compensatory Damages Amendment (CDA),
which, among other things, permitted victims of intentional discrimination to recover compensatory damages in an action under § 2000e-16 (42 USCS
§ 1981a(a)(1)) and added that any party in such an

227

action could demand a jury trial (42 USCS § 1981a(c)). Thereafter, the EEOC began to grant compensatory damages awards in Federal Government employment discrimination cases. An individual filed a complaint which charged that the Federal Department of Veterans Affairs had discriminated against him by denying him a promotion on the basis of his gender. The EEOC found in his favor and awarded him the promotion plus backpay. The individual then filed suit in a Federal District Court asking for compensatory damages and other relief, but the District Court dismissed the complaint. The United States Court of Appeals for the Seventh Circuit, in reversing the District Court's dismissal, (1) rejected the argument of the Department of Veterans Affairs that because the individual had failed to exhaust his administrative remedies with respect to an award of compensatory damages, he could not bring that claim in court, and (2) expressed the view that (a) the EEOC lacked the legal power to award compensatory damages, and (b) consequently there was no administrative remedy to exhaust (137 F3d 992).

On certiorari, the United States Supreme Court vacated the judgment of the Court of Appeals and remanded the case. In an opinion by BREYER, J., joined by STEVENS, O'CONNOR, SOUTER, and GINSBURG, JJ., it was held that (1) the EEOC possessed the legal authority to require the federal agency to pay compensatory damages as (a) read literally, the language of the 1972 extension of Title VII and of the CDA is consistent with such a grant of authority to the EEOC because, after the enactment of the CDA, an award of compensatory damages is a remedy which is appropriate; (b) an examination of the purposes of the 1972 Title VII extension shows that this reading of the language is the correct reading, as the general purpose of § 717 (42 USCS § 2000e-16) is to remedy discrimination in federal employment, which it does in part by creating a dispute resolution system that requires a complaining party to pursue administrative relief prior to court action, and to deny that an award of compensatory damages by the EEOC to a claimant is appropriate would undermine this remedial scheme; and (c) the history of the CDA reinforces an interpretation that Congress wanted the EEOC to consider compensatory damages; (2) the Federal Government's sovereign immunity was waived, under the CDA, in respect to an award of compensatory damages, and the CDA permitted the EEOC to consider the matter; and (3) the Supreme Court would leave it to the Court of Appeals on remand (a) to determine whether the individual properly raised a claim that, even if the EEOC had the legal power to award compensatory damages, he had exhausted his administrative remedies, and, if so, (b) to decide the issue.

KENNEDY, J., joined by REHNQUIST, Ch. J., and SCALIA, and THOMAS, JJ., dissenting, expressed the view that the EEOC could not have awarded compensatory damages against the United States under § 717 (42 USCS § 2000e-16) because the statute did not authorize such awards in express and unequivocal terms, and, as a consequence, § 717(b) did not provide the required waiver of the United States' sovereign immunity.

COUNSEL

Barbara B. McDowell argued the cause for petitioner. Timothy M. Kelly argued the cause for respondent.

NATIONAL AERONAUTICS AND SPACE ADMINIS-
TRATION, et al., Petitioners

v

FEDERAL LABOR RELATIONS AUTHORITY et al.

527 US —, 144 L Ed 2d 258, 119 S Ct 1979

[No. 98-369]

Argued March 23, 1999.
Decided June 17, 1999.

Decision: Investigator from Office of Inspector General
of National Aeronautics and Space Administration
(NASA) held to be "representative" of NASA for
purposes of 5 USCS § 7114(a)(2)(B), giving right
to union representation at certain examinations of
employee by representative of agency.

SUMMARY

In 1978, Congress enacted the Inspector General Act
(IGA) (5 USCS Appx §§ 1 et seq.), which created an
Office of Inspector General (OIG) in each of several
federal agencies, including the National Aeronautics
and Space Administration (NASA). On the next day,
Congress enacted a Federal Service Labor-Management
Relations Statute (FSLMRS) provision (5 USCS
§ 7114(a)(2)(B)) which gives an employee of a union-
ized unit in an agency a right to union representation at
any examination of the employee by a "representative
of the agency" in connection with an investigation, if
the employee (1) reasonably believes that an examination may result in disciplinary action against the employee, and (2) requests representation. During an
investigation by NASA's OIG of some allegedly threat-

ening activities by an employee at a NASA facility in Alabama, an OIG investigator agreed that a union representative could attend an interview of the employee, but the investigator's conduct of the interview gave rise to a complaint by the union representative that the investigator had improperly limited the representative's participation. The union filed with the Federal Labor Relations Authority (FLRA) a charge alleging that NASA and its OIG had committed an unfair labor practice. An Administrative Law Judge, in ruling for the union, concluded that (1) the OIG investigator was a representative of the agency within the meaning of § 7114(a)(2)(B), and (2) certain aspects of the investigator's behavior had violated the right to union representation under § 7114(a)(2)(B). On review, the FLRA (1) agreed that the investigator (a) was a representative of the agency for such purposes, and (b) had improperly prevented the union representative from actively participating in the interview; and (2) issued an enforcement order (50 FLRA 601). The United States Court of Appeals for the Eleventh Circuit, in denying a NASA petition for review and in granting an application by the FLRA for enforcement of its order, expressed the view that the FLRA had correctly concluded that the investigator was a representative of the agency within the meaning of § 7114(a)(2)(B) (120 F3d 1208, 1997 US App LEXIS 22959).

On certiorari, the United States Supreme Court affirmed. In an opinion by STEVENS, J., joined by KENNEDY, SOUTER, GINSBURG, and BREYER, JJ., it was held that an investigator from NASA's OIG is considered to be a representative of NASA when the investigator is conducting an employee examination covered by § 7114(a)(2)(B), for (1) when the ordinary tools of statutory construction are combined with the FLRA's position on the matter, the application of

§ 7114(a)(2)(B) is not limited to agency investigators representing an "entity" that collectively bargains with the employee's union; (2) the proper operation of the IGA does not require nullification of § 7114(a)(2)(B) in all OIG examinations; and (3) some broader policy arguments to the contrary by NASA and its OIG were unpersuasive.

THOMAS, J., joined by REHNQUIST, Ch. J., and O'CONNOR and SCALIA, JJ., dissenting, expressed the view that (1) in light of the independence guaranteed Inspectors General by the IGA, investigators employed in an OIG will not represent agency management in the typical case; and (2) there was no basis for concluding, as the FLRA had, that in the case at hand, the investigator from NASA's OIG was a representative of the agency within the meaning of § 7114(a)(2)(B).

COUNSEL

David C. Frederick argued the cause for petitioners.

David M. Smith argued the cause for respondent Federal Labor Relations Authority.

Stuart Kirsch argued the cause for respondent American Federation of Government Employees.

TOMMY DAVID STRICKLER, Petitioner

v

FRED W. GREENE, Warden

527 US —, 144 L Ed 2d 286, 119 S Ct 1936

[No. 98-5864]

Argued March 3, 1999.
Decided June 17, 1999.

Decision: Federal habeas corpus relief denied—and rule of Brady v Maryland (1963) 373 US 83, 10 L Ed 2d 215, 83 S Ct 1194, and its progeny held not violated by failing to disclose exculpatory evidence to accused—where accused, who was sentenced to death, could not show prejudice.

SUMMARY

An accused was charged in a Virginia state court with capital murder and other crimes. The accused's counsel did not file a pretrial motion for discovery of possible exculpatory evidence. At the accused's trial, a witness gave detailed testimony about the crimes and about the accused's role as one of the perpetrators. The prosecuting attorney, who maintained an open file policy which gave the accused access to all of the evidence in the prosecutor's files, failed to disclose exculpatory information contained in police files. The exculpatory information, consisting of notes taken by a detective during interviews with the witness, and letters written by the witness to the detective, cast serious doubt on significant portions of the witness' testimony. The jury found the accused guilty, and he was sentenced to death. Virginia's highest court affirmed the verdict and the death sentence (241 Va 482, 404 SE2d 227). After new counsel had been appointed to represent the accused in subsequent state habeas corpus proceedings, the accused advanced an ineffective assistance of counsel claim based, in part, on his trial counsel's failure to file a motion under the rule of Brady v Maryland (1963) 373 US 83, 10 L Ed 2d 215, 83 S Ct 1194—that the suppression by prosecutors of evidence favorable to an accused violates due process if the evidence is material either to guilt or to punishment, irrespective of the good faith or bad faith of the prosecution—for disclosure of all exculpatory evidence known to the prosecution or in its possession. In response, the state asserted that such a motion was unnecessary because of the prosecutor's open file policy. The trial court denied relief. Virginia's highest court affirmed the denial of relief (249 Va 120, 452 SE2d 648). The accused filed a federal habeas corpus petition in the United States District Court for the Eastern District of Virginia and was granted access to the exculpatory information for the first time. The District Court vacated the accused's capital murder conviction and death sentence on the grounds that the state had failed to disclose the exculpatory information and that petitioner had not, in consequence, received a fair trial. The United States Court of Appeals for the Fourth Circuit reversed the District Court's decision and remanded the case with instructions to dismiss the petition, holding that (1) the accused had procedurally defaulted his Brady claim by not raising it at his trial or in the state collateral proceedings, and (2) because of the absence of prejudice, the claim was, in any event, without merit (149 F3d 1170).

On certiorari, the United States Supreme Court affirmed. In an opinion by STEVENS, J., joined by REHNQUIST, Ch. J., and O'CONNOR, SCALIA, and GINS-

BURG, JJ., and joined in pertinent part by THOMAS, J., it was held that the accused was not entitled to federal habeas corpus relief, because (1) he did not show that there was a reasonable probability that his conviction or sentence would have been different had the suppressed information been disclosed, and (2) he thus did not show that (a) under the Brady rule, the suppressed information was material or prejudice ensued, or (b) he suffered prejudice sufficient to excuse his procedural default.

SOUTER, J., joined by KENNEDY, J., as to (2) below, concurring in part and dissenting in part, expressed the view that (1) the Supreme Court should characterize the Brady materiality standard as requiring a significant possibility of a different result in a verdict or sentence, and (2) there is a significant possibility in the present case that disclosure of the suppressed material would have led the jury to recommend a life sentence, instead of the death sentence, and therefore the sentence should be vacated.

COUNSEL

Miguel A. Estrada argued the cause for petitioner.
Pamela A. Rumpz argued the cause for respondent.

GRUPO MEXICANO de DESARROLLO, S. A., et al.,
Petitioners

v

ALLIANCE BOND FUND, INC., et al.

527 US —, 144 L Ed 2d 319, 119 S Ct 1961

[No. 98-231]

Argued March 31, 1999.
Decided June 17, 1999.

Decision: Federal District Court held to lack authority,
in action for money damages, to issue preliminary
injunction preventing note issuer from disposing
of assets in which note holders who sought injunction claimed no lien or equitable interest.

SUMMARY

Some American investment funds purchased unsecured, guaranteed notes from a Mexican holding company. After the holding company encountered financial
troubles and missed an interest payment on the notes,
the investment funds accelerated the principal amount
of the notes and filed suit, on the theory of breach of
contract, for damages representing the amount allegedly due, in the United States District Court for the
Southern District of New York, to the personal jurisdiction of which the holding company had consented. The
funds, alleging that the holding company was at risk of
insolvency, if not already insolvent, and that the company's planned transfer of certain assets would frustrate
any judgment that the funds could obtain against the
company, requested, while the breach-of-contract action was pending, a preliminary injunction restraining

the company from transferring these assets. After issuing a temporary restraining order preventing transfer of the assets, the District Court preliminarily enjoined the company from disposing of the assets. The United States Court of Appeals for the Second Circuit affirmed (143 F3d 688).

On certiorari, the United States Supreme Court reversed and remanded. In an opinion by SCALIA, J., joined in pertinent part by REHNQUIST, Ch. J., and O'CONNOR, KENNEDY, and THOMAS, JJ., it was held that the District Court lacked the authority to issue, pursuant to Rule 65 of the Federal Rules of Civil Procedure, the preliminary injunction, as (1) substantially, the equity jurisdiction of the federal courts was the jurisdiction in equity exercised by the High Court of Chancery in England at the time of the adoption of the Federal Constitution and the enactment of the Judiciary Act of 1789 (1 Stat 73), which confers on the federal courts jurisdiction over all suits in equity, (2) the substantive prerequisites for obtaining an equitable remedy as well as the general availability of injunctive relief were not altered by Rule 65 and depended on traditional principles of equity jurisdiction, (3) the general rule that a judgment establishing a debt was necessary before a court of equity would interfere with the debtor's use of the debtor's property was not changed by the merger of law and equity under the Rules, (4) the Court of Chancery did not provide a prejudgment injunctive remedy until 1975, and (5) the debate concerning the remedy sought by the funds ought to be conducted and resolved by Congress.

GINSBURG, J., joined by STEVENS, SOUTER, and BREYER, JJ., dissenting, expressed the view that (1) absent immediate judicial action, the funds would have been left with a multimillion dollar judgment on which they could not collect a penny, (2) the District Court properly invoked its equitable power to avoid that manifestly unjust result and to protect its ability to render an enforceable final judgment, and (3) where, as in the instant case, legal remedies were not practical and efficient, the federal courts had to rely on their flexible jurisdiction in equity to protect all rights and do justice to all concerned.

COUNSEL

Richard A. Mescon argued the cause for petitioners. Drew S. Days, III argued the cause for respondents.

BILL MARTIN, Director, Michigan Department of
Corrections, et al., Petitioners

v

EVERETT HADIX et al.

527 US —, 144 L Ed 2d 347, 119 S Ct 1998

[No. 98-262]

Argued March 30, 1999.
Decided June 21, 1999.

Decision: Section 803(d)(3) of Prison Litigation Reform Act of 1995 (42 USCS § 1997e(d)(3)) held to
limit attorneys' fees for postjudgment monitoring
services performed after Act's effective date, but
not to limit fees for monitoring services performed
before effective date.

SUMMARY

In 1977 and 1980, two groups of prisoners filed
federal class actions, under 42 USCS § 1983, challenging the conditions of confinement in the Michigan
prison system. The defendants in both suits were prison
officials. The prisoners prevailed in both suits, and, in
each case, the United States District Court for the
Eastern District of Michigan ruled that the prisoners
were "prevailing parties" entitled to attorneys' fees,
under the Civil Rights Attorney's Fees Award Act of
1976 (42 USCS § 1988), for postjudgment monitoring
of the defendants' compliance with remedial decrees.
Systems were established for awarding those fees on a
semiannual basis, and the District Court established
specific market rates for awarding fees. On April 26,
1996, the Prison Litigation Reform Act of 1995 (PLRA)

239

became effective, and § 803(d)(3) of the PLRA (42 USCS § 1997e(d)(3)) placed a cap on the size of fees that could be awarded to attorneys who litigated prisoner lawsuits. On the effective date of the PLRA, the prevailing market rate in both cases was $150 per hour, but, under the PLRA, fees in the Eastern District were capped at a maximum hourly rate of $112.50. In both cases, the District Court, in considering fee requests for postjudgment monitoring performed before the PLRA was enacted, concluded that the PLRA cap did not limit attorneys' fees in these cases for services performed prior to, but still unpaid by, the PLRA's effective date. The United States Court of Appeals for the Sixth Circuit affirmed these decisions. Fee requests next were filed in both cases for services performed between January 1, 1996, and June 30, 1996, a period encompassing work performed both before and after the PLRA's effective date. In each case, in nearly identical orders, the District Court reiterated its earlier conclusion that the PLRA did not limit fees for work performed before the effective date, but concluded that the PLRA cap did limit fees for services performed after the effective date. The Court of Appeals consolidated the appeals from these orders, and affirmed in part and reversed in part. The Court of Appeals held that the PLRA's fee limitation did not apply to cases which were pending on the enactment date, and that if the fee limitation did so apply, it would have an impermissible retroactive effect, regardless of when the work was performed (143 F3d 246).

On certiorari, the United States Supreme Court affirmed in part and reversed in part. In an opinion by O'CONNOR, J., joined by REHNQUIST, Ch. J., and KENNEDY, SOUTER, THOMAS, and BREYER, JJ., and joined by SCALIA, J., as to all but holdings (1)(b) and (2)(b) below, and by STEVENS and GINSBURG, JJ., as to holding

(1) below, it was held that (1) § 803(d)(3) did not limit
attorneys' fees for postjudgment monitoring services
which were performed before the PLRA's effective
date, as (a) Congress did not clearly express an intent
that § 803(d)(3) apply retroactively, and (b) attorneys
had a reasonable expectation that work they performed
prior to the effective date of the PLRA would be
compensated at the pre-PLRA rates; but (2)
§ 803(d)(3) did limit fees for monitoring services performed after the PRLA's effective date, as (a) Congress
did not clearly express an intent that § 803(d)(3) apply
prospectively only, and (b) the attorneys were then on
notice that the hourly rate had been adjusted, and any
expectation, after the effective date, of compensation at
the pre-PLRA rates was unreasonable.

SCALIA, J., concurring in part and concurring in the
judgment, expressed the view that (1) the determination as to retroactive application ought to be made with
reference to the activity which a statute was intended to
regulate, not with reference to expectations, (2) the
purpose of the provision at issue in the present case was
to reduce the incentive for lawyers to work on prisoner's civil rights cases, and (3) therefore the relevant
retroactivity event is the doing of the work for which the
incentive was offered.

GINSBURG, J., joined by STEVENS, J., concurring in
part and dissenting in part, expressed the view that
§ 803(d) does not, in cases commenced before the
PLRA became law, limit attorneys' fees with respect to
postjudgment monitoring services performed after the
PLRA's effective date, as there is not a satisfactory basis
in the PLRA's text or history for concluding that
Congress meant to order a midstream change which
placed such cases under the new fee regime.

241

COUNSEL

Thomas L. Casey argued the cause for petitioners.

Deborah A. La Belle argued the cause for respondents.

––––––––––––

LOUIS JONES, Petitioner

v

UNITED STATES

527 US —, 144 L Ed 2d 370, 119 S Ct 2090

[No. 97-9361]

Argued February 22, 1999.
Decided June 21, 1999.

Decision: Accused facing possible death sentence held not entitled to instruction as to effect of sentencing jury deadlock; alleged error, where death sentence was imposed, in allowing jury to consider aggravating factors that allegedly violated Eighth Amendment held harmless.

SUMMARY

After the accused had kidnapped a member of the Armed Forces from an air force base and had killed her, the accused was charged with kidnapping with death resulting to the victim, in violation of 18 USCS § 1201(a)(2), an offense punishable by life imprisonment or death. The government, exercising its discretion under the Federal Death Penalty Act of 1994 (18 USCS §§ 3591 et seq.), decided to seek the death penalty. After the accused was tried in the United States District Court for the Northern District of Texas and found guilty by the jury, the District Court conducted a separate sentencing hearing pursuant to 18 USCS § 3593. Under 18 USCS § 3593(c), for any aggravating factor to be weighed in determining whether to impose the death penalty, a jury must unanimously agree that the government has established the existence of the

243

aggravating factor beyond a reasonable doubt. In addition to unanimously finding aggravating factors that under 18 USCS § 3592(c) made the accused death-eligible, the sentencing jury (1) unanimously found that two nonstatutory aggravating factors—one that set forth victim impact evidence and the other that set forth victim vulnerability evidence—had been proved beyond a reasonable doubt, and (2) after weighing the aggravating and mitigating factors, unanimously recommended the death penalty. The District Court—which had refused the accused's request to include in the jury instructions an instruction to the effect that in the event of a jury deadlock concerning what sentence, either death or life imprisonment without possibility of release, to impose, the District Court would impose a sentence of life imprisonment without possibility of release, rather than any lesser sentence—imposed sentence in accordance with the jury's recommendation. The United States Court of Appeals for the Fifth Circuit affirmed (132 F3d 232).

On certiorari, the United States Supreme Court affirmed. In an opinion by THOMAS, J., joined by REHNQUIST, Ch. J., and O'CONNOR and KENNEDY, JJ., and joined in pertinent part by SCALIA, J., it was held that (1) the accused was not entitled to an instruction as to the effect of jury deadlock, as (a) the Federal Constitution's Eighth Amendment did not require such an instruction, and (b) the Supreme Court declined to exercise its supervisory powers to require such an instruction in every capital case; (2) there was no reasonable likelihood that the jury had been led to believe that the accused would receive a court-imposed sentence less than life imprisonment in the event that the jury could not reach a unanimous sentence recommendation; and (3) even if it was assumed that the District Court had erred by allowing the jury to consider nonstatutory aggravating factors that were vague, overbroad, and duplicative in violation of the Eighth Amendment, the error was harmless beyond a reasonable doubt.

GINSBURG, J., joined by STEVENS and SOUTER, JJ., and joined in pertinent part by BREYER, J., dissenting, expressed the view that (1) accurate sentencing information is an indispensable prerequisite to a jury's determination whether a defendant shall live or die, (2) that indispensable prerequisite was not satisfied in this case, and (3) the jury instructions introduced a level of uncertainty and unreliability into the factfinding process that cannot be tolerated in a capital case.

COUNSEL

Timothy Crooks argued the cause for petitioner.

Michael R. Dreeben argued the cause for respondent.

JEFFERSON COUNTY, ALABAMA, Petitioner

v

WILLIAM M. ACKER, JR., Senior Judge, United
States District Court, Northern District of Alabama,
and U. W. CLEMON, Judge, United States District
Court, Northern District of Alabama

527 US —, 144 L Ed 2d 408, 119 S Ct 2069

[No. 98-10]

Argued March 29, 1999.
Decided June 21, 1999.

Decision: Alabama county's suits to collect occupational tax from federal judges held properly removed to federal court under 28 USCS
§ 1442(a)(3); federal adjudication held not barred
by Tax Injunction Act (28 USCS § 1341); imposition of tax held consented to by 4 USCS § 111.

SUMMARY

Pursuant to the authority granted by an Alabama
state statute, an Alabama county enacted an ordinance
which (1) imposed a tax—variously referred to as an
occupational, license, or privilege tax—on persons
engaged in any vocation, occupation, calling, or profession in the county who were not otherwise required by
law to pay any license or privilege tax to either the state
or the county; (2) declared it to be "unlawful . . . to
engage in" a covered occupation without paying the
ordinance's tax; (3) included, among those subject to
the tax, any federal, state, county, or city officer or
employee where the services of such officer or employee were rendered within the county; (4) measured
246

the tax due as one-half percent of the gross receipts of
the person subject to the tax; and (5) defined "gross
receipts" as having the same meaning as "compensation" and as including all salaries, wages, commissions,
and bonuses. The county instituted two suits in Alabama small claims court to collect the county tax from
two judges of the United States District Court for the
Northern District of Alabama who held court in the
county. The judges removed the suits to the District
Court under 28 USCS § 1442(a)(3), which authorizes
the removal of a civil action or criminal prosecution
commenced in a state court against any "officer of the
courts of the United States, for any act under color of
office or in the performance of his duties." The District
Court denied the county's motions to remand and
consolidated the suits. Eventually, the District Court
granted summary judgment for the two judges, as the
court, among other matters, ruled that under the
doctrine of intergovernmental tax immunity, the
county tax violated the Federal Constitution to the
extent that the tax reached the compensation of federal judges (850 F Supp 1536, 1994 US Dist LEXIS
4415). On appeal, a panel of the United States Court of
Appeals for the Eleventh Circuit initially reversed the
District Court's judgment (61 F3d 848, 1995 US App
LEXIS 23313). However, on rehearing en banc, the
Court of Appeals affirmed the District Court's disposition, as the Court of Appeals expressed the view that
(1) the county tax, as applied to federal judges,
amounted to a direct tax on the Federal Government
or its instrumentalities in violation of the doctrine of
intergovernmental tax immunity; and (2) Congress had
not consented to the county tax under various statutes
including the Public Salary Tax Act of 1939 (4 USCS
§ 111), which allows a state and its taxing authorities to
tax the pay or compensation for personal service that a

federal employee receives if the taxation does not discriminate against the employee because of the source of the pay or compensation (92 F3d 1561, 1996 US App LEXIS 22399). The United States Supreme Court granted certiorari, vacated the Court of Appeals' judgment, and remanded the case for further consideration in light of a 1997 Supreme Court decision in another case involving the Tax Injunction Act (TIA) (28 USCS § 1341), which restricts District Courts from enjoining, suspending, or restraining the assessment, levy, or collection of state taxes (520 US 1261, 138 L Ed 2d 191, 117 S Ct 2429). On remand, the en banc Court of Appeals (1) expressed the view that (a) the county's suits were properly removed to federal court under § 1442(a)(3), and (b) the TIA did not operate to bar federal jurisdiction in the case at hand; (2) reinstated the prior en banc opinion on the merits, and (3) again affirmed the District Court's ruling (137 F3d 1314, 1998 US App LEXIS 5999).

On certiorari, the Supreme Court reversed the Court of Appeals' judgment and remanded the case for further proceedings. In an opinion by GINSBURG, J.—expressing the unanimous view of the court as to holding 2 below, joined by STEVENS, O'CONNOR, KENNEDY, and BREYER, JJ., as to holding 1 below, and joined by REHNQUIST, Ch. J., and STEVENS, SCALIA, KENNEDY, SOUTER, and THOMAS, JJ., as to holding 3 below—it was held that (1) the county's tax collection suits were properly removed by the two judges to the District Court under § 1442(a)(3), because the judges had (a) presented a colorable federal defense, and (b) shown the essential nexus between the judges' activities under color of office and the county's demands for payment of the tax; (2) the TIA, as indicated by its terms and purpose, did not (a) bar a federal court from adjudicating suits, such as the suits in question, for the collection of taxes, or (b) prevent taxpayers from urging defenses in such suits that the taxes for which collection was sought were invalid; and (3) the federal constitutional doctrine of intergovernmental tax immunity did not shield the two judges from paying the county tax in question, because the tax operated as a nondiscriminatory tax on the judges' compensation to which § 111 consented.

SCALIA, J., joined by REHNQUIST, Ch. J., and SOUTER and THOMAS, JJ., concurring in part and dissenting in part, joined holdings 2 and 3 above in view of the Supreme Court's decision to reach the merits, but expressed the opinion that the county's suits had been improperly removed under § 1442(a)(3), as the two judges had failed to show a causal connection between the charged conduct and asserted official authority.

BREYER, J., joined by O'CONNOR, J., concurring in part and dissenting in part, agreed that the Supreme Court had jurisdiction to hear the merits of the case, but expressed the view that the county's tax (1) amounted to a tax imposed directly upon a federal official's performance of official duties, rather than an income tax on federal employees; and (2) thus, was (a) unconstitutional under the doctrine of intergovernmental tax immunity, and (b) not consented to by federal statutes including § 111.

COUNSEL

Jeffrey M. Sewell argued the cause for petitioner.

Kent L. Jones argued the cause for the United States, as amicus curiae, by special leave of court.

Alan B. Morrison argued the cause for respondents.

MARYLAND, Petitioner

v

KEVIN DARNELL DYSON

527 US —, 144 L Ed 2d 442, 119 S Ct 2013

[No. 98-1062]

Decided June 21, 1999.

Decision: Automobile exception to warrant requirement of Federal Constitution's Fourth Amendment held not to require separate finding of
exigency in addition to finding of probable cause.

SUMMARY

Acting on a tip from a reliable confidential informant and subsequent investigation, sheriff's deputies
from a Maryland county stopped and searched an
automobile that was being rented by an accused, who
was a known drug dealer. The deputies found 23 grams
of crack cocaine in a duffel bag in the trunk of the
automobile and arrested the accused. The accused was
tried and convicted, in a Maryland court, of conspiracy
to possess cocaine with intent to distribute. On appeal,
the Maryland Court of Special Appeals reversed, holding that (1) in order for the automobile exception to
the warrant requirement—under the Federal Constitution's Fourth Amendment—to apply, there must be not
only probable cause to believe that evidence of a crime
is contained in the automobile, but also a separate
finding of an exigency which precluded the police from
obtaining a warrant, and (2) although there was abun-
dant probable cause, the search violated the Fourth
Amendment because there was no exigency that pre-

vented or even made it significantly difficult for the police to obtain a search warrant (122 Md App 413, 712 A2d 573). The Maryland Court of Appeals denied certiorari (351 Md 287, 718 A2d 235).

Granting certiorari, the United States Supreme Court reversed. In a per curiam opinion expressing the view of REHNQUIST, Ch. J., and O'CONNOR, SCALIA, KENNEDY, SOUTER, THOMAS, and GINSBURG, JJ., it was held that the holding of the Maryland Court of Special Appeals rested upon an incorrect interpretation of the automobile exception to the warrant requirement of the Fourth Amendment, as (1) the automobile exception has no separate exigency requirement, and where there is probable cause to search an automobile, a search is not unreasonable if based on facts that would justify the issuance of a warrant, even though a warrant is not actually obtained, and (2) the holding that the automobile exception required such a finding of exigency was squarely contrary to past holdings of the Supreme Court.

BREYER, J., joined by STEVENS, J., dissenting, expressed the view that the Supreme Court's per curiam opinion correctly stated the law, but that because the accused's counsel, who was not a member of the Supreme Court's bar and who did not wish to become one, had not filed a brief in opposition to the state's petition for certiorari, the Supreme Court should not have summarily reversed without first inviting an attorney to file a brief, as amicus curiae, in response to the petition for certiorari.

MARY KOEGEL FERTEL-RUST, Petitioner

v

MILWAUKEE COUNTY MENTAL HEALTH CENTER
et al.

527 US —, 144 L Ed 2d 447, 119 S Ct 1997

[No. 98-8952]

Decided June 21, 1999.

Decision: Person who filed eight frivolous petitions in
Supreme Court denied leave to proceed in forma
pauperis on certiorari petition; order entered barring person's future in forma pauperis filings of
noncriminal certiorari petitions.

SUMMARY

An individual sought leave to proceed in forma
pauperis in the United States Supreme Court under
Supreme Court Rule 39 with respect to a petition for
certiorari. According to the court, which four times in
the last 5 years had invoked Supreme Court Rule
39.8—which authorizes the court to deny leave to
proceed in forma pauperis with respect to frivolous
petitions—to deny the individual in forma pauperis
status, the instant petition was the individual's eighth
frivolous filing in the court.

In a per curiam opinion expressing the view of
REHNQUIST, Ch. J., and O'CONNOR, SCALIA, KENNEDY,
SOUTER, THOMAS, GINSBURG, and BREYER, JJ., the Supreme Court (1) invoked Rule 39.8 to deny the individual's request for leave to proceed in forma pauperis
on the instant petition, and (2) directed the Clerk of
the Supreme Court not to accept any further petitions

for certiorari in noncriminal matters from the individual unless she complied with Supreme Court Rules 33.1 and 38.

STEVENS, J., dissented for reasons expressed in some previous Supreme Court cases involving some similar issues.

KAREN SUTTON and KIMBERLY HINTON, Petitioners

v

UNITED AIR LINES, INC.

527 US —, 144 L Ed 2d 450, 119 S Ct 2139

[No. 97-1943]

Argued April 28, 1999.
Decided June 22, 1999.

Decision: Severely myopic individuals who were denied
employment as global airline pilots held not disabled, within meaning of Americans with Disabilities Act, where corrective lenses allowed individuals to function identically to people without similar
impairment.

SUMMARY

The Americans with Disabilities Act (ADA) (42 USCS
§§ 12101 et seq.) provided that no covered employer
shall discriminate against a qualified individual with a
disability and included in the definition of disability (1)
a physical impairment that substantially limits one or
more major life activities, or (2) being regarded as
having such an impairment (42 USCS § 12102(2)). Two
individuals applied for employment as global airline
pilots with a major commercial airline. Each of the
individuals was severely myopic and had uncorrected
visual acuity of 20/200 or worse. However, the visual
acuity of each was correctable to 20/20 or better with
eyeglasses or contact lenses. The airline required a
minimum uncorrected visual acuity of 20/100 or better
for global airline pilots, and because the individuals did

not meet this requirement, neither was offered employment. The individuals filed suit in the United States District Court for the District of Colorado alleging that the airline had violated the ADA by discriminating against them either on the basis of their disability or because the airline regarded the individuals as having a disability. The District Court dismissed the complaint for failure to state a claim upon which relief could be granted, holding that the individuals did not (1) state a claim that they were disabled within the meaning of the ADA, as (a) their visual impairment could be fully corrected, and (b) they were therefore not actually substantially limited in any major life activity; or (2) make allegations sufficient to support a claim that they were regarded by the airline as having an impairment that substantially limited a major life activity, as the individuals alleged only that the airline regarded them as unable to satisfy the requirements of a particular job. The United States Court of Appeals for the Tenth Circuit affirmed the District Court's judgment (130 F3d 893).

On certiorari, the United States Supreme Court affirmed. In an opinion by O'CONNOR, J., joined by REHNQUIST, Ch. J., and SCALIA, KENNEDY, SOUTER, THOMAS, and GINSBURG, JJ., it was held that the individuals' complaint failed to state a claim upon which relief can be granted, as (1) the determination of whether an individual is disabled, under the ADA, should be made with reference to measures that mitigate the individual's impairment, including eyeglasses and contact lenses, (2) since the individuals, with corrective measures, could function identically to individuals without a similar impairment, the individuals did not properly allege that they possessed a physical impairment that substantially limited them in any major life activity, and (3) the individuals did not properly

255

allege that the airline regarded them as having a such an impairment, because (a) the individuals alleged only that the airline regarded the individuals' poor vision as precluding them from holding positions as global airline pilots, and (b) since there were a number of other positions utilizing the individuals' skills, such as regional pilots and pilot instructors, the individuals' allegations did not support the claim that the airline regarded the individuals as having an impairment that substantially limited them in the major life activity of working.

GINSBURG, J., concurring, expressed the view that the ADA does not reach the legions of people with correctable disabilities, as Congress' legislative finding that individuals with disabilities are a discrete and insular minority is a telling indication of Congress' intent to restrict the ADA's coverage to a confined and historically disadvantaged class.

STEVENS, J., joined by BREYER, J., dissenting, expressed the view that the individuals had a disability covered by the ADA, as (1) the threshold question whether an individual is disabled, within the meaning of the ADA, should focus on his or her past or present physical condition without regard to mitigation that has resulted from rehabilitation, self-improvement, prosthetic devices, or medication, and (2) to be faithful to the remedial purpose of the ADA, the Supreme Court should give the statute a generous, rather that a miserly, construction.

BREYER, J., dissenting, expressed the view that (1) the ADA's language, structure, basic purposes, and history, should require the Supreme Court to draw a statutory line that includes within the category of persons authorized to bring suit under the ADA some whom Congress may not have wanted to protect, such as those who wear ordinary eyeglasses, and (2) if such a construction leads to too many lawsuits that ultimately prove without merit, the Equal Employment Opportunity Commission can, through regulation, draw finer definitional lines and exclude some of those who wear eyeglasses.

COUNSEL

Van Aaron Hughes argued the cause for petitioners.

Edwin S. Kneedler argued the cause for the United States, as amicus curiae, by special leave of court.

Roy T. Englert, Jr. argued the cause for respondent.

VAUGHN L. MURPHY, Petitioner

v

UNITED PARCEL SERVICE, INC.

527 US —, 144 L Ed 2d 484, 119 S Ct 2133

[No. 97-1992]

Argued April 27, 1999.
Decided June 22, 1999.

Decision: Under Americans with Disabilities Act, determination whether impairment substantially limits major life activities held properly made with reference to mitigating measures, and individual with high blood pressure held not disabled.

SUMMARY

The Americans with Disabilities Act (ADA) (42 USCS §§ 12101 et seq.) provides that no covered employer shall discriminate against a qualified individual with a disability (42 USCS § 12112(a)) and includes in the definition of disability (1) a physical impairment that substantially limits one or more major life activities, or (2) being regarded as having such an impairment (42 USCS §§ 12102(2)(A), 12102(2)(C)). An individual—who was fired from his mechanic's job which required him to drive commercial motor vehicles—brought suit against his former employer in the United States District Court for the District of Kansas, alleging that his firing was in violation of the ADA. The individual was fired because the employer believed that the individual's blood pressure exceeded the requirements imposed by the Federal Department of Transportation (DOT) for drivers of commercial motor vehicles. The District Court granted the employer summary judgment, holding that (1) the individual's impairment should be evaluated in its medicated state, (2) the individual was not disabled under the ADA, and (3) the individual was not regarded as disabled under the ADA, as the employer regarded him as only not certifiable under the DOT regulations (946 F Supp 872). The United States Court of Appeals for the Tenth Circuit affirmed the District Court's judgment (141 F3d 1185).

On certiorari, the United States Supreme Court affirmed. In an opinion by O'CONNOR, J., joined by REHNQUIST, Ch. J., and SCALIA, KENNEDY, SOUTER, THOMAS, and GINSBURG, JJ., it was held that (1) the determination whether an individual's impairment substantially limits one or more major life activities is made with reference to the mitigating measures which he employs; (2) because, with medication, the individual's hypertension did not significantly restrict his activities, and because he could function normally and engage in activities that other persons normally do, he did not have an impairment which substantially limited him in any major life activity; and (3) the individual was not regarded as having a substantially limiting impairment because (a) a person is regarded as disabled within the meaning of the ADA if a covered entity mistakenly believes that the person's actual, nonlimiting impairment substantially limits one or more major life activities, (b) to be regarded as substantially limited in the major life activity of working, an individual must be regarded as precluded from more than a particular job, and (c) the individual was generally employable in mechanic jobs which did not call for driving a commercial motor vehicle and which thus did not require DOT certification.

STEVENS, J., joined by BREYER, J., dissenting, expressed the view that the individual's severe hypertension was an impairment which substantially limited his ability to perform several major life activities.

COUNSEL

Stephen R. McAllister argued the cause for petitioner.

James A. Feldman argued the cause for the United States, as amicus curiae, by special leave of court.

William J. Kilberg argued the cause for respondent.

CAROLE KOLSTAD, Petitioner

v

AMERICAN DENTAL ASSOCIATION

527 US —, 144 L Ed 2d 494, 119 S Ct 2118

[No. 98-208]

Argued March 1, 1999.
Decided June 22, 1999.

Decision: Award, under 42 USCS § 1981a, of punitive damages in employment discrimination action under Title VII (42 USCS §§ 2000e et seq.) held not to require showing of independently "egregious" conduct, but plaintiff held required to impute liability for punitive damages to employer.

SUMMARY

Under a provision of the Civil Rights Act of 1991 (42 USCS § 1981a), punitive damages are available in employment discrimination actions under Title VII of the Civil Rights Act of 1964 (42 USCS §§ 2000e et seq.) if an employer (1) under 42 USCS § 1981a(a)(1), has engaged in intentional discrimination, and (2) under 42 USCS § 1981a(b)(1), has done so with malice or reckless indifference to federally protected rights. A woman who was formerly employed by a professional association—and who had applied unsuccessfully for a promotion—filed an action against the association in the United States District Court for the District of Columbia and alleged that the decision by association officers to promote a male applicant constituted employment discrimination in violation of Title VII. The District Court denied the woman's request for a jury

instruction on punitive damages and submitted the
case to the jury, which (1) found that the association
had discriminated against the woman on the basis of
sex, and (2) awarded her backpay. A panel of the
United States Court of Appeals for the District of
Columbia Circuit (1) reversed the District Court's
decision regarding a punitive damages instruction, and
(2) ruled that because the jury could reasonably have
found intentional discrimination by the association, the
jury should have been permitted to consider punitive
damages (108 F3d 1431). On rehearing en banc,
however, the Court of Appeals affirmed the District
Court's decision and expressed the view that before the
question of punitive damages can go to the jury in a
Title VII case, the evidence must show not only intentional discrimination, but also some further egregious
misconduct by the defendant (139 F3d 958).

On certiorari, the United States Supreme Court
vacated and remanded. In an opinion by O'CONNOR, J.,
joined by SCALIA and KENNEDY, JJ., joined in part (as to
holding 1 below) by STEVENS, SOUTER, GINSBURG, and
BREYER, JJ., and joined in part (as to holding 2 below)
by REHNQUIST, Ch. J., and THOMAS, J., it was held that
(1) in an action claiming employment discrimination
in violation of Title VII, an employer's conduct need
not be "egregious," independent of the required state
of mind, in order to satisfy the requirements of § 1981a,
although evidence of such conduct can be used to meet
the plaintiff's burden of proof as to malice or reckless
indifference; but (2) in the context of punitive damages, (a) it is not sufficient to show that certain
individuals have exhibited the malice or reckless indifference required under § 1981a(b)(1), as the plaintiff
employee must also impute liability for punitive damages to the employer under the principles of agency
law, and (b) an employer may not be held vicariously

liable for the discriminatory employment decisions of managerial agents where those decisions are contrary to the employer's good-faith efforts to comply with Title VII.

REHNQUIST, Ch. J., joined by THOMAS, J., concurred in part and dissented in part, expressing the view that there should be an egregiousness requirement that would reserve punitive damages in Title VII cases for only the worst cases of intentional discrimination.

STEVENS, J., joined by SOUTER, GINSBURG, and BREYER, JJ., concurred in part and dissented in part, expressing the view that (1) egregious behavior was not a prerequisite to proving the wrongful motives required by § 1981a(b)(1); (2) the case should be remanded to the District Court for a trial on punitive damages, because the record contained evidence from the employer could be found to have acted with reckless indifference to the woman's federally protected rights; and (3) the Supreme Court should not have commented on issues of vicarious liability that were neither briefed by the parties nor presented by the facts of the case.

COUNSEL

Eric Schnapper argued the cause for petitioner.
Seth P. Waxman argued the cause for the United States, as amicus curiae, by special leave of court.
Raymond C. Fay argued the cause for respondent.

———————

ALBERTSON'S, INC., Petitioner

v

HALLIE KIRKINGBURG

527 US —, 144 L Ed 2d 518, 119 S Ct 2162

[No. 98-591]

Argued April 28, 1999.
Decided June 22, 1999.

Decision: Employer held entitled under Americans with Disabilities Act (42 USCS §§ 12101 et seq.) to enforce federal visual acuity standard against employee truckdriver who had obtained waiver of standard under experimental federal program.

SUMMARY

A truckdriver who had been hired by a grocery store chain was examined to see whether he met basic visual acuity standards set by the Federal Department of Transportation (DOT) for commercial truckdrivers (49 CFR § 391.41(b)(10)). Although the driver had amblyopia—an uncorrectable condition that left him with 20/200 vision in his left eye and thus effectively monocular vision—and his vision as measured did not in fact meet the DOT minimum requirement, a physician erroneously certified that the driver met the DOT standards, and the driver started to work for the store chain. After the driver's vision was correctly assessed at a subsequent physical and the driver was denied DOT certification, he applied for a waiver pursuant to a DOT program under which some drivers who had deficient vision but who met various conditions could be given certification. However, the store chain fired the driver for failing to meet the DOT standards and refused to rehire him after he received a waiver from the DOT. In a suit brought against the store chain in the United States District Court for the District of Oregon, the driver claimed that his firing violated the Americans with Disabilities Act of 1990 (ADA) (42 USCS §§ 12101 et seq.), which includes provisions that (1) no covered employer shall discriminate against a "qualified employee with a disability" (42 USCS § 12112(a)), and (2) a "qualified individual with a disability" is an individual with a disability who, with or without reasonable accommodation, can perform the essential functions of the employment position that such individual holds or desires (42 USCS § 12111(8)). In granting summary judgment for the store chain, the District Court concluded that for purposes of the ADA, (1) because the driver could not meet the basic DOT vision standards, the driver was not "qualified" for his job without an accommodation, and (2) giving the driver time to get a DOT waiver was not a required "reasonable accommodation." The United States Court of Appeals for the Ninth Circuit, in reversing and remanding, expressed the view that (1) the driver had established a disability—under an ADA provision (42 USCS § 12102(2)(A)) which defines a disability as an impairment which substantially limits a major life activity—by demonstrating that the manner in which he saw differed significantly from the manner in which most people saw; (2) compliance with DOT regulations could not be used as the justification for the store chain's vision standard, as the waiver program was a legitimate part of the DOT's regulatory scheme; and (3) although the store chain was free to set a vision standard different from the DOT's if such an independent standard could be justified under the ADA, such justification could not be shown under the circumstances presented (143 F3d 1228, 1998 US App LEXIS 9439).

On certiorari, the United States Supreme Court reversed. In an opinion by SOUTER, J., joined by REHNQUIST, Ch. J., and O'CONNOR, SCALIA, KENNEDY, THOMAS, and GINSBURG, JJ., and expressing the unanimous view of the court in part (as to points 2 and 3 below), it was held that (1) the Court of Appeals erred in finding that the driver had a disability under § 12102(2)(A) without identifying the degree of visual loss suffered by the driver; (2) under the ADA, an employer who requires as a job qualification that the employee meet an otherwise applicable federal safety regulation that tends to exclude persons with disabilities does not have to justify enforcing the regulation solely because the standard may be waived experimentally in an individual case; and (3) with respect to the driver's ADA rights, the regulations establishing the DOT's waiver program did not modify the content of the basic visual acuity standards in a way that disentitled the store chain to insist on the basic standards, for (a) the general standard was based on a considered determination about the level of visual acuity needed for safe operation of commercial motor vehicles in interstate commerce, while the waiver program was simply a means of obtaining information bearing on the justifiability of revising the existing standards, and (b) it was not credible that Congress enacted the ADA with the understanding that employers choosing to respect the government's sole substantive visual acuity regulation in the face of an experimental waiver might be burdened with an obligation to defend the regulation's application according to the regulation's own terms.

THOMAS, J., concurring, (1) agreed that the store chain was entitled to summary judgment under the

Supreme Court's approach, as the ADA was not to be interpreted to require the store chain to defend the application of the government's regulation to the driver when the store chain had an unconditional obligation to enforce the regulation; (2) expressed the view that it would have been preferable to hold that the driver, as a matter of law, was not qualified within the meaning of the ADA to perform the job in question; and (3) the Supreme Court's opinion left open the argument that federal laws such as DOT's visual acuity standards might be critical in determining whether a plaintiff is a "qualified individual with a disability" for ADA purposes.

COUNSEL

Corbett Gordon argued the cause for petitioner.

Scott N. Hunt argued the cause for respondent.

Edward C. DuMont argued the cause for the United States, as amicus curiae, by special leave of court.

TOMMY OLMSTEAD, Commissioner, Georgia Department of Human Resources, et al., Petitioners

v

L. C., by JONATHAN ZIMRING, Guardian Ad Litem and Next Friend, et al.

527 US —, 144 L Ed 2d 540, 119 S Ct 2176

[No. 98-536]

Argued April 21, 1999.
Decided June 22, 1999.

Decision: Title II of Americans with Disabilities Act (42 USCS §§ 12131 et seq.) held to require states, under some circumstances, to provide persons with mental disabilities with community-based treatment rather than placement in institutions.

SUMMARY

Two women with mental retardation—one of whom was also diagnosed with schizophrenia, and the other with a personality disorder—were voluntarily admitted to a Georgia state hospital, where they were confined for treatment in a psychiatric unit. Although treatment professionals eventually concluded that each of the women could be cared for appropriately in a community-based program, the women remained institutionalized at the hospital. One of the women, filing suit in the United States District Court for the Northern District of Georgia against various Georgia officials under 42 USCS § 1983 and Title II of the Americans with Disabilities Act of 1990 (42 USCS §§ 12131 et seq.), (1) alleged that Georgia had violated Title II in failing to place her in a community-based program once her

treating professionals had determined that such placement was appropriate, and (2) requested, among other
things, that the state place her in a community care
residential program. The other woman, intervening,
stated an identical claim. The District Court, in granting partial summary judgment for the women, (1)
rejected Georgia's argument that inadequate funding,
rather than discrimination against the women by reason of their disabilities, accounted for their retention at
the hospital; (2) concluded that under Title II, unnecessary institutional segregation of persons with disabilities constituted discrimination per se which could not
be justified by a lack of funding; and (3) rejected the
argument that immediate transfers in cases such as the
one at hand would fundamentally alter the state's
activity and thus were not required under a federal
regulation   implementing   Title   II   (28   CFR
§ 35.130(b)(7)), which regulation required public entities to make reasonable modifications but not fundamental alterations in existing programs in order to
avoid discrimination (1997 US Dist LEXIS 3540). After
the District Court issued judgment in the case, the
women were placed in community-based programs.
The United States Court of Appeals for the Eleventh
Circuit (1) affirmed the District Court's judgment, but
(2) remanded the case for consideration of the question whether the additional cost of the women's treatment in community-based care would be unreasonable
given the demands of Georgia's mental health budget
(138 F3d 893, 1998 US App LEXIS 6878, reh, en banc,
den 149 F3d 1197, 1998 US App LEXIS 20760). After
the United States Supreme Court granted certiorari to
review the Court of Appeals' judgment, the District
Court, on remand, issued a decision concluding that
the annual cost to the state of providing community-

based treatment to the women was not unreasonable in relation to Georgia's overall mental health budget.

On certiorari, the United States Supreme Court affirmed the Court of Appeals' judgment in part, vacated that judgment in part, and remanded for further proceedings. GINSBURG, J., announced the judgment of the court. In those portions of an opinion by GINSBURG, J., which constituted the opinion of the court and were joined by STEVENS, O'CONNOR, SOUTER, and BREYER, JJ., it was held that under Title II of the ADA, states are required to provide persons with mental disabilities with community-based treatment rather than placement in institutions, where (1) the state's treatment professionals have determined that community placement is appropriate; (2) the transfer from institutional care to a less restrictive setting is not opposed by the affected individual; and (3) the community placement can be reasonably accommodated, taking into account the resources available to the state and the needs of others with mental disabilities. Also, GINSBURG, J., joined by O'CONNOR, SOUTER, and BREYER, JJ., expressed the view that (1) the Court of Appeals had wrongly construed 28 CFR § 35.130(b)(7) to permit Georgia a cost-based defense only in the most limited of circumstances; and (2) the fundamental-alteration component of § 35.130(b)(7), sensibly construed, would allow Georgia to show, on remand, that in the allocation of available resources, immediate relief for the women would be inequitable, given the responsibility undertaken by Georgia for the care and treatment of a large and diverse population of persons with mental disabilities.

STEVENS, J., concurring in part and concurring in the judgment, (1) expressed the view that (a) if the District Court's rejection, on remand, of Georgia's fundamental-alteration defense was wrong, that arguable error would properly be corrected either by the Court of Appeals or by the Supreme Court in review of that decision, and (b) the Supreme Court thus should simply affirm the Court of Appeals' judgment; and (2) agreed to join the Supreme Court's judgment and parts of the opinion of GINSBURG, J., because there were not five votes for a simple affirmance.

KENNEDY, J., joined in part (as to points 1 and 2 below) by BREYER, J., concurring in the judgment, expressed the view that (1) it would be unreasonable to interpret the ADA so that states had some incentive to drive those in need of medical care and treatment out of appropriate care and into settings with too little assistance and supervision; (2) it would be important for courts to apply the Supreme Court's decision with deference to the decisions of responsible treating physicians and state policymakers; and (3) remand was necessary for a determination of (a) questions posed in the opinion of GINSBURG, J., and (b) whether an ADA violation could be shown based on the summary judgment materials on file or any further pleadings and materials properly allowed.

THOMAS, J., joined by REHNQUIST, Ch. J., and SCALIA, J., dissenting, expressed the view that for purposes of the ADA, Georgia did not discriminate against the women by reason of their disabilities, for (1) temporary exclusion from community placement does not amount to discrimination, and (2) continued institutional treatment of persons who—though deemed treatable in a community placement—must wait their turn for such placement does not establish that the denial of such placement occurred by reason of the persons' disability.

COUNSEL

Beverly P. Downing argued the cause for petitioners.

Michael Gottesman argued the cause for respondents.

Irving L. Gornstein argued the cause for the United States, as amicus curiae, by special leave of court.

―――――――

FLORIDA PREPAID POSTSECONDARY EDUCA-
TION EXPENSE BOARD, Petitioner

v

COLLEGE SAVINGS BANK and UNITED STATES

527 US —, 144 L Ed 2d 575, 119 S Ct 2199

[No. 98-531]

Argued April 20, 1999.
Decided June 23, 1999.

Decision: Abrogation, under Patent Remedy Act (35
USCS §§ 271(h), 296(a)), of states' sovereign immunity from patent infringement suits held not to
be valid legislation enacted to enforce Fourteenth
Amendment's due process clause.

SUMMARY

The Patent Remedy Act (35 USCS §§ 271(h), 296(a))
expressly provides in § 271(h) that the entities subject
to a patent infringement suit under 35 USCS § 271(a)
include states, state instrumentalities, and state officers
and employees. In § 296(a), the Act expressly abrogates
the immunity, under the Federal Constitution's Eleventh Amendment, of states, state instrumentalities, and
state officers and employees from patent infringement
suits under 35 USCS § 271. A New Jersey chartered
bank brought, in the United States District Court for
the District of New Jersey, an action under § 271(a)
alleging that a Florida state agency had willfully infringed the bank's patent on the financing methodology used in the bank's annuity contracts for financing
future college expenses, as well contributed to and
induced infringement. The state agency moved to

273

dismiss the action on the grounds that the Act was an unconstitutional attempt by Congress to use its powers under the Constitution's Article I to abrogate state sovereign immunity, but the bank responded that Congress had properly exercised its power pursuant to § 5 of the Constitution's Fourteenth Amendment to enforce the guarantees of the due process clause in the Fourteenth Amendment's § 1. After the United States intervened to defend the constitutionality of the statute, the District Court denied the motion to dismiss (948 F Supp 400). The United States Court of Appeals for the Federal Circuit, in affirming, expressed the view that Congress had clearly expressed its intent to abrogate the states' immunity from suit in federal court for patent infringement, and that Congress had the power under § 5 to do so (148 F3d 1343).

On certiorari, the United States Supreme Court reversed and remanded. In an opinion by REHNQUIST, Ch. J., joined by O'CONNOR, SCALIA, KENNEDY, and THOMAS, JJ., it was held that Congress' abrogation under the Act of the states' sovereign immunity under the Eleventh Amendment from patent infringement suits in federal court was invalid, because the statute could not be sustained as legislation enacted pursuant to Congress' authority under § 5 to enforce the due process clause, since (1) in enacting the Act, Congress identified no pattern of patent infringement by the states, (2) the legislative record provided little support for the proposition that Congress sought to remedy a Fourteenth Amendment violation in enacting the Act, (3) the legislative record suggested that the Act did not respond to a history of widespread and persisting deprivation of constitutional rights of the sort Congress had faced in enacting proper prophylactic § 5 legislation, (4) the Act's provisions were so out of proportion to a supposed remedial or preventive object that they could not be understood as responsive to, or designed to prevent, unconstitutional behavior, and (5) the Act's indiscriminate scope offended the principle that congressional limitations on statutes such as the Act tended to insure that Congress' means were proportionate to ends legitimate under § 5.

STEVENS, J., joined by SOUTER, GINSBURG, and BREYER, JJ., dissenting, expressed the view that given the absence of effective state remedies for patent infringement by states and the statutory pre-emption of such state remedies, the Act was an appropriate exercise of Congress' power under § 5 to prevent state deprivation of property without due process of law.

COUNSEL

Jonathan A. Glogau argued the cause for petitioner.

Kevin J. Culligan argued the cause for respondent College Savings Bank.

Seth P. Waxman argued the cause for respondent United States.

———

COLLEGE SAVINGS BANK, Petitioner

v

FLORIDA PREPAID POSTSECONDARY EDUCA-
TION EXPENSE BOARD et al.

527 US —, 144 L Ed 2d 605, 119 S Ct 2219

[No. 98-149]

Argued April 20, 1999.
Decided June 23, 1999.

Decision: Federal courts held to lack jurisdiction over
suit under 15 USCS § 1125(a) against state agency,
because state's sovereign immunity was neither (1)
validly abrogated by Trademark Remedy Clarification Act (106 Stat 3567), nor (2) voluntarily waived
by state's activities in interstate commerce.

SUMMARY

The Lanham Act's § 43(a) (15 USCS § 1125(a))
created a private right of action against any person who
uses false descriptions or makes false representations in
commerce. The Trademark Remedy Clarification Act
(TRCA) (106 Stat 3567) (1) amended § 43(a) by defining "any person" to include states and state instrumentalities, and (2) in 15 USCS § 1122, expressly abrogated
the sovereign immunity, under the Federal Constitution's Eleventh Amendment or under any other sovereign immunity doctrine, of such state entities from suit
in federal court under § 43(a). A New Jersey chartered
bank that held a patent on the methodology of administering its certificates of deposit that were designed to
finance the costs of college education filed, in the
United States District Court for the District of New

Jersey, an action alleging that a Florida state agency had violated § 43(a) by making misstatements about its own tuition savings plans in its brochures and annual reports. The state agency, arguing that the TRCA had not validly abrogated sovereign immunity, moved to dismiss the action on the ground that it was barred by sovereign immunity. The United States intervened to defend the constitutionality of the TRCA. Both the United States and the bank argued that the agency had constructively waived its immunity by engaging in the interstate marketing and administration of its programs after the TRCA made clear that such activity would subject the agency to suit. However, the District Court granted the motion to dismiss (948 F Supp 400), and the United States Court of Appeals for the Third Circuit affirmed the District Court judgment (131 F3d 353).

On certiorari, the United States Supreme Court affirmed. In an opinion by SCALIA, J., joined by REHNQUIST, Ch. J., and O'CONNOR, KENNEDY, and THOMAS, JJ, it was held that federal courts were without jurisdiction to entertain the suit against an arm of the state of Florida, because the TRCA neither (1) validly abrogated the state's sovereign immunity under the Eleventh Amendment pursuant to the power of Congress under § 5 of the Constitution's Fourteenth Amendment to remedy and prevent state deprivation of property without the due process of law guaranteed by § 1 of the Fourteenth Amendment, nor (2) operated as an invitation to waiver of such immunity which was automatically accepted by a state's engaging in activities regulated by the Lanham Act (15 USCS §§ 1051 et seq.).

STEVENS, J., dissenting, expressed the view that (1) the activity of doing business or the activity of making a profit is a form of property, and (2) the validity of a congressional decision to abrogate sovereign immunity in a category of cases does not depend on the strength of the claim asserted in a particular case within that category.

BREYER, J., joined by STEVENS, SOUTER, and GINSBURG, JJ., dissenting, expressed the view that (1) when a state engages in ordinary commercial ventures, it acts (a) like a private person, (b) outside the area of the state's core responsibilities, and (c) in a way unlikely to prove essential to the fulfillment of a basic governmental obligation; (2) Congress possesses the authority to abrogate a state's sovereign immunity where necessary and proper to the exercise of a congressional power under the Constitution's Article I; and (3) Congress had the constitutional power to provide that the bank could bring a Lanham Act suit in the circumstances of the instant case.

COUNSEL

David C. Todd argued the cause for petitioner.

Seth P. Waxman argued the cause for respondent United States.

William B. Mallin argued the cause for respondents Florida Prepaid Postsecondary Education Expense Board, et al.

JOHN H. ALDEN, et al., Petitioners

v

MAINE

527 US —, 144 L Ed 2d 636, 119 S Ct 2240

[No. 98-436]

Argued March 31, 1999.
Decided June 23, 1999.

Decision: Congress held not to have power, under
Article I of Federal Constitution, to subject nonconsenting states to private suits for damages in
states' own courts; Maine held not to have consented to private Fair Labor Standards Act suit in
Maine court.

SUMMARY

The Fair Labor Standards Act (FLSA) (29 USCS
§§ 201 et seq.), which has been said to have been
enacted under the Federal Constitution's commerce
clause (Art I, § 8, cl 3), regulates matters including
overtime and (1) in 29 USCS § 203(x), defines a
covered "[p]ublic agency" to include the government
or any agency of a state; (2) in 29 USCS § 216(b),
authorizes a private right of action, in any federal or
state court of competent jurisdiction, for items including unpaid overtime compensation and liquidated
damages; and (3) in 29 USCS § 216(c), alternatively
authorizes an action, in any court of competent jurisdiction, by the United States Secretary of Labor to
recover, on behalf of employees, items including unpaid overtime compensation and liquidated damages.
A group of probation officers (1) filed suit against their

employer, the state of Maine, in the United States District Court for the District of Maine, (2) alleged that the state had violated the FLSA's overtime provisions, and (3) sought compensation and liquidated damages. While the suit was pending, the United States Supreme Court held in Seminole Tribe v Florida (1996) 517 US 44, 134 L Ed 2d 252, 116 S Ct 1114, that "the background principle of state sovereign immunity embodied in" the Constitution's Eleventh Amendment—which expressly refers to only federal courts—prevented congressional authorization, under the commerce clause's provision concerning commerce with "the Indian Tribes," of private suits in federal court against nonconsenting states. Upon consideration of this decision, the District Court dismissed the officers' suit (1996 US Dist LEXIS 9985) and the United States Court of Appeals for the First Circuit affirmed (118 F3d 37, 1997 US App LEXIS 16545). The officers then filed essentially the same FLSA suit in the Superior Court of Maine, but (1) the state court dismissed the suit on the basis of the state's sovereign immunity, and (2) the Supreme Judicial Court of Maine affirmed on the same basis (715 A2d 172, 1998 Me LEXIS 197).

On certiorari, the Supreme Court affirmed. In an opinion by KENNEDY, J., joined by REHNQUIST, Ch. J., and O'CONNOR, SCALIA, and THOMAS, JJ., it was held that (1) the sovereign immunity of the states from suit neither derives from nor is limited by the terms of the Eleventh Amendment, but rather—as the Constitution's structure, its history, and the Supreme Court's authoritative interpretations make clear—is a fundamental aspect of the sovereignty which the states enjoyed before the Constitution's ratification and which they retain at the present time, except as altered by the plan of the constitutional convention or by certain constitutional amendments; (2) in light of history, practice, precedent, and the structure of the Constitution, the powers delegated to Congress under Article I of the Constitution do not include the power to subject nonconsenting states to private suits for damages in the states' own courts; and (3) the judgment sustaining the dismissal in the case at hand would be affirmed, as (a) the state of Maine had not consented to the officers' FLSA suit in the state's own courts, and (b) the Federal Government, despite specific authorization in § 216(c), had apparently found the asserted federal interest insufficient to justify sending an attorney to Maine to prosecute this FLSA litigation.

SOUTER, J., joined by STEVENS, GINSBURG, and BREYER, JJ., dissenting, expressed the view that the Supreme Court was mistaken on each point that it raised, as among other matters (1) it was implausible to argue that a substantial—let alone a dominant—body of thought at the time of the Constitution's framing understood sovereign immunity to be an inherent right of statehood that was adopted or confirmed by the Constitution's Tenth Amendment; (2) there was no evidence that any concept of inherent sovereign immunity was understood historically to apply when the sovereign sued was not the font of the law; (3) the Supreme Court's federalism ignored the accepted authority of Congress to bind states under the FLSA and to provide for enforcement of federal rights in state court; and (4) enforcement of the FLSA by the Secretary of Labor alone under § 216(c), without a private right of damages, was not likely to prove adequate to assure compliance with the FLSA in the multifarious circumstances of some 4.7 million employees of the 50 states.

COUNSEL

Laurence S. Gold argued the cause for petitioners.

Seth P. Waxman argued the cause for the United States, as amicus curiae, by special leave of court.

Peter J. Brann argued the cause for respondent.

ESTEBAN ORTIZ, et al., Petitioners

v

FIBREBOARD CORPORATION et al.

527 US —, 144 L Ed 2d 715, 119 S Ct 2295

[No. 97-1704]

Argued December 8, 1998.
Decided June 23, 1999.

Decision: Mandatory settlement class in asbestos personal injury litigation held not certifiable on limited fund theory under Rule 23(b)(1)(B) of Federal Rules of Civil Procedure.

SUMMARY

From 1967 onward, plaintiffs filed a stream of personal injury claims against an asbestos manufacturer that swelled to thousands of new claims for compensation each year. Beginning in 1979, the manufacturer was also litigating against two insurance companies over coverage for the personal injury claims. Eventually, negotiations involving the manufacturer, the insurers, and a group of asbestos plaintiffs' lawyers led to the settlement of some 45,000 pending claims. The parties then agreed upon $1.535 billion as the key term of a global settlement agreement, under which the insurers would contribute $1.525 billion and the manufacturer would contribute $10 million, all but $500,000 of which would come from other insurance proceeds. At the insistence of the plaintiffs' counsel, the manufacturer and its insurers reached a backup settlement of the coverage dispute called the trilateral settlement agreement, under which the insurers agreed to provide the manufacturer with $2 billion to defend against asbestos claimants and pay the winners, should the global settlement agreement fail to win court approval. Subsequently, a group of plaintiffs filed, in the United States District Court for the Eastern District of Texas, an action seeking certification for settlement purposes of a mandatory class that comprised three groups—(1) claimants who had not yet sued the manufacturer, (2) claimants who had dismissed such claims and retained the right to sue in the future, and (3) relatives of class members—but excluded claimants who had actions pending against the manufacturer or who had filed and, for negotiated value, dismissed such claims, and whose only retained right was to sue the manufacturer upon development of an asbestos-related malignancy. After allowing a group of objectors to intervene, the District Court determined that the threshold requirements of Rule 23(a) of the Federal Rules of Civil Procedure were met and that the settlement was fair, adequate, and reasonable under Rule 23(e). The District Court then certified the class under Rule 23(b)(1)(B). In response to the intervenors' objection that the absence of a limited fund precluded certification under Rule 23(b)(1)(B), the District Court ruled that both the disputed insurance asset liquidated by the $1.535 billion global settlement—and, alternatively, the sum of the value of the manufacturer plus the value of its insurance coverage, as measured by the insurance funds' settlement value—were relevant limited funds. The United States Court of Appeals for the Fifth Circuit (1) affirmed both the class certification and the adequacy of the settlement, and (2) approved the class certification, under Rule 23(b)(1)(B), on a limited fund rationale based on the threat to other class members' ability to receive full payment from the manufacturer's limited assets (90 F3d 963). Following

284

the United States Supreme Court's decision in the asbestos litigation case of Amchem Products, Inc. v Windsor (1997) 521 US 591, 138 L Ed 2d 689, 117 S Ct 2231, the Supreme Court granted certiorari, vacated the Court of Appeals' judgment, and remanded for further consideration in light of that decision (521 US 1114, 138 L Ed 2d 1008, 117 S Ct 2503). On remand, the Court of Appeals again affirmed the District Court's judgment with similar reasoning (134 F3d 668).

On certiorari, the Supreme Court reversed and remanded. In an opinion by SOUTER, J., joined by REHN-QUIST, Ch. J., and O'CONNOR, SCALIA, KENNEDY, THOMAS, and GINSBURG, JJ., it was held that (1) applicants for contested certification of a mandatory settlement class under Rule 23(b)(1)(B) on a limited fund theory in an asbestos personal injury case must show—assuming for the sake of argument that a mandatory and limited fund rationale could under some circumstances be applied to a settlement class of tort claimants—that the fund is limited by more than the agreement of the parties and that the fund has been allocated to claimants belonging within the class by a process addressing any conflicting interests of class members; and (2) the District Court erred in certifying the mandatory settlement class in the present case, because the essential premises of a mandatory limited fund action—that (a) the totals of the aggregated liquidated claims and the fund available for satisfying them, set definitely at their maximums, demonstrate the inadequacy of the fund to pay all the claims, (b) the whole of the inadequate fund is to be devoted to the overwhelming claims, and (c) the claimants identified by a common theory of recovery are treated equitably among themselves—were not supported in the record on which the certification rested, as among other factors (a) the limit of the fund was determined by treating the global settlement agreement as dispositive, (b) class members were represented by counsel who also negotiated the separate settlement of pending claims by excluded plaintiffs whose settlements would be funded fully upon settlement of the class action on any terms that could survive final fairness review, and (c) the class excluded myriad claimants with causes of action, or foreseeable causes of action, arising from exposure to the manufacturer's asbestos.

REHNQUIST, Ch. J., joined by SCALIA and KENNEDY, JJ., concurring, expressed the view that (1) the Supreme Court is not free to devise an ideal system for adjudicating asbestos-related claims, and (2) unless and until the Federal Rules of Civil Procedure are revised, the Supreme Court's opinion correctly stated the existing law.

BREYER, J., joined by STEVENS, J., dissenting, expressed the view that (1) in the special background circumstances of the case at hand, the Supreme Court should (a) allow a District Court full authority to exercise every bit of discretionary power that the law provides, and (b) be reluctant to overturn a fact-specific or circumstance-specific exercise of that discretion; (2) the case at hand fell within the language of Rule 23(b)(1)(B) as long as there was significant risk that the total assets available to satisfy the claims of the class members would fall well below the likely total value of those claims; and (3) in the present case, the three additional conditions which the Supreme Court set forth—as sufficient to justify binding absent members of a class from which no one had a right to secede—were satisfied.

COUNSEL

Laurence H. Tribe argued the cause for petitioners.
Elihu Inselbuch argued the cause for respondents.

————

RONALD DWAYNE WHITFIELD, Petitioner

v

TEXAS

RONALD DWAYNE WHITFIELD, Petitioner

v

TEXAS

RONALD DWAYNE WHITFIELD, Petitioner

v

TEXAS

527 US —, 144 L Ed 2d 764, 119 S Ct 2333

[No. 98-9085]

Decided June 24, 1999.

Decision: Person who filed nine frivolous petitions in Supreme Court denied leave to proceed in forma pauperis on certiorari petition; order entered barring person's future in forma pauperis filings of petitions for certiorari or for extraordinary writs in noncriminal matters.

SUMMARY

An individual sought leave to proceed in forma pauperis in the United States Supreme Court under Supreme Court Rule 39 with respect to a petition for certiorari. According to the court, which previously had invoked Supreme Court Rule 39.8—which authorizes the court to deny leave to proceed in forma pauperis with respect to frivolous petitions—to deny the individual in forma pauperis status with respect to a petition for certiorari, the instant petition was the individual's ninth frivolous filing in the court, six of which were petitions for certiorari and three of which were petitions for extraordinary writs.

In a per curiam opinion expressing the view of REHNQUIST, Ch. J., and O'CONNOR, SCALIA, KENNEDY, SOUTER, THOMAS, GINSBURG, and BREYER, JJ., the Supreme Court (1) invoked Rule 39.8 to deny the individual's request for leave to proceed in forma pauperis on the instant petition, and (2) directed the Clerk of the Supreme Court not to accept any further petitions for certiorari or for extraordinary writs in noncriminal matters from the individual unless he complied with Supreme Court Rules 33.1 and 38.

STEVENS, J., dissented for reasons expressed in some previous Supreme Court cases involving some similar issues.

GLOSSARY OF COMMON LEGAL TERMS

Abatement
The extinguishment of a lawsuit.

Abstention doctrine
The doctrine whereby a federal court may decline to exercise, or may postpone the exercise of, its jurisdiction, where a case involves a controlling question of state law.

Action
A lawsuit.

Administrative determination
A decision by a government board, agency or official, rather than by a court.

Administrator
One appointed by a court to settle the estate of a deceased person. The feminine form is "administratrix."

Admiralty
The body of law governing maritime cases.

Affidavit
A sworn written statement.

Amicus curiae
One who, not being a party to a lawsuit, assists the court in deciding the case.

Antitrust laws
Laws prohibiting restrictions on competition.

Appealable
That which may be taken to a higher court for review.

Appellant
One who appeals to a superior court from the order of an inferior court.

Appellee
A party against whom a case is appealed from an inferior court to a superior court.

Arbitration
The submission of a dispute to a selected person—not a court—for decision.

Arraign
To call a person before a judge or commissioner to answer criminal charges made against him.

Array
The whole body of persons, summoned to attend court, from whom a jury will be selected.

Assignee
One to whom property or a right is transferred.

Assignor
The transferor of property or a right.

Bill of Rights
The first ten amendments to the United States Constitution.

Brief
A written legal argument submitted to the court deciding the case.

Calendar
A list of cases awaiting decision in a court.

Capital crime
An offense punishable by death.

Cause of action
A right to legal redress.

Cease-and-desist order
An order to stop doing specified acts.

Certiorari
A superior court's order to a lower court to send up the record of a case for review by the superior court.

Choice of remedies
An election of which form of legal redress to seek.

Civil
Not criminal, as a civil lawsuit.

Class action
A lawsuit on behalf of persons too numerous to participate actively therein.

Commerce clause
The provision of the United States Constitution giving Congress power to regulate commerce with foreign nations, among the states.

Common law
The body of the law apart from constitutions, treaties, statutes, ordinances, and regulations.

Contempt
An exhibition of scorn or disrespect toward a judicial or legislative body.

Continuance
A postponement of proceedings.

Copyright
The exclusive privilege of publishing literary or artistic productions.

Coram nobis
A means of challenging a court's judgment, especially in criminal cases.

293

Court of Appeals
See United States Court of Appeals.

Cross Appeal
An appeal filed by the person against whom an appeal is taken.

De novo
Anew or over again, such as a trial de novo.

Devise
A will provision making a gift of land.

Disputes clause
A provision in a government contract for the settlement of disputes between the contractor and the government by decision of a government board or official.

District court
See United States District Court.

Diversity case
A case decided by a federal court because the parties are citizens of different states.

Double jeopardy
Placing a person twice in jeopardy of conviction for the same offense.

Due process clause
The provision of the United States Constitution that no person shall be deprived of life, liberty, or property without due process of law.

En banc
With all the judges of the court sitting.

Equal protection
The guaranty of the United States Constitution that no person or class of persons shall be denied the same protection of the laws that is enjoyed by other persons or classes of persons in like circumstances.

Establishment clause
The provision of the United States Constitution that Congress shall make no law respecting an establishment of religion.

Federal District Court
See District court.

Federal question jurisdiction
The jurisdiction of federal courts over cases presenting questions of federal law.

Felony
A crime punishable by death or by imprisonment in a state prison.

Forma pauperis
Without the payment of legal fees in advance.

Full faith and credit clause
The provision of the United States Constitution that full faith and credit shall be given in each state to the public acts, records, and judicial proceedings of every other state.

Habeas corpus
A judicial inquiry into the legality of the restraint of a person.

Indictment
A grand jury's accusation of crime.

Interlocutory
That which settles an intervening matter but does not decide a case.

Intestate
One who dies without leaving a valid will.

Jurisdiction of subject matter
The power to decide a certain type of case.

Just compensation clause
The provision of the United States Constitution that no private property may be taken for public use without just compensation.

Laches
Delay barring the right to special forms of relief.

Legatee
One to whom personal property is given by will.

Lessee
A tenant.

Lessor
A landlord.

Libel
Written defamation; in maritime cases, a suit in court.

Lien
A charge upon property for the payment of a debt.

Local action
A lawsuit, especially one involving rights to land, which can be brought only in the place where the wrong was committed.

Maintenance and cure
The legal duty of a seaman's employer to care for him during his illness.

Mandamus
A judicial command to perform an official duty.

Misdemeanor
Any crime not punishable by death or by imprisonment in a state prison.

296

Patent
The exclusive right of manufacture, sale, or use secured by statute to one who invents or discovers a new and useful device or process.

Per curiam
By the court as a whole.

Per se
By itself.

Plaintiff
A person who brings a lawsuit.

Plenary
Full or complete.

Police power
The power inherent in the states as sovereigns and not derived under any written constitution.

Prima facie
At first sight; with regard to evidence, that which, if unexplained or uncontradicted, is sufficient to establish a fact.

Privileges and immunities clause
The provision of the United States Constitution that no state shall make or enforce any law which abridges the privileges or immunities of citizens of the United States.

Pro hac vice
For this occasion.

Pro se
For himself; in his own behalf.

Proximate cause
The immediate cause of injury.

Public defender
A lawyer employed by the public to defend persons accused of crime.

Recognizance
A bail bond.

Remand
To order to be sent back.

Res judicata
The doctrine that a final judgment is binding on the parties to the lawsuit and the matter cannot be relitigated.

Respondent
The defendant in an action; with regard to appeals, the party against whom the appeal is taken.

Sanction
The penalty to be incurred by a wrongdoer.

Saving clause
A statutory provision preserving rights which would otherwise be annihilated by the statute.

Seaworthy
The reasonable fitness of a vessel to perform the service which she has undertaken to perform.

Statute of frauds
A statute rendering certain types of contracts unenforceable unless in writing.

Statute of limitations
A statute fixing a period of time within which certain types of lawsuits or criminal prosecutions must be begun.

Subpoena
Legal process to require the attendance of a witness.

Substantial federal question
A question of federal law of sufficient merit to warrant decision of the case by a federal court.

Substantive offense
An offense which is complete in itself and does not depend on the establishment of another offense.

Summary judgment
A judgment without a trial.

Supremacy clause
The provision of the United States Constitution that the Constitution, federal laws enacted pursuant thereto, and federal treaties shall be the supreme law of the land, binding the judges in every state, notwithstanding any state law to the contrary.

Surety
One who binds himself with another, called the principal, for the performance of an obligation with respect to which the principal is already bound and primarily liable.

Surrogate
The judge of a court dealing largely with wills and decedents' estates.

Tort
A wrong independent of contract; a breach of duty which the law, as distinguished from a mere contract, has imposed.

Tortfeasor
One who commits a tort; a wrongdoer.

Transitory action
An action which may be brought wherever the defendant may be served with process.

Trespass
An injury intentionally inflicted on the person or property of another.

Trier of fact
One who decides questions of fact.

United States Code
The official compilation of statutes enacted by Congress.

United States Court of Appeals
The intermediate level of federal courts above the United States District Courts but below the Supreme Court of the United States.

United States District Court
A federal trial court.

Unseaworthy
See Seaworthy.

USC
See United States Code.

USCS
The abbreviation for United States Code Service, Lawyers Edition, which is a publication annotating the federal laws, arranged according to the numbering of the United States Code.

Venue
The place where a case may be tried.

Writ of certiorari
See Certiorari.

Writ of error coram nobis
See Coram nobis.

TABLE OF CASES

TABLE OF CASES

TABLE OF CASES

TABLE OF CASES

TABLE OF CASES

INDEX

A

ABDUCTION AND KIDNAPPING.
Kidnapping does not end until victim is free, 143 L Ed 2d 388.

ABSTENTION DOCTRINE.
Indians.
Tribal court exhaustion doctrine as not requiring Federal District Court to let tribal court decide whether tribe members' causes of action against urarium mine operators were claims under Price-Anderson Act, 143 L Ed 2d 635.

ADMINISTRATIVE LAW.
Civil service employees.
Right to union representation at examinations by NASA representative, 144 L Ed 2d 258.
Customs regulations.
Statutory interpretation, 143 L Ed 2d 480.
Federal Communications Commission jurisdiction.
Local service providers, rules regarding local competition and pricing, 142 L Ed 2d 834.
Medicare reimbursement determinations.
Review of refusal to reopen determination, 142 L Ed 2d 919.
Primary jurisdiction.
National Labor Relations Board, claim regarding NLRA § 8(a)(3), 142 L Ed 2d 242.

ADMINISTRATIVE PROCEDURE ACTS.
Meaning of "other money damages."
Sovereign immunity waiver under § 10(a).
Subcontractor suing U.S. Army for default by prime contractor, seeking equitable lien, 142 L Ed 2d 718.

ALL WRITS ACT OR STATUTE.
Court of Military Appeals, writs in aid of jurisdiction.
Enjoining dropping of major from Air Force, 143 L Ed 2d 720.

AMERICANS WITH DISABILITIES ACT.
Arbitration and award.
Collective bargaining agreements, arbitration requirements, 142 L Ed 2d 361.
Claim of employment discrimination under act as not inherently conflicting with social security disability claim.
Rebuttable presumption of disability not created by SSDI claim, 143 L Ed 2d 966.

ATTORNEYS AT LAW —Cont'd
Sanctions for failure to comply with discovery.
> Not final order appealable under 28 USCS § 1291, 144 L Ed 2d
> 184.

ATTORNEYS' FEES.
Retroactivity of fees under Prison Litigation Reform Act, 144 L Ed
2d 347.

AUTOMOBILES AND HIGHWAY TRAFFIC.
Search and seizure.
> Exigency exception where abundant probable cause exists and
> warrant justified although not issued, 144 L Ed 2d 442.
> Full search after citation issued for traffic violation and no arrest
> made.
>> Justification not found for search under historical
>> interpretation of Fourth amendment, 142 L Ed 2d 492.
> Warrants, not required when there is probable cause to believe
> automobile is forfeitable contraband, 143 L Ed 2d 748.

AVIATION.
Warsaw convention.
> Personal injury sustained aboard international air carrier, claim
> denied, 142 L Ed 2d 576.

B

BONDS AND UNDERTAKINGS.
Miller Act, right of subcontractor to sue on surety bond posted by
prime contractor.
> Subcontractor suing U.S. Army for default by prime contractor,
> seeking equitable lien, 142 L Ed 2d 718.

BOYCOTTS.
Telephone company change of supplier as not constituting group
boycott.
> Where change unjustified in terms of ordinary competitive
> objectives, 142 L Ed 2d 510.

BRIBERY.
Illegal gratuity statute.
> Conviction under to require link between thing of value conferred
> upon public official and specific official act for which it was
> given, 143 L Ed 2d 576.

C

CAPITAL OFFENSES AND PUNISHMENT.
Habeas corpus claim, lethal gas violating prohibition of cruel and
unusual punishment.
> Denial where state provided choice between lethal gas and lethal
> injection and claimant chose lethal gas, 143 L Ed 2d 196.

INDEX

CAPITAL OFFENSES AND PUNISHMENT —Cont'd
Instructions to jury.

Appeal of instructions, test to be applied by courts, 142 L Ed 2d 521.

Refusal of instruction regarding deadlocked jury in federal capital sentencing hearing, 144 L Ed 2d 370.

Stay of execution, order issued by International Court of Justice.

Germany's motion to enforce order to stay is tardy and United States has not waived sovereign immunity, 143 L Ed 2d 192.

CARJACKING.
Intent to kill or harm, 143 L Ed 2d 1.
Three separate offenses, 143 L Ed 2d 311.

CARRIERS.
Mental injury, Warsaw Convention held not to allow recovery if unaccompanied by physical injury.

Intrusive search leading to claim of personal injury, 142 L Ed 2d 576.

CENSUS.
Statistical sampling.

Prohibited in determining population for use for apportionment, 142 L Ed 2d 797.

CERTAINTY AND DEFINITENESS.
Gang-congregation municipal ordinance prohibiting loitering in public places.

Held impermissibly vague and in violation of due process clause of Fourteenth Amendment, 144 L Ed 2d 67.

CERTIORARI.
Dismissal.

Death of defendant after certiorari granted, 142 L Ed 2d 500.

Frivolous petitions.

Denial of appeals under Rule 39.8 where previous 34 of 35 petitions deemed frivolous, 143 L Ed 2d 203.

Extraordinary writs, appeal denied under Rule 39.8, 142 L Ed 2d 573.

Order entered barring person's future in forma pauperis filings, 143 L Ed 2d 16, 235.

CIVIL RIGHTS AND DISCRIMINATION.
Americans with Disabilities Act.

Labor agreement containing arbitration clause, applicability to disabilities claim, 142 L Ed 2d 361.

At-will employment termination, action under 42 USCS § 1985, 142 L Ed 2d 502.

Intercollegiate athletics.

Title IX suit against private organization, federal funds "received" through member dues, 142 L Ed 2d 929.

Ind-5

DAMAGES —Cont'd

Mental injury under Warsaw Convention.

    Personal injury sustained aboard international air carrier, claim denied, 142 L Ed 2d 576.

DEBTOR AND CREDITOR.

Claim for injunction preventing transfer of assets as frustrating payment of debt.

    Establishment of prior judgment of debt required, even under equity jurisdiction, 144 L Ed 2d 319.

DEPORTATION OR EXCLUSION OF ALIENS.

Construction and interpretation.

    Federal Court of Appeals as not according deference to Board of Immigration Appeals interpretation of 8 USCS § 15903(h) with respect to alien's entitlement to withholding of deportation, 143 L Ed 2d 590.

Judicial review of Attorney General's decision to commence proceedings, 142 L Ed 2d 940.

DISCOVERY.

Sanctions for failure to comply.

    Not final order appealable under 28 USCS § 1291, 144 L Ed 2d 184.

DISTRICT AND PROSECUTING ATTORNEYS.

Habeas corpus.

    Exculpatory evidence withheld; whether open file policy of prosecutor broad enough not to violate due process, 144 L Ed 2d 286.

DISTRICT COURTS AND JUDGES.

Removal or transfer of causes.

    Addressing personal jurisdiction before subject matter jurisdiction, 143 L Ed 2d 760.

DRUGS AND NARCOTICS.

Continuing criminal enterprise.

    Elements of crime include series of violations and individual violations that make up continuing series, 143 L Ed 2d 985.

DUE PROCESS.

Employment at will as protected property.

    Termination, action brought under 42 USCS § 1985, 142 L Ed 2d 502.

Fourteenth Amendment.

    Seizure of property, notice to owners of methods for obtaining return not mandated under, 142 L Ed 2d 636.

Gang-congregation municipal ordinance prohibiting loitering in public places.

    Held impermissibly vague and in violation of due process clause of Fourteenth Amendment, 144 L Ed 2d 67.

Habeas corpus.

    Exculpatory evidence withheld; whether open file policy of prosecutor broad enough not to violate due process, 144 L Ed 2d 286.

DUE PROCESS —Cont'd

Sovereign immunity abrogated to enforce Fourteenth Amendment due process.

Patent Remedy Act not valid for this purpose, 144 L Ed 2d 575.

Trademark Clarification Act held to be valid legislation for this purpose, 144 L Ed 2d 605.

Workers' compensation benefits subject to utilization review by private insurer.

Determination of reasonable and necessary expenses does not violate property interest of employee in receiving benefits, 143 L Ed 2d 130.

Withholding of payment not considered state action under Fourteenth Amendment, 143 L Ed 2d 130.

E

EIGHTH AMENDMENT.

Waiver of rights under.

Lethal gas chosen over lethal injection precludes claim of cruel and unusual punishment for using lethal gas, 143 L Ed 2d 196.

ELECTIONS AND VOTING.

Preclearance.

Application of requirement to discretionary actions of covered jurisdiction, 142 L Ed 2d 728.

ELEVENTH AMENDMENT.

Citizens of one state suing another state, 143 L Ed 2d 258.

EMERGENCY MEDICAL TREATMENT AND ACTIVE LABOR ACT.

Failure to stabilize patient before transferring between facilities, improper motive need not be shown, 142 L Ed 2d 648.

EMINENT DOMAIN.

Regulatory taking as violation of Fifth Amendment takings clause.

Propriety of jury trial and submission of liability issue to jury for consideration, 143 L Ed 2d 882.

EMOTIONAL INJURY.

Warsaw Convention held not to allow recovery for mental injury which is unaccompanied by physical injury.

Intrusive search leading to claim of personal injury, 142 L Ed 2d 576.

EQUAL FOOTING.

States: retention of hunting, fishing and gathering rights on ceded land, 143 L Ed 2d 270.

EQUAL PROTECTION.

Collective bargaining.

Exemption of faculties' instructional workload standards from. Held not to violate clause, 143 L Ed 2d 227.

FREEDOM OF SPEECH AND PRESS.
Advertising.
Radio and television broadcasts regarding gambling where
gambling not prohibited by law.
Violation of First Amendment to prohibit such broadcasts, 144
L Ed 2d 161.
Political speech, protection under First Amendment.
Circulators of initiative petitions required to wear name badges
and disclose certain information, 142 L Ed 2d 599.

FRIVOLOUS MATTERS.
Clerk of Supreme Court not to accept petitions in forma pauperis in
noncriminal matters, 143 L Ed 2d 203, 235, 384, 982.
Previous petitions deemed frivolous, 142 L Ed 2d 573.
Rule 39.8 of Supreme Court controlling, 144 L Ed 2d 447, 764.

G

GAMBLING.
Advertising where gambling not prohibited by law.
Violation of First Amendment to prohibit such broadcasts, 144 L
Ed 2d 161.

GERRYMANDERING.
Racial gerrymandering, 143 L Ed 2d 731.

GIFTS.
Illegal gratuity statute.
Conviction under held to require link between thing of value
conferred upon public official and specific official act for
which it was given, 143 L Ed 2d 576.

GRAND JURY.
Counsel.
Witness has no right to have counsel present, 143 L Ed 2d 399.

H

HABEAS CORPUS.
Exhaustion of remedies.
Under rule of 28 USCS § 2254(c), petitioner must present federal
constitutional claims to state courts, 144 L Ed 2d 1.
Harmless or prejudicial error.
Capital sentencing instructions, application of harmless error test
required, 142 L Ed 2d 521.

HARMLESS OR PREJUDICIAL ERROR.
Criminal offense, element omitted from jury instructions.
Harmless error analysis on appeal, 144 L Ed 2d 35.
Instructions to jury.
Refusal of instruction regarding deadlocked jury in federal capital
sentencing hearing, 144 L Ed 2d 370.

I

INJUNCTIONS —Cont'd
Claim for injunction preventing transfer of assets as frustrating
payment of debt.
Prior judgment establishing debt required, even under equity
jurisdiction, 144 L Ed 2d 319.

INSTRUCTIONS TO JURY.
Appeal and review.
Capital sentencing instructions, test to be applied on habeas
corpus appeal, 142 L Ed 2d 521.
Criminal offense, instruction omitting element subject to
harmless error analysis on appeal, 144 L Ed 2d 35.
Deadlocked jury in federal capital sentencing hearing.
Refusal to give instruction regarding effect of deadlock, 144 L Ed
2d 370.
Job discrimination case, instruction on punitive damages denied
under Title VII of Civil Rights Act.
Whether egregious conduct required for consideration of punitive
damages, 144 L Ed 2d 494.

INSURANCE.
RICO application to insurance business.
Impairment of Nevada state law for purposes of
McCarran-Ferguson Act not found, 142 L Ed 2d 753.

INTENT OR MOTIVE.
Criminal intent.
Carjacking, intent to kill or harm, 143 L Ed 2d 1.

J

JOB DISCRIMINATION.
Correctable disabilities; what constitutes impairment under
Americans with Disabilities Act.
Denial of employment due to high blood pressure preventing
certification as commercial vehicle driver, 144 L Ed 2d 484.
Correctable disabilities; what constitutes impairment under
Americans with Disabilities Act.
Denial of employment due to monocular vision preventing
certification as commercial truck driver, 144 L Ed 2d 518.
Denial of employment due to severe myopia correctable to certain
standards, 144 L Ed 2d 450.
Equal Employment Opportunity Commission's power to require
federal agencies to award compensatory damages for claim
under Title IV, 144 L Ed 2d 106.
Jury instruction on punitive damages denied in case under Title VII
of Civil Rights Act.
Whether egregious conduct required for consideration of punitive
damages, 144 L Ed 2d 494.

JURISDICTION.
Addressing personal jurisdiction without first addressing subject
matter jurisdiction, 143 L Ed 2d 760.

MEDICARE.
Reimbursement.
Review of refusal to reopen determination, 142 L Ed 2d 919.

MENTAL HOSPITALS.
Public mental health services.
Denial of community-based treatment rather than institutional placement where community placement appropriate, 144 L Ed 2d 540.

MONTREAL AGREEMENT.
Construction and application of Warsaw Convention, pertaining to international air transportation.
Claim for recovery for mental injury unaccompanied by physical injury, 142 L Ed 2d 576.

N

NATIONAL LABOR RELATIONS ACT.
Union security clause as violating duty of fair representation and claim regarding NLRA § 8(a)(3), 142 L Ed 2d 242.

NATIONAL LABOR RELATIONS BOARD.
Primary jurisdiction.
Union security clause as violating duty of fair representation and claim regarding NLRA § 8(a)(3), 142 L Ed 2d 242.

O

ORDINANCES.
Gang-congregation municipal ordinance prohibiting loitering in public places.
Held impermissibly vague and in violation of due process clause of Fourteenth Amendment, 144 L Ed 2d 67.

ORIGINAL JURISDICTION.
Supreme Court declination to exercise original jurisdiction for foreign bill of complaint to prevent execution of German citizen, 143 L Ed 2d 192.

P

PARTIES.
Standing to sue.
Census 2000, use of statistical sampling prohibited for use for apportionment, 142 L Ed 2d 797.

PARTNERSHIP.
Bankruptcy.
Debtor's prebankruptcy equity holders disqualified from contributing new capital and receiving interests in reorganized entity under nonconsensual reorganization plan giving exclusive ownership, 143 L Ed 2d 607.

TREATIES —Cont'd
Warsaw Convention.
Personal injury sustained aboard international air carrier, claim
denied, 142 L Ed 2d 576.

TRUSTS.
Wasting trust defined, 142 L Ed 2d 881.

U

UNIONS.
Administrative agency employees.
Right to union representation at examinations by representative
of agency, 144 L Ed 2d 258.

V

VENUE.
Using or carrying firearm during and in relation to crime of
violence, 143 L Ed 2d 388.

VOTING RIGHTS ACT.
Covered jurisdictions, designating.
Requiring federal approval for implementing noncovered state's
law, 142 L Ed 2d 728.
Preclearance.
Application of requirement to discretionary actions of covered
jurisdiction, 142 L Ed 2d 728.

W

WEAPONS AND FIREARMS.
Venue.
Crime of violence in multiple districts, 143 L Ed 2d 388.

WELFARE AND WELFARE LAWS.
Domicile or residence.
Travel from state to state as inhibited by statute imposing
residency requirements on welfare recipients, 143 L Ed 2d
689.

WITNESSES.
Self-incrimination.
Guilty plea not waiver of privilege, 143 L Ed 2d 424.

WORKERS' COMPENSATION.
Private insurer decision to withhold payment and seek utilization
review.
Permitted under state workers' compensation law, which bars
reimbursement for excessive medical payments, 143 L Ed 2d
130.

9376